Key Aspects of German Business Law

Springer
*Berlin
Heidelberg
New York
Barcelona
Hong Kong
London
Milan
Paris
Tokyo*

Bernd Tremml · Bernard Buecker (Eds.)

Key Aspects of German Business Law

A Practical Manual

Second Edition

Springer

Dr. jur. M.C.J. Bernd Tremml
Wendler Tremml Rechtsanwälte
Martiusstraße 5
80802 München
Germany
munich@law-wt.de

Bernard Buecker
2201 Tower Life Building
310 S. St. Mary's
San Antonio, Texas 78205
USA

The information contained herein is general information and is not intended to provide legal advice. Should you require legal advice, you should seek the assistance of counsel.

Copyright © 2002 Bernd Tremml, Bernard Buecker

ISBN 3-540-43411-9 Springer-Verlag Berlin Heidelberg New York
ISBN 3-540-65251-5 1st edition Springer-Verlag Berlin Heidelberg New York

Library of Congress Cataloging-in-Publication Data applied for
Die Deutsche Bibliothek – CIP-Einheitsaufnahme
Key aspects of German business law: a practical manual / Bernd Tremml; Bernard Buecker ed. – 2. ed. – Berlin; Heidelberg; New York; Barcelona; Hong Kong; London; Milan; Paris; Tokyo: Springer, 2002
   ISBN 3-540-43411-9

This work is subject to copyright. All rights are reserved, whether the whole or part of the material is concerned, specifically the rights of translation, reprinting, reuse of illustrations, recitation, broadcasting, reproduction on microfilm or in any other way, and storage in data banks. Duplication of this publication or parts thereof is permitted only under the provisions of the German Copyright Law of September 9, 1965, in its current version, and permission for use must always be obtained from Springer-Verlag. Violations are liable for prosecution under the German Copyright Law.

Springer-Verlag Berlin Heidelberg New York
a member of BertelsmannSpringer Science+Business Media GmbH

http://www.springer.de

© Springer-Verlag Berlin · Heidelberg 1999, 2002
Printed in Germany

The use of general descriptive names, registered names, trademarks, etc. in this publication does not imply, even in the absence of a specific statement, that such names are exempt from the relevant protective laws and regulations and therefore free for general use.

Hardcover-Design: Erich Kirchner, Heidelberg
SPIN 10874671   64/2202-5 4 3 2 1 0 – Printed on acid-free paper

Preface

This book presents a clear and precise overview of the key aspects of German business law. It was written by attorneys involved in the daily practice of business law in Germany and is aimed at people who wish to orient themselves quickly with the German legal system and the manner in which it impacts business purchases, establishment, operations and liquidations.

The first section of the book is devoted to an explanation of the major issues to be considered in acquiring or establishing a business in Germany, whereas the second section focuses on areas of special consideration. In both sections special attention has been paid to highlighting and explaining the differences between the German legal system and that of the United States, though the intention is to provide information that will prove valuable to all foreigners, particularly business men and women and lawyers advising clients with an interest in doing business in Germany.

Though it is the object of this book to present readers with a general orientation and the foundation for making informed decisions concerning business transactions in Germany, it cannot possibly function as a substitute for case-specific professional advice and by no means purports to do so. Those readers who wish to follow up on any decisions they may have formed on the basis of the material presented here are well advised to seek the guidance of qualified attorneys and tax advisors before entering into any binding obligations.

This holds particularly true in light of the fact that all information here is based on the laws that were in effect in the Federal Republic of Germany on the first of January 2002.

THE EDITORS

Bernd Tremml
Attorney at Law
Munich, Germany

Bernard Buecker
Attorney at Law
San Antonio, Texas

Contents

Introduction: Overview of the German Legal System 1

PART I
HOW TO ESTABLISH OR ACQUIRE A BUSINESS IN GERMANY

Recognized Forms of Business Organizations..7
BERND TREMML and BERNARD BUECKER

The Acquisition of Closely Held Companies...31
BERND TREMML

Valuation of Business Enterprises..49
BERND TREMML

PART II
SPECIALIZED LAWS IMPACTING THE FORMATION, ACQUISITION AND OPERATION OF A BUSINESS IN GERMANY

Key Aspects of German Tax Law..57
HANS J. GORISS

Aspects of German Labor Law...69
WOLF D. SCHENK

Residence Work and Permits..81
MICHAEL WENDLER

Distribution Agreements..89
MICHAEL BIHLER

Computer Law..103
MICHAEL KARGER

Electronic Commerce..109
RAIMUND E. WALCH

Protection of Internet Domain Names..115
WOLFGANG C. LEONTI

Notaries in Germany..121
CHRISTIAN R. WOLF

Real-Estate Property Law in Germany..133
CHRISTIAN R. WOLF

The Law of Bankruptcy and Security Interests....................................145
REINHARD NACKE

Enforcement of Rights and Claims / Arbitration..................................155
REINHARD NACKE

Institutions of the European Community..163
BERND TREMML

Antitrust Law in the European Community..177
BERND TREMML and ANDREAS MEISTERERNST

Unfair Terms in Consumer Contracts in the European Community...............191
BERND TREMML and ANDREAS MEISTERERNST

The PCT and the Enforcement of Patents in Europe.................................203
KAY RUPPRECHT

Trademark Protection in Germany and Europe..253
EUGEN POPP

List of Authors..327

Glossary of German Terms and Abbreviations....................................329

Introduction

Overview of the German Legal System and its Role in Light of Germany´s Membership in the European Community

Foreigners interested in starting a business or investing in Germany are generally attracted by the prospect of expanding into other European markets from there because of Germany's membership in the EC, but have concerns about the implications of the dual European and German legal systems. They may wonder whether or not a German venture requires familiarization with two, often conflicting bodies of law, or if businesses in Germany frequently have to deal with administrative authorities at both the national and international levels with regard to the same transaction. The answer to such questions is "no". Given the structure of the European Community (EC) and particularly the manner in which EC institutions pass laws, an investment in Germany does not involve investments in a legal quagmire.

As a fundamental principle, the European Community and its institutions possess the power to pass legislation concerning only those areas in which an express delegation of national authority exists. For this reason alone, large numbers of regulatory areas remain outside of EC control. For example, most civil, criminal and administrative laws remain the sole province of the Member States. In general, EC authority is limited to those regulatory areas which are essential to the establishment of a common market. Furthermore, the laws the EC has passed have tended to take the form of "directives". As will be explained in detail in the Chapter Institutions of the European Community, directives do not, as a general principal, take effect until after they have been incorporated into national law. This special characteristic of directives is intended to give the Member States the flexibility of choosing the manner in which the objectives of a directive become law in their own country, the manner that is most compatible with their particular legal system. For individuals and business enterprises alike, it is often not easy to recognize whether or not a national law is based on a European directive. In sum, EC directives do *not* constitute an overlay of regulations which investors must familiarize themselves with separately, but rather comprise an integral part of a Member State's national law.

Much the same applies to those areas in which the EC has enacted a type of legislation known as a "regulation". A regulation does not require incorporation into national law in order to be effective, but as a rule is implemented by the national authorities. For example, if a German administrative authority applies an EC regulation in its dealings with German residents and they feel an error has been made, they can take action only against the national authority and, in doing so, usually operate solely within the German administrative or judicial systems.

For these reasons, the direct effect of European Community law on German residents or businesses is relatively small. However, that is not to say that the EC's influence should be downplayed. The numerous areas of law impacting the establishment and operation of businesses in Germany are often reflective of EC law. Nevertheless, for the most part EC laws have been incorporated into national law and are subject to Germany's legal system. And it is within this system that foreign investors will predominantly conduct their business transactions.

For the most part, Germany's legal system is stable and smooth working. It is based on the Continental European legal tradition as opposed to Anglo-Saxon law upon which the U.S. legal system is based. The primary difference between the two systems is that the Continental European legal system is based on the codification of laws as opposed to "case law". In accordance with the Continental tradition, the German legal system consists essentially of written laws. Nearly all potential regulatory areas are the subject of formal and detailed codification. Many of Germany's legal codes are the final product of literally decades of careful deliberation and refinement. This offers foreign entrepreneurs and investors considerable advantages. German law is so clearly structured and transparent that contract terms can be standardized to a very large extent. Since all the standard practices and regulations governing the conduct of business are codified in the German Civil Code (BGB or "Bürgerliches Gesetzbuch"), the terms and provisions of the BGB automatically apply, if no special terms are agreed upon between the parties. In other words, contracts drafted in the United States typically contain detailed statements of all the terms agreed to by the parties and more; contracts in Germany tend to be considerably shorter, which lowers their drafting costs accordingly.

As in the United States, it is the task of the courts to interpret the written law. Because a number of German codes are more than a hundred years old, the case law pertaining to certain individual provisions of them is very extensive. The courts have the primary task of interpreting the statutes, regulations and Constitution, and they also play a role in filling in the gaps of laws where necessary. However, the reliance on precedence or case law plays a much smaller role in the German legal system than in American jurisprudence, since German laws are so explicitly detailed and codified.

The sharp differentiation between the various areas of law in Germany and the separate codification of them have led to a strict division of subject-matter jurisdiction among the different types of courts. As in the United States, there are separate civil courts responsible for deciding legal disputes among private persons, and there are criminal courts for ruling on criminal prosecutions brought by the State against individuals. In contrast to the U.S. legal system, there are also separate court systems for administrative matters or legal disputes involving measures taken by public authorities against residents and for labor-law and financial matters. Germany has a special body of law governing taxation and a court system specialized in trying tax cases as well. It should also be noted that, in contrast to the judicial system in the United States, there is no duality between state and federal courts. In Germany, their areas of jurisdiction are clearly kept separate. Each of the various court systems has its own supreme court. The Constitutional Court is the final authority above each of them.

The judges who serve on the courts are judges by profession and are specialized in one type of law. They do not rotate from one type of court to another as U.S. judges do, but generally serve on only one type of court throughout their careers. They are not elected but rather appointed by the government of the particular state of Germany where the court is located. Germany does not make use of the jury process. In certain cases, however, the judges are assisted in making their decisions by common citizens who do not necessarily have a legal background of any kind ("Laienrichter"), and who are chosen to serve on the court for a limited time period.

Regardless of which type of court is handling a particular dispute, the parties' trial preparation consists primarily in the drafting and presentation of legal briefs in which evidence is presented and the issues in dispute are argued. In so doing, the parties rely on the court's special procedural rules. Each type of court has its own rules determining its case procedure, the kind of evidence it will admit, etc. The courts make extensive use of independent public-appointed experts ("Sachverständiger"), whose professional input almost always influences the ruling to a very large extent and often determines the outcome of a case. Due in part to the judicial system's reliance on the parties' briefs, the reports of independent experts and other written submissions, the trial itself (in particular the in-court presentation of live testimony and other evidence) takes considerably less time and involves less costs than U.S. court proceedings. This will be discussed extensively in the Chapter "Unfair Terms in Consumer Contracts in the European Community". With the exception of criminal cases, most trials last no longer than one or two days.

An overview of Germany's legal system would not be complete without a few comments about the governmental administrative apparatus. The Federal Republic of Germany is, as its name expresses, a federal state. That means that legislative powers are divided between the federal government and each of the country's sixteen states. The most important areas of law are the exclusive domain of the federal government. However, because the individual states of Germany are generally vested with the authority to enforce federal laws and the majority of the administrative offices necessary to accomplish this task are established by the states, the states have an important influence on the interpretation and development of federal laws. Similar to the state subdivisions in the U.S., the states of Germany are comprised of districts ("Bezirke"), counties ("Landkreise") and communities ("Gemeinde"), whereby a striking difference between the two administrative systems is in many cases the higher degree of authority and competence exercised by the more local and regional units in Germany, which often allows them to take action and make decisions affecting both residents and businesses more efficiently and quickly.

In conclusion, it can be said that the legal system in Germany is precisely structured. Its areas of court jurisdiction are clearly defined and its laws so explicitly codified that overlapping and ambiguities are largely ruled out. This makes it relatively easy for foreigners to orient themselves within the system. They will find the drafting of business contracts to be a relatively swift and inexpensive process as opposed to the process in the U.S., where effort and costs generally tend to be considerably higher, because its laws allow a vastly wider degree of interpretation and all the terms of agreement must be contained in the contract itself. In contrast, the terms of the German Civil Code (BGB) regulating contracts automatically come into effect in the absence of other terms. Contracts between business partners are necessary only if and insofar as the parties wish to agree to terms that differ from the standard provisions of the BGB. As it pertains to business operations, the clearly structured German system encourages fair, free trade and the minimization of conflicts.

PART I

HOW TO ESTABLISH OR ACQUIRE A BUSINESS IN GERMANY

Recognized Forms of Business Organizations

Bernd Tremml and Bernard Buecker

I. Overview of Business Forms Available

The Federal Republic of Germany recognizes a variety of business organizational forms. Each of them has its own particular justification for existence based on specific economic considerations. It is therefore important for foreign business people who intend to establish a company in Germany to evaluate the various business forms available – for instance, in terms of their organizational structure, liability and methods of taxation – and determine which of them is most suitable for the enterprise they have in mind.

German law basically differentiates between business organizational forms which have the characteristic of a partnership ("Personengesellschaft" is the general term for partnership) and those which have the characteristics of a corporation. In contrast to the partnership forms, the corporate ones each possess the status of a separate legal entity. Another major distinction is that, as a general rule, the shareholders of businesses organized as corporations possess limited liability equal to the amount of capital they have invested in the business, whereas a partnership's creditors can lay claim to the personal assets of each of the partners if necessary.

The corporate forms are:

- the GmbH, which is an abbreviation for "Gesellschaft mit beschränkter Haftung" and means "limited liability company,"
- the AG, which is an abbreviation for "Aktiengesellschaft" and means "stock corporation."

The partnership forms are:

- the GbR, which is an abbreviation for "Gesellschaft des bürgerlichen Rechts" and possesses characteristics of a joint venture,
- the OHG, which is an abbreviation for "Offene Handelsgesellschaft" and possesses characteristics of a general partnership,
- the KG, which is an abbreviation for "Kommanditgesellschaft" and possesses characteristics of a limited partnership,"
- the "Einzelunternehmen," or "sole proprietorship,"
- the "Stille Gesellschaft," or "silent partnership."

In addition, Germany recognizes two types of business organizational forms which are a mixture of the corporate and partnership forms:

- the GmbH & Co. KG
- and -
- the KGaA, which is an abbreviation for "Kommanditgesellschaft auf Aktien" and is a type of limited partnership combined with stock.

The most common business form used in Germany today is the GmbH (limited liability company). This is due to the fact that a GmbH is relatively easy to establish and operate and is an appropriate organizational form for almost all types of business. There are a comparatively smaller number of stock corporations in Germany since this form is more suitable for very large enterprises such as banks and insurance companies. The partnership forms are less often found among larger enterprises because their owners or participants wish to avoid being personally and fully liable for all of the debts of the business.

II. Corporate Forms of Business Organizations

A. Limited liability company ["Gesellschaft mit beschränkter Haftung" (GmbH)]

1. Nature

The legal basis for the limited liability company (GmbH) is contained in the GmbH Act (GmbHG), first adopted in 1898 and substantially revised in 1980. As an incorporated business entity, the GmbH itself possesses rights and obligations and is liable for all of its debts to the full extent of its corporate assets. It also may pursue and defend legal actions in its own name (Par. 13 GmbHG).

In the GmbH's articles of incorporation ("Gesellschaftssvertrag"), the shareholders set the amount of nominal capital which is to be paid into the corporation by each of them. The individual shareholders are then liable for the company's obligations only in the amount of their committed capital investment. The GmbH cannot enforce an obligation against any shareholder in excess of that amount. Under German law, the shares of a GmbH cannot be quoted on stock exchanges.

The articles of incorporation can make special regulations for the individual needs and requirements of the company and its owners to the extent they do not conflict with the provisions of the GmbH Act.

2. Regular formation procedure

A GmbH can be established for any lawful purpose by one or more people. Its founder(s), or initial shareholders, may be natural persons or legal entities, residents or non-residents, German or foreign citizens. The law does not limit the number of shareholders who may participate in a GmbH.

The structure and operations of a GmbH are governed by its articles of incorporation. The first step in the process of forming a GmbH is the drafting of its articles by its founders (shareholders). The articles must be signed by each of the shareholders and approved by a notary. In addition to a statement of the name, location and purpose of the company, the articles must state the total amount of the nominal capital ("Stammkapital") and the percent or share of it that each shareholder has agreed to pay in return for shares in the business. The name chosen for the company must directly relate to the company's purpose or contain the names of at least one of the shareholders. It is further required that the company name contain the designation "GmbH" ["company with limited liability." (See Par. 4 GmbHG)].

The company comes into actual existence and is able to reap the benefits of having its liabilities limited to its assets only after it has been registered in the commercial register ("Handelsregister") located in the district court of the company's place of business. Before that time, the founding partners are personally liable for their own business transactions during the GmbH's "formation stage" (Par. 11 GmbHG).

Entry into the commercial register requires the submission of a formal application by the managing director(s) with all the necessary attachments, including:

- the articles of incorporation,
- original documents expressing the authority of any person to act on behalf of the founding shareholders (power of attorney) or a certified copy of the same,
- a confirmation of the appointment of the managing director(s) if the appointment(s) are not stated in the articles of incorporation,
- specimen signatures of the managing director(s),
- a statement as to whether the managing director(s) are personally empowered to represent the company or whether they can do so only in conjunction with others,
- a list of the shareholders, including their full name, profession and address as well as the share amount of the nominal capital investment guaranteed by each of them,
- the assurance that the combined amount of cash and non-cash assets required by law before the GmbH can be legally registered has indeed been paid into the company and is available for use by its management. (The law requires that at least 25% of each share and 50% of the nominal capital must be paid in before the company can be registered unless non-cash investments have been arranged and agreed upon).
- In the case of a one-person-GmbH the cash and non-cash contained in the company must equal € 25,000.-- [twenty-five thousand Euro] at the time of registration.
- Assurance that the total amount of investment shares (the nominal capital of the business, or "Stammkapital") equals at least € 25,000.--.

- A special non-cash investment report verifying the actual value of any non-cash investments.

If all of the above requirements are met, the GmbH will be registered and the registration automatically announced in a nation-wide publication.

3. Capital Structure

a)   Share capital

The 1980 reform of the GmbH Act raised the statutory minimum amount of capital that must be invested by the owners in return for shares to € 25,000.-- and the minimum that each single shareholder must invest to € 500.--.

The capital may be paid in cash, in kind (non-cash) or in a combination of the two. When a non-cash investment has been agreed to, a special report has to be presented so that the actual worth of the non-cash capital investments can be evaluated by the registry court.

It is not required that the nominal capital (upwards of € 25,000.--) be divided into equal amounts. Each share can be ascribed a value equal to the investment the individual shareholder has agreed to make and must be stated in the articles of incorporation. Shares can be subsequently split into units of less value and transferred to others, however, only with the approval of the company (Par. 17 GmbHG).

b)   Transfer of shares

The shares of a GmbH are freely transferable and inheritable (Par. 15 GmbHG). However, the articles of incorporation can stipulate that the transfer is conditional upon the consent of the GmbH or the other shareholders. A change of shareholders does not affect the continuing existence of the company. The company can acquire its own shares only if the share capital is fully paid-up, sufficient funds beyond the stated share capital exist, and the statutory reserves for its own shares can be maintained. In order to be valid, the transfer of a share (in whole or in part) must be executed before a notary.

c)   Increase and reduction of nominal capital

The shareholders can increase or reduce the nominal capital figure as cited in the articles of incorporation, however, only in so far as they do not reduce it below the legally required minimum of € 25,000.--. The decision to raise or lower the capital value of a company requires a vote of three-fourths of the shareholder votes cast unless the articles of incorporation provide otherwise. The amendment to the articles of incorporation must be filed with the court so that the corresponding changes can be made in the commercial register (Par. 54 GmbHG).

In the event that the nominal capital amount is to be increased, each of the shareholders must present a notarized statement that they are willing to raise their personal investments proportionate to the overall increase and according to the new value of their shares (Par. 55 GmbHG). Moreover, new shareholders may be added to the GmbH at the time of an increase in the GmbH's nominal capital value.

In order that a reduction in the nominal amount of share capital take effect, the shareholder resolution authorizing it must be announced in the public journals officially responsible for publishing commercial-register matters. Any creditors who oppose the reduction are entitled to have their outstanding claims satisfied. The law proscribes that one year must have elapsed after the final public announcement before the GmbH can file an application to have the decreased capital amount officially noted in the commercial register (Par. 58 GmbHG).

4. Representation and management

Representation and management of a GmbH result from the cooperation of the following official corporate bodies: managing director(s), shareholders and supervisory board.

a) Managing director ("Geschäftsführer")

Because the managing director is the only person entitled to represent the company in and out of court (Par. 35 GmbHG), the GmbH must - either in the articles of incorporation or by separate resolution - appoint one or more managing director(s) in order for the company to be able to act. The managing director must be a natural person with unlimited capacity to enter into legal transactions (Par. 6 GmbHG) and may but need not be a shareholder of the company.

German corporate law differentiates between the external authority of the managing director and his or her internal rights and obligations. This means that, although the authority of the managing director may be and often is restricted by the provisions of the articles of incorporation, shareholder resolutions or the managing director's employment contract, such restrictions are of no effect concerning the managing director's interactions with third parties.

The managing director of a GmbH has the legal obligation to perform his or her duties with the "diligence of a prudent businessperson." And even though the business transactions of the managing director(s) are valid with respect to third parties, if the directors violate their obligations to perform their duties carefully, they are jointly and severally liable to the company for any resulting damage. Under the general provisions of German tort law, the managing director's personal liability for wrongful acts committed against third persons is limited to situations in which he or she has personally acted.

The other situations in which the managing director can be held personally liable to third parties are:

1. if in the registration of a newly formed company the managing director has officially stated that one-fourth (or more) of the share capital has been paid by the shareholders and this is not the case (Par. 64 GmbHG) or
2. the managing director fails to declare bankruptcy within three weeks after he or she has learned or could have learned that the company is either unable to pay its debts and/or that its liabilities exceed its assets.

If the managing director has been appointed by a shareholder resolution, the appointment can be withdrawn by a new resolution. If the managing director has been appointed in the articles of incorporation, then, based on the rule that every change of the articles requires a 75% majority vote, he or she can be removed only by a three-quarters vote of the voting shareholders. Entry into the commercial register is necessary for all changes affecting the identity or representation authority of the managing director(s) (Par. 39 GmbHG).

b)   *Shareholders ("Gesellschafter")*

The rights of the shareholders within the corporation, particularly with respect to the management of the business, derive from the articles of incorporation in so far as they are consistent with statutory provisions (Par. 45 GmbHG). All shareholder resolutions must be adopted in a general meeting. Unless otherwise provided in the articles of incorporation, the managing director calls the shareholder meetings by sending registered letters to the shareholders at least one week in advance of the meeting. In their meetings, the shareholders are entitled to reach decisions which concern and impact the day-to-day operations of the business and to exercise complete discretion in issuing management instructions. There are particular issues which can be resolved only in a shareholder meeting. They include the appointment and dismissal of management, the granting and cancellation of "Prokuras" (full powers of attorney as defined in Par. 48 HGB, the Commercial Code), the institution of claims for damages against the managing director or shareholders, the approval of financial statements and the agreement to the manner in which any dividends are to be distributed.

In order to be effective, shareholder decisions require a majority approval of those shareholders who participated in the vote (Par. 47 GmbHG). Proxy voting is allowed. If all company shares are controlled by one shareholder, that shareholder must prepare and sign minutes without undue delay following the passage of a resolution.

Shareholders have the right, upon request, to be informed of business affairs by the company's management and to inspect the company books and records (Par. 51 a GmbHG). If management believes, however, that providing specific information could substantially impair business operations or otherwise be detrimental to the company, it can refuse the request. Any shareholder who has not been given the requested information or permission to inspect the books is entitled to file a court action seeking judicial resolution of the conflict.

c) *Supervisory board ("Aufsichtsrat")*

German law does not always require that a GmbH has a supervisory board. Any decision to establish such a board, however, must be reflected in the articles of incorporation. A GmbH must have a supervisory board if it is a capital-investment company. There are also cases in which the "Co-Determination Law" ("Mitbestimmungsgesetz") makes such a board mandatory. This law, which requires that certain companies allow employee participation in management, will be described in more detail later. One variation of it is the Coal-and-Steel Co-Determination Law ("Montan-Mitbestimmungsgesetz"), which applies to GmbHs that are engaged in coal or steel production. The supervisory board must consist of an equal number of shareholder and labor representatives and a neutral person. The neutral person may but need not be the chairman of the board.

Under the German Co-Determination Law, GmbHs with more than 2,000 employees must have a supervisory board consisting of an equal number of shareholder and labor representatives.

Par. 76 of the Business Unit Constitution Law ["Betriebsverfassungsgesetz (BetrVG) 1952"] requires that GmbHs with more than five hundred employees install a supervisory board comprised of a two-third majority of shareholder-elected members and a one-third minority of employee-elected members. This Paragraph of the BetrVG 1952 is still in force (Par. 129, sec. 1 BetrVG).

Whether a supervisory board has been created at the discretion of the shareholders or is required by law, its primary role is to represent the GmbH when dealing with the managing director(s).

5. Accounting and auditing

The managing director is responsible for ensuring that the GmbH has proper account books and balance sheets. Accounting and auditing laws pertaining to GmbHs are contained in the Commercial Code (HGB), the GmbH Act (GmbHG) and the tax laws as modified in 1986 by the Accounting Directives Act ("Bilanzrichtliniengesetz").

In accordance with sound accounting principles, the company must keep proper account books showing all transactions, assets and liabilities. At the date of the GmbH's formation and at the end of each financial year, an inventory and a balance sheet must be prepared. These financial records must be kept for ten years; commercial correspondence and invoices must be kept for six years.

In terms of the exact type of accounting requirements, German law differentiates between small, medium and large companies. Which of these size categories a company falls into depends on its profit, sales and number of employees. If the company is a so-called "large company," its accounts must be audited by a certified public accountant ("Wirtschaftsprüfer"), and its annual financial statement, its management report as well as the proposals and decisions on the distribution of profits must be made public according to the Accounting Directives Act. Mid-sized companies, on the other hand, may obtain the services of a certified bookkeeper ("vereidigter Buchprüfer"). There are no laws requiring audits in small companies.

6. Liquidation

a)   *Reasons for dissolution*

A GmbH can be dissolved at any time by a resolution passed by three-fourths of the shareholders participating in the vote unless otherwise stipulated in the articles of incorporation. Furthermore, upon the application of shareholders holding at least 10 % of the share capital, the company can be dissolved by court order. The issuance of such an order requires that the court finds either that it has become impossible for the GmbH to accomplish its purpose or that other substantial reasons stemming from the prevailing conditions in the company exist which are substantial enough to justify its dissolution.

Bankruptcy proceedings are another cause of the dissolution of a GmbH. If, however, the bankruptcy proceedings are terminated after the conclusion of a compulsory settlement or upon motion of a debtor, then the shareholders may elect not to dissolve the company.

b)   *Insolvency and liquidation*

When a GmbH becomes insolvent and the managing director has filed a declaration of bankruptcy, the court appoints liquidators. When a GmbH is dissolved for a reason other than the initiation of bankruptcy proceedings, the managing director automatically assumes the role of liquidator. During the process of liquidation, the company must be clearly identified and recognizable as being in a state of liquidation.

The liquidator's duties are to terminate current business, discharge all obligations of the dissolved company, collect its accounts receivable and convert all assets into cash. It is also his or her duty to prepare a balance sheet at the beginning of the liquidation process, once every year thereafter and at the conclusion of the process.

Except in the case of bankruptcy proceedings, the dissolution of the company must be registered in the commercial register, and a notice requesting creditors to file any claims must be published three times. The GmbH's assets may not be distributed to the shareholders until the expiration of one year following the third publication. At this time (and assuming the liquidation process has otherwise reached the point where the assets can be distributed), all remaining assets are to be distributed among the shareholders in proportion to their share interests.

As mentioned above, all the books and records of a company must be retained for ten years. Following a liquidation process, those documents are to be delivered to a former shareholder or third party for safe-keeping.

7. Conclusion

The limited liability company with its simple formation procedure and structure is the most suitable legal form for foreign businesses wanting to limit the risks of their activities to the amount of capital they are willing to invest in the Federal Republic of Germany.

B. Stock corporations ["Aktiengesellschaft" (AG)]

1. Nature

The formation and constitution of an AG are governed by legislation entitled the "Aktiengesetz" (AktG). Similar to the GmbH, an AG is an incorporated business entity with its own legal personality. Only its corporate assets are available to satisfy the liability of the company to its creditors. The stockholders ("Aktionäre") bear no personal liability.

The nominal capital ("Grundkapital") of an AG is divided into stocks ("Aktien") which, unlike the shares of a GmbH, may but need not be quoted on the stock exchange. The stocks are freely transferable, which makes the occupations and backgrounds of the individual stockholders completely irrelevant.

The stock corporation is the best business organizational form in Germany for large enterprises. It offers the best legal basis for an international business.

2. Formation and registration

An AG can be formed by one or more persons who are willing to subscribe for stock in return for their capital investment. These persons may be individuals or corporate entities, residents of Germany or non-residents.

At the beginning of the formation procedure, the founders have to draft articles of incorporation ("Satzung") which primarily must include: the AG's name, location, business objective and amount of stock capital (face amount as well as the number of stock certificates issued and their initial subscription price). The company's name usually reflects its activities and must be followed by the acronym "AG." In most cases, the designated seat of the corporation must be the place where the company intends to maintain an establishment, where its management is to be located or from where the administration of the company will be conducted.

The articles of incorporation must have been recorded by a German notary before the corporation can be officially formed and registered. The founders appoint the first supervisory board ("Aufsichtsrat"), which is then empowered to appoint the initial board of management ("Vorstand"). In addition to these two organs, the stockholders themselves, who are empowered to take action in general meetings known as "Hauptversammlungen," comprise the third organ of an AG. The members of the supervisory board and initial board of management are charged with examining the act of formation and rendering a written formation report. The formation must also be examined by one or more court-appointed formation auditors if one of the following circumstances exist:

- a member of the board of management or the supervisory board is also one of the founders of the corporation,
- a member of the board of management or supervisory board had stock earmarked for him- or herself, either directly or indirectly, during the formation stage,
- a member of the board of management or the supervisory board will receive a special advantage
- or the formation involves non-cash investments or related non-cash acquisitions.

The AG must apply for registration in the commercial register ("Handelsregister") of the local court responsible for the district in which the company is located. The application must be signed by all the founders as well as by each member of the board of management and the supervisory board. All underlying documents, including the articles of incorporation, must accompany the application for registration.

The registration will be granted only if the required percentage of the initial stock subscription has been duly paid-in. That amounts to at least 25% of the par value of the stocks in the case of cash subscriptions and 100% in the case of non-cash investments.

The AG comes into existence as a legal entity upon entry in the commercial register (Par. 41 AktG). Until that time, anyone who acts on behalf of the corporation is personally liable.

3. Capital structure

a) Stock capital

The statutory minimum capital amount, which must be paid-in at the time of registration, is fifty-thousand Euro (€ 50,000.--). The capital is divided into par value shares, which can have a nominal value of at least € 1.-- and each share has to be named in a full Euro amount. The face value of the shares and their total amount must be expressed in Euro.

Membership in an AG is documented by stock certificates. Both common stock ("Stammaktien") and preferred stock ("Vorzugsaktien") may be issued either as bearer stock certificates ("Inhaberaktien") or as registered stock certificates ("Namensaktien"). In general, one share of stock entitles its owner to one vote on issues addressed in the stockholder meeting ("Hauptversammlung"). Preferred stock, however, may be stipulated as non-voting stock. Bearer stock is the most common type of stock issued by German stock corporations. The shares cannot be issued before they have been registered and the purchaser has paid-in the full issue price.

b)   Transfer of stockholdings

Bearer stock can be freely transferred and any attempt to limit that transferability is strictly prohibited. The transfer of registered stock, however, can be limited with the consent of the company, provided its articles of incorporation explicitly allow for such regulation in order to guarantee that the company maintains control and influence over its members and thus over its own operations.

In practice, bearer stock is usually offered by banks and the original certificates left deposited with them. The banks then collect the dividends on behalf of the investors. Stockholders who own a relatively small number of a corporation's total shares generally tend to give proxies to their banks to exercise their voting rights. Such proxies are valid for a maximum of fifteen months at a time and can be withdrawn at any time within that period (Par. 135 AktG).

c)   Increase and decrease of nominal capital

An increase or decrease in the nominal capital amount requires a resolution passed by a three-fourth majority of the votes cast at a stockholder meeting. An application for an increase or decrease must be filed with the commercial register. The new nominal capital amount becomes effective at the moment of registration.

The easiest way to increase the share capital is by issuing new shares against contributions, which may be in cash or non-cash. In the case of non-cash investments, the property, the name of the person from whom the AG acquires it and the nominal amount of the stock shares granted in return for it must be noted in the shareholder resolution to increase the company's nominal capital value on (Par. 183 AktG).

Other ways to acquire new capital are through the issuance of convertible bonds, profit-sharing bonds or profit participating certificates.

4.   Representation and management

a)   Board of management ("Vorstand")

The board of management consists of one or more persons. The management board of a AG with a stock capital of more than three million Euro generally must consist of at least two persons. In order to maintain the independence of both of the boards, a member of the board of management cannot serve as a member of the supervisory board and vice versa. The members of the board of management are usually appointed by the supervisory board for a period of five years.

The board of management is responsible for managing the business, handling all general administrative matters and representing the corporation in its dealing with third parties as well as in all judicial actions. The power of its authority may not be limited in its dealings with third parties. It is possible, however, to provide in the article of incorporation that certain actions require the approval of another organ of the AG.

The members of the board of management are each required to act with the diligence and care of a prudent and conscientious manager. Transactions entered into in violation of this standard of care, while valid and binding on the AG, make the members of the board of management personally liable to the corporation for any damage it has sustained as a result of their careless behavior. Board members cannot be held responsible for having breached their standard of care, however, if they have acted on a valid resolution of the stockholders.

b)   Supervisory board ("Aufsichtsrat")

In contrast to the law governing the GmbH (GmbHG), the law pertaining to the AG (AktG) requires that every AG establish a supervisory board. This board's primary functions are the appointment and dismissal of board of management ("Vorstand"), supervision of executive management, approval of the financial statements prepared by the executive managers and approval of any special transactions enumerated in the articles of incorporation.

The size of the supervisory board may vary between three and twenty-one members, depending on the size of the corporation. In AGs which employ less than 2,000 persons, the size of the board depends on the nominal value of share capital of the company. If the value of share capital is 1.5 million Euro or less, the law requires a board consisting of three but no more than nine members. If the capital value lies between 1.5 and ten million Euro, the law requires that between nine and fifteen members be appointed. Corporations with a capital value of more than ten million Euro are required to appoint between fifteen and twenty-one members.

German law gives employees of larger corporations the right to vote for a portion of the supervisory board and/or to serve on it through representation. The membership of employees on the supervisory board is generally dependent on the overall number of people employed by the corporation. Certain industries have special regulations governing employee participation.

c) *Stockholder meeting ("Hauptversammlung")*

The general meeting of the stockholders must be held annually and within eight months after the end of the business year. The meeting must take place in Germany and generally at the place where the AG has its registered office. In addition to the general meeting, extraordinary stockholder meetings can be called by the supervisory board or by stockholders holding at least five per cent of the common stock.

The stockholders, acting in concert at their general meeting, are responsible for the appointment and removal of their supervisory board representatives, the election of auditors, the formal approval of actions taken by the supervisory board and the board of management during the preceding business year and decisions concerning the distribution of profits. The most important of the statutory powers that are the exclusive rights of the stockholders are the rights to

- amend the articles of incorporation,
- reduce or increase the stock capital,
- liquidate the AG.

5. Accounting and auditing

Legal requirements imposed on an AG's accounting system are primarily found in the Commercial Code (HGB, part two), the AktG and the tax laws. The second part of Commercial Code came into effect in 1986 through the Accounting Directives Act ("Bilanzrichtliniengesetz"), which was instituted in compliance with the European Community law stipulating that the Fourth, Seventh and Eighth EC Directives be incorporated into national law.

Books and records must be kept in accordance with the principles of proper accounting ("Grundsätze ordnungsgemässer Buchführung"). These principles are derived from a variety of sources and are constantly being developed, expanded and interpreted. Requirements of the Commercial Code include:

- the maintenance of books and records in a modern language and the notation of currency figures in Euro,
- the preparation of annual financial reports,
- the retention of account books, other financial records, invoices and correspondences for a certain prescribed period of time.

The tax laws require that the AG's accounting system be maintained in such a way that an independent expert can obtain an overview of its assets, liabilities and business operations within a reasonably short time. The account records must be kept and archived in Germany. Usually the company's goods must be inventoried and the results of the inventory recorded in the balance sheet with validity as of the date on which the balance sheet is legally due.

Further requirements contained in the HGB as well as the AktG regarding the preparation and presentation of financial reports include:

- maintenance and reflection in the balance sheet of a statutory reserve fund equal in amount to the value of at least ten per cent of the common stock,
- use of a prescribed format for the balance sheet and income statement,
- compliance with certain rules pertaining to the valuation of assets, liabilities, and stockholder equities; for example, the whole share capital must be stated at par value and liabilities must be indicated in terms of the amounts due,
- and compliance with specific depreciation rules.

The Commercial Code requires that the financial statements of mid-size and large stock corporations be audited by a Certified Public Accountant appointed by the stockholders. Following the audit, the accountant must issue an opinion whether the accounting system, the financial statements and the annual report comply with the law and the corporation's own articles of incorporation. In small stock corporations, the financial statements must be approved only by the supervisory board.

6. Liquidation

a) Reasons for dissolution

Stock corporations may be dissolved

- when a pre-planned period of existence set forth in the articles of association expires,
- upon decision of a three-forth majority of the voting stockholders
- or if an adjudication of bankruptcy is declared.

Further grounds for dissolution include:

- court denial of a bankruptcy petition stemming from its estimation that the corporation lacks enough assets to cover the costs of bankruptcy proceedings,
- a determination by the court of registry that a defect in the articles of incorporation exist
- or the corporation is uncapitalized.

The articles of incorporation may state yet further reasons and conditions under which the corporation is to be dissolved. When a ground for dissolution exists, the board of management must apply for the registration of the dissolution of the corporation in the commercial register.

The following extraordinary circumstances may also result in a formal end to the AG's existence:

- corporate merger ("Verschmelzung"),
- and the transformation of the AG into another type of business organization ("Umwandlung").

In contrast to the grounds for dissolution discussed above, however, the occurrence of one of these types of extraordinary circumstances does not result in the liquidation of the AG, which continues to pursue its original purpose, albeit in another form.

b)   Insolvency and liquidation

The liquidation procedure of an AG is clearly prescribed by law. Basically, two kinds of liquidation proceedings are recognized. When insolvency is the cause for the dissolution, the liquidation procedures to be followed are those set forth in the Insolvency Act ["Insolvenzordnung" (InsO), Par. 174 f.]. This law grants special protections to creditors. For example, if the board of management determines that the losses of an AG exceed its stated capital or the corporation cannot meet its obligations because of insolvency, it must file a petition in bankruptcy with the local court within three weeks. Failure of the board to do so can make its members personally liable and subject to criminal prosecution. Creditors of the corporation also have the right to file a petition for its bankruptcy. The liquidators are appointed by the court. If insolvency is not the basis for the corporation's dissolution, the AG must be liquidated according to the procedures delineated in the Stock Corporation Law (Par. 264 AktG). In accordance with these procedures, the members of the board of management serve as liquidators unless the articles of incorporation or a resolution of the stockholders provide otherwise.

The liquidators have to advise creditors of the dissolution of the AG by way of a notice published three consecutive times in the required newspaper or periodical. In the notice they must clearly request that any and all creditors submit their claims. All creditor claims including those of the tax authorities must be settled before any of the corporation's assets can be distributed among its stockholders. The distribution of remaining assets cannot occur earlier than one year after the third public notice to the creditors. Once the liquidation is complete and the final financial statements have been prepared, the liquidators must apply for the entry of the closing of the corporation in the commercial register.

III. Partnership Forms of Business Organizations

A. Civil-law partnership ["Gesellschaft des bürgerlichen Rechts" (also referred to as "GbR" or "BGB-Gesellschaft")]

The civil-law partnership does not possess the status of a separate legal entity and is not registered in the commercial register. It must act, sue or be sued by naming all its members. But following a decision of the German Supreme Court a civil-law partnership can also be sued under the companies' name.

The GbR may not be used as the organizational form for a business which falls under the definition of a "Handelsgewerbe," or commercial trade enterprise owned and operated by individuals who are merchants by profession. It is most often used to govern relationships between several partners in a professional society engaged in the provision of professional services, such as a law office or any other group of independent professionals working in a joint office.

To form a GbR, at least two partners must enter into a partnership agreement ("Gesellschaftsvertrag"). This agreement need not be in writing, and the parties are usually free to agree to the terms they see fit, even if such terms are different from the provisions of the Civil Code (BGB) pertaining to this type of business. The law requires only that the partners agree to the purpose to be promoted and combine their efforts in pursuance of a common economic objective (Par. 705 BGB).

The assets of a GbR are held by all partners jointly ("Gesamthandsvermögen", i.e., "joint ownership"). The assets cannot be disposed of without agreement between all the partners (Par. 719 BGB). The partners cannot convey their membership and share of the assets to another person without the agreement of the other partners or unless provisions to the contrary were made in the partnership agreement.

All of the partners normally have the same rights. They jointly share in the profits and losses and equally participate in any liquidation proceedings. All partners have equal voting rights in the partnership meetings and are able to represent the partnership as a whole in their dealings with third parties only through joint participation of the other partners unless the partnership agreement provides for another form of representation. For example, if the partnership agreement so allows, the partners may appoint one or more managing partners and invest them with the authority to act on behalf of the partnership as a whole, according to the standard principles of representation, and to enter agreements with third parties that bind the company. According to the principle of self-organization, which applies here, a fully authorized manager must be a partner in the business.

The liability for obligations resulting from transactions conducted in the name of the partnership is carried by all the partners jointly and severally. Unless a contract with a given creditor provides otherwise, creditors with unsatisfied claims are entitled to sue the partners both as members of the GbR and as private individuals. In this manner, creditors can tap the assets of both the partnership and its individual members. Debtors of the partnership, however, may not set off any claims they might have against a single partner, against their liability to the partnership as a whole.

B. General partnership ["Offene Handelsgesellschaft"(OHG)]

The Commercial Code ("Handelsgesetzbuch" or HGB) makes provisions for the establishment of a partnership among merchants who wish to pursue a common commercial purpose under a common name (Par. 105 HGB). That organizational form is the simplest among merchants engaged in trade and is the counterpart of the GbR—it is to merchants what the GbR is to professionals. It can be chosen by merchants only, or by people who intend to operate a commercial trade ("Handelsgewerbe"). The Commercial Code clearly defines what constitutes a commercial trade and what types of business endeavors can be organized as one.

The OHG is structured similarly to the GbR and is not a separate legal entity. The partners own the partnership property jointly ("Gesamthandsvermögen"), and all of the partners, or "general partners," are subject to personal liability for the company's debts (Par. 128 HGB). The partners may be natural persons or legal entities. A legal entity may be partner in an OHG, however, only if it, too, is engaged in merchant trading and corresponds in all respects to what the law defines as a "Handelsgewerbe."

Persons forming an OHG do so typically out of a desire to achieve a true co-partnership, to which the partners devote both their labor and financial resources. Normally each partner has the authority to act on behalf of the business and enter binding agreements in its name, which allows for flexible operations. The unlimited liability of all the partners, which is a mandatory characteristic of partnerships, improves the chances of these types of companies receiving bank credit if and when required.

The intense nature of the relationship of the partners in an OHG requires that each partner have confidence and trust in the reliability and abilities of the other partner(s). When such confidence and mutual trust are present, the OHG is a good form in which to organize a small or a mid-size enterprise.

The OHG comes into existence through its registration in the commercial register. Even in the event that it is not registered, however, and a creditor issues a claim against it, the courts will rule that an OHG does indeed exist if a partnership agreement has been entered into and a transaction with a third party has taken place. The general provisions of the Commercial Code (HGB) apply to partnership agreements unless they contain contrary terms which are allowed under the Commercial Code.

The general partnership must be filed in the commercial register in notarized form. The application for the filing of the OHG must include the name, address and occupation of each partner, the company name and location as well as the date on which business will be commenced. All the partners must submit specimen signatures.

The company name of an OHG must contain the appendix "OHG" or „offene Handelsgesellschaft". Descriptive additions to the name are admissible, but they cannot be either misleading or confusing. Any change in the company name or location or in the identity of its partners must be registered in the commercial register.

Although it is not a legal entity, a general partnership can sue and be sued (Par. 124 HGB). Thus, a creditor of the OHG may sue the partnership itself under the company name as well as each of the partners individually. A private creditor of one of the partners, however, cannot file suit against the OHG itself.

At the end of each business year, the managing partners must prepare a balance sheet and have it approved and signed by all of the partners. The partnership agreement may require that this annual statement of accounts be approved at a meeting of the partners and/or examined by a public accountant. An OHG, like all other business enterprises, is obliged to conduct proper bookkeeping in accordance with the regulations of the Commercial Code (HGB).

Under the Commercial Code, reasons for dissolution of an OHG include a unanimous resolution of the partners, bankruptcy or a court decision. The partners can stipulate in their agreement other conditions under which the company can be dissolved. Should the stipulated conditions arise, any of the partners has the right to initiate dissolution proceedings by way of regular notice.

In the event that circumstances arise which make it unreasonable for the partnership to continue in existence, the law provides for the possibility to give extraordinary notice and subsequently file for special legal action seeking a dissolution order (Par. 133 HGB). The partner's right to seek such an order under extraordinary conditions cannot be restricted in the partnership agreement. Regardless of the reason for dissolution, the partnership agreement may contain a provision which allows the remaining partners to perpetuate the business.

C. Limited partnership ["Kommanditgesellschaft" (KG)]

The KG is a special form of an OHG. It, too, is formed by merchant partners for the purpose of operating a commercial business enterprise under a single company name. The rules governing the OHG (Par. 105 ff. HGB) are generally applicable to the KG unless modified by subsequent provisions of the Commercial Code (Par. 161 ff. HGB).

The main and most important difference between an OHG and a KG is that the KG consists of two different kinds of partners: personally liable partners ("Komplementäre") and limited partners ("Kommanditisten"). As their designations clearly indicate, the personally liable partners are liable for the debts of the company without any limitation. Their rights and duties correspond to those of an OHG partner. Normally, because they devote their labor and are subject to greater financial risk, the personally liable partners are responsible for the company's management and representation. The liability of the limited partners, on the other hand, is limited to the amount of their capital investments in the partnership. These contributions can be cash, non-cash equivalents or even in the form of a substantiated claim against the company.

A KG must consist of at least one personally liable partner and at least one limited partner. Other rules regarding the KG's formation are similar to the requirements for the establishment of an OHG except that the different rights and duties of the two types of partners must be observed, particularly in the partnership agreement.

German law strictly differentiates between the external representation of a company and its internal management. As a rule, the power of the personally liable partners to represent the firm externally cannot be restricted to certain types of transactions or by general limitations. The only type of restriction which is effective vis à vis third parties is a joint-representation provision in the partnership agreement, which can provide either that the signatures of two or more personally liable partners is required in order to bind the KG or the signatures of two or more personally liable partners and the signature of another (such as a "Prokurist") is necessary before the KG is bound. A KG which wishes to be governed by such a provision must file an application for the entry of it in the commercial register .

While it is not possible to deprive the personally liable partners of their rights of representation and the corresponding right of third parties to rely on them (external management rights), just the opposite is true of the limited partners. Due to their limited liability, the limited partners are not entitled to represent the firm unless they have been granted a full power of attorney ("Prokura," or "Handlungsvollmacht").

With regard to the internal management of the KG, however, German law allows greater flexibility. For example, the partnership agreement may allocate certain types of responsibilities to different partners, exclude a partner completely from management or allow management participation of limited partners.

The obligation to prepare the annual balance sheet lies with the personally liable partners. However, the partnership agreement may also provide for the participation of the limited partners. A KG is subject to the same accounting, auditing and dissolution requirements as an OHG (see section B. above).

D. Silent partnership ("Stille Gesellschaft")

A silent partnership is formed by a partnership agreement. No registration or other disclosure is required. The silent partnership, therefore, remains a genuine internal affair between the silent partner and the principal who owns the business.

As a rule, the sole obligation of silent partners is to make a capital investment in accordance with the partnership agreement. Management rights are vested in the principal. Generally, silent partners have no more right to control the business than do the limited partners of a KG. Silent partners participate in the profits of the partnership, but usually do not share the losses. Silent partners usually have no claim to the hidden reserves of the business.

Silent partners are able to lay claim for repayment of their investments upon dissolution of the partnership. Unless the partnership agreement provides otherwise, silent partners possess the same rights as a creditors. This holds true even in the case of bankruptcy.

It is possible for the parties to agree that any silent partner(s) will participate in profits and losses upon liquidation and in the hidden reserves. Such an arrangement results in the creation of a "non-typical" silent partnership.

Foreign companies with German subsidiaries are often confronted with a situation in which their subsidiaries require additional funds. The silent partnership can be used to acquire such funds.

IV. Mixed Corporate / Partnership Organizational Forms

A. GmbH & Co. KG

The GmbH & Co. KG is a form that combines the limited liability company (GmbH) with a limited partnership (KG) and is frequently used in Germany. The advantage of this form of business organization is the fact that a GmbH may (and usually does) participate as the only personally liable partner of the KG, thus limiting the liability of the only personally liable partner. The GmbH can be held liable for its business debts only to the extent of its assets. Its liability cannot be extended to the private property of its shareholders. Therefore, there is no real unlimited liability of any of the partners in a GmbH & Co. KG.

When the GmbH is the sole personally liable partner, it has the duty of managing and representing the GmbH & Co. KG. The GmbH fulfills its responsibilities in this regard through the efforts of its own managing director(s).

B. Limited partnership with stock ["Kommanditgesellschaft auf Aktien" (KGaA)]

The KGaA is another mixed type of partnership / corporate form available for use in Germany. Though it is relatively rare, some of the largest enterprises in Germany have chosen to use it. It possess attributes of both a limited partnership as well as a stock corporation. Like a corporation, it is a separate legal entity. Yet like a limited partnership, at least one of its personally liable partners must bear the full liability for all the debts of the company. The other partners (limited stockholders) own stock in the company but are not personally liable to the company's creditors (Par. 278 AktG).

The limited stockholders are entitled to participate in the corporation's affairs only through concerted action taken at stockholder meetings. The personally liable partner(s) are responsible for the management and representation of the company.

V. Other Business Organizational Forms

A. Sole proprietorship ("Einzelunternehmen")

The sole proprietorship is one of the most popular organizational forms for small businesses due to the comparative ease with which it can be formed and operated.

Sole proprietors, like the general partners of an OHG, are subject to personal liability for all the debts of the business. Consequently, their private assets can be impounded if necessary in order to satisfy the claims of creditors. If sole proprietors are engaged in the types of merchant trade listed in section 1 par. 1 of the Commercial Code (HGB), then they are considered to be operating "Handelsgewerbe" and must register the business.

B. Branch office ("Zweigniederlassung")

Instead of or in addition to the formation of a new enterprise, it is often advisable for a foreign company to set up a branch office ("Zweigniederlassung") in Germany. Tax advantages often play an important role in such a decision. The corporate income tax rate applied to the profits of a branch office are 46% compared to 50% for a subsidiary. On the other hand, a parent company is liable to the full extent of its own assets for creditors' claims filed against the branch.

A branch has no legal personality of its own and thus derives its rights and obligations from the status of the head office of the parent company. It may sue or be sued only through the parent company. By virtue of its local presence, however, a foreign company operating as a branch office in Germany can have action taken against it by any local creditor through the local judicial system.

German law makes a distinction between dependent and independent branches. If a branch can be considered to be a separate or independent entity, then it has to be registered in the commercial register (Par. 13 HGB). An independent branch can be established only if it has its own assets, bank accounts and bookkeeping system and would be able to continue in operation even if the head office were to close down. In addition, an independent branch must be represented by a manager who has the power to enter contracts and agreements that legally bind the branch. A smaller branch that cannot be considered to be self-supporting and independent need not be registered in the commercial register.

An independent branch may operate and be listed in the commercial register under its own company name. This name must consist of the name of the parent association and may contain an additional distinguishing term. The application for entry of the branch in the commercial register must be signed by all the officers of the company in the presence of a notary. Normally, their signatures must be submitted to the German consulate but, according to the Hague Convention of October 5th, 1961, this requirement can be met through the attachment of an "Apostille."

The application for registration must include the company's name, registered location and purpose in addition to a description of its financial basis and legal structure. Documents required in the application process must be notarized and accompanied by a German translation.

The founders of either type of branch office must notify the local Trade Supervision Office ("Gewerbeaufsichtsamt") in order to enable the authorities to determine whether a license is necessary or not. The notification is required by par. 14 of the Trade Supervision Law ["Gewerbeordnung" (GewO)]. Usually, no special license is required unless the branch's planned enterprise falls into a special category of business. Such special categories include, to cite the most common ones, banks, restaurants, hotels, bars, insurance companies and commercial transportation enterprises. Failure to provide the required notification can result in a substantial fine.

VI. Corporate Succession and Changes of Organizational Form

The business development of an AG, GmbH or KGaA can result in the need or desire for a transformation of the company ("Formwechsel"), a merger with at least one other corporation ("Verschmelzung durch Aufnahme") or a consolidation with another corporation for the purpose of forming a new corporation ("Verschmelzung durch Neugründung"). This transformation is ruled by the Transformation Act [„Umwandlungsgesetz" (UmwG)].

A. Merger and consolidation

A merger takes place under German law when the total assets and liabilities of one corporate enterprise are transferred to another in return for shares in it. As a result of a merger, the transferee company is terminated and its shareholders become shareholders in the acquiring corporation [i.e., merger by take over ("Verschmelzung durch Aufnahme")].

A consolidation occurs when the assets and liabilities of two or more corporations are transferred to a newly formed corporation in return for shares in this new corporation ("Verschmelzung durch Neugründung").

The following types of enterprises can be fused through either a merger or a consolidation:

- general or limited partnerships (OHGs/KGs)
- stock corporations (AGs),
- limited partnerships with stock (KGaAs)
- GmbHs.

B. Transformation

In contrast to a merger or consolidation, a transformation impacts only one business by changing its organizational form. Under the provisions of the UmwG, an AG may be transformed into GbR, an OHG, a KG, a GmbH or another AG.

A transformation of an AG into a KG requires a resolution passed by a three-fourth majority vote of the stockholders. A transformation of an AG to a GbR or an OHG, however, generally requires the unanimous approval of all the voting stockholders. In the first case, the transformation must be approved by the personally liable partners.

To effect a transformation of a GmbH into an AG or a KGaA, the shareholders must approve an amendment of the articles of incorporation reflecting the change. An application must be made to have the names of the members of the board of management of the newly created stock corporation and the transformation itself noted in the commercial register. At the time the registration of the transformation occurs, the GmbH still continues to exist, though now in the form of the new company: a stock corporation (AG) or a limited partnership with stock (KGaA). The share capital becomes stock capital, and shares or ownership interests become stock.

Under the provisions of the Transformation Act ("Umwandlungsgesetz"), GmbHs, AGs, and KGaAs may be transformed into general partnerships (OHGs) or limited partnerships (KGs).

The Acquisition of Closely Held Companies

Bernd Tremml

I. Introduction

The basic reason behind the acquisition of a company is the same in all countries - the purchaser wishes to acquire the value of another enterprise. As is obvious but too often forgotten, the legal system of the country where the purchase will take place has a considerable impact on the consummation of an acquisition. Of particular importance is the local corporate law, especially the provisions of it that govern business organizations and structures.

The structure as well as the content of the rules and regulations of German law may appear strange to a person more familiar with Anglo-American law. For example, in Germany, whenever parties have no written agreement on a particular issue, the law, as it is interpreted by the courts, will apply or impose a solution. Thus, a party that might have forgotten to address a particular issue does not remain completely unprotected.

Such judicially imposed contract terms are, however, often viewed as very unsatisfactory by either the purchaser or seller of a business enterprise. In the absence of an agreement to the contrary, the law holds the seller liable only in disputes of material significance, which shifts the weight of risk in all other cases to the shoulders of the purchaser. To clarify matters from the onset and avoid such judicial impositions as well as the hassles and high costs of litigation, it has meanwhile become common practice for the parties in an acquisition transaction to agree to specific terms that are within the range of the law and clearly lay them out in the form of a written contract.

An acquisition involves such diverse areas of law as contract, commercial, corporate, labor, and tax law and sometimes even inheritance or domestic-relations law. Through a contract, the laws can be tailored to meet the needs of a specific case, which offers both the seller and purchaser considerably better protection. It is imperative that significant attention be focused on the drafting of the acquisition contract.

II. Types of Acquisition

As discussed in the previous chapter, German law provides for a variety of business organizational forms, which can be divided into sole proprietorships, partnerships, corporations and forms that are a mixture of the latter two. Only a relatively small number of German companies issue stock and trade it on the open market. As mentioned, the stock corporation (AG) is chosen by only a handful of large and mainly international enterprises, and because its stock is freely traded, there is nothing its management can do to prevent a purchaser bent on acquiring a majority of stocks from getting them. Therefore, in terms of acquisition, it has a unique status. All the other types of enterprises are customized to meet the needs of their owners, and as a general rule, their equity holdings are not openly traded or even freely transferable. They can, therefore, be described as privately or closely held enterprises. This chapter will deal primarily with the acquisition of GmbHs, the legal form of a closely held company that is most commonly chosen by mid-sized German enterprises.

There are two ways in which to acquire any kind of already existing German enterprise: the acquisition of ownership interests (the equity holdings of a GmbH or the stock of an AG, for instance) or the acquisition of all or some of its assets and liabilities. In either of these ways, an enterprise can be acquired in whole or in part.

A. Acquisition of ownership interests

As a rule, all the rights of ownership are transferred from the seller of a GmbH to the buyer on the date of purchase. It's important to know exactly what that entails.

Prior to the acquisition, an interim balance sheet must be prepared, which shows the expected profits to the date of sale, as of which the equity holdings of the GmbH together with the right to receive future profits are transferred to the buyer. Any necessary adjustments to the interim balance sheet must be made in accordance with the final financial report.

B. Sale of assets

The sale of assets is quite complex because a great degree of specificity is required and detailed attention must be given to the matter to avoid the possibility of error. Each item of property, as well as all the rights and liabilities associated with it, needs to be accurately and clearly listed in the acquisition agreement.

1. Real estate

The conditions of ownership and a detailed description of any real estate property can be conclusively determined from the information contained in the real estate register. Buildings constitute an integral part of the real estate. Appurtenances such as machines are included in the sale of real estate unless otherwise agreed. The transfer to the purchaser occurs when an agreement by both the seller and the purchaser has been entered into before a German notary public and the transfer has been officially noted in the real estate register.

2. Purchase of current moveable assets or groups of moveable assets

If current moveable assets or groups of moveable assets are sold, the individual items must be accurately and clearly listed in the acquisition agreement. With groups of assets, a purely quantitative description (i.e., "100 units") is not sufficient. Assets must be identified according to time and place, which is achieved by applying the so-called "All-Formula" rule in such a manner as to signify for example that all the items located in a particular stockroom or warehouse on the date of purchase will be conveyed to the purchaser.

Current moveable assets and groups of moveable assets are often encumbered by third-party security rights. It is important to treat such items separately in the agreement since they could, of course, be excluded from the transfer. However, it can also be agreed that the sellers' right to have such an item released or conveyed to them upon satisfaction of the claim for which it was offered as security, is transferred to the purchaser. The transfer of title to movable objects is effected by conveyance, or if a third party is in possession of the object, by surrender of the right to possession.

3. Claims

Claims can be transferred if it is possible to substantiate them, for example, through a designation of the underlying transaction or the name of the debtor. If the purchaser intends to continue to operate the business of the seller after acquisition of it, the designation "all claims of the seller resulting from operations of the business" effectively serves the purpose. Such claims then become the enforceable claims of the purchaser. To avoid unpleasant surprises, the purchaser should, as in the case of the purchase of movable objects described above, insist on a detailed record of all outstanding claims. As a further security measure, the purchaser should obtain a personal guarantee from the seller that those claims will be satisfied by the seller in the event of default.

4. Company name and special industrial property rights

A company name can be transferred along with the sale of the company as a whole. The express agreement of the seller is, however, necessary for the continued use of the company name by the purchaser. Applications for change of registration and notarized transfer registrations should be made at the time of the closing of the sale.

Patents can be transferred separately, and as a rule they are transferred whenever the assets of the firm are transferred as a whole. If the rights resulting from a patent or design should need to be asserted against a third party, the transfer must have been previously registered. Often patents or designs are registered in the name of the previous owner. Therefore, verification is indispensable.

5. Additional rights and obligations

All remaining rights and obligations, any contracts which are to be assumed and any intangible assets such as know-how, customers, good will and so on should be listed in as accurate a manner as possible. When the transfer of a right is not regulated by applicable law, the pertinent details must be agreed upon. Also, the extent of any corresponding guarantees and indemnities of the seller should be set forth as clearly as possible in the sale's contract because they may be a purchaser's only recourse in case of a failure in the transfer of any such right. Of course, an accurate description of the right or obligation also serves to provide a dependable basis for the calculation of the purchase price. Because the transfer of a contract containing an assumption of debt requires the agreement of the creditor, a three-party agreement among the seller, the purchaser and the creditor will have to be made, or consent of the creditor to the transfer will otherwise have to be secured.

III. Contract Formalities

A. Letter of intent, negotiation contracts and preliminary contracts

1. Liability during contract negotiations

Acquisition contract negotiations cost both time and energy. Expenses prior to and in anticipation of the execution of the contract are often incurred, and more often than not business secrets are revealed. Thus, the question of how the relationship between the parties should be regulated during the preliminary stages of contract negotiations arises.

As a general rule, negotiations alone do not obligate the parties to enter into a acquisition contract. In theory, the negotiations can be broken off without any justifiable reason, and it is possible to engage in parallel negotiations with other parties. Nonetheless, the law imposes a fiduciary relationship between the negotiating parties, which obliges them to observe and respect the just interests of the other.

A foreign purchaser may be surprised that even before any contractual obligations are incurred, a negotiating partner is liable for damages in accordance with the rules of *culpa in contrahendo* (anticipatory breach) [Par. 311 sec. 2, 3; Par. 280 sec. 1 German Civil Code (BGB)]. For example, if a potential purchaser makes personal use of a business secret that he or she becomes aware of during the course of negotiations, he or she is liable for any damages. Also, even in the absence of any intent to cause a loss, if a purchaser or a seller breaks off the negotiations, he may be liable for damages the other party sustains through "detrimental reliance." Such damages might be, for instance, the irreversible expenditures the other party incurred by relying on the probable execution of the contract, expenditures which, upon the breaking off of the contract negotiations, constitute a definite loss.

2. Letter of intent and negotiation contracts

German business practice uses a letter of intent as part of preliminary contract negotiations. According to German law, such a letter is in principle a pure declaration of intent. It is meant to preclude adverse legal consequences and not to obligate a party to execute a final contract, even if a party states that under certain circumstances it is willing to be bound to do so. It should be noted, however, that the negotiating parties may rely on the probable execution of a final contract if the wording of the letter of intent seems to assume that a final contract will be entered into. The possibility of liability for reliance injury is obvious in such a case.

In order to preclude the risk and uncertainty of being sued for damages based on "detrimental reliance" in the event the contract negotiations are terminated, it is highly advisable to contractually determine the relationship the parties will have during the negotiation stage.

A preliminary agreement can include certain performance or disclosure obligations and/or a unilateral obligation on the part of the seller not to conduct any negotiations with third parties up to a certain point in time (according to German law, such a unilateral obligation is enforceable without the providing of consideration by the purchaser). The parties' agreement regarding their obligations during the negotiation stage can be laid out in the letter of intent.

However, a letter of intent which is used this way and contains provisions concerning certain performance or other obligations during the on-going contract negotiations, constitutes a binding offer to perform in accordance with the obligations. Its acceptance results in a so-called negotiation contract. Thus, in this way the parties can, for example, agree to and be bound by the following obligations:

- performance obligations (such as the conduction of preliminary investigations, marketing and location analyses, duty of disclosure),
- disclosure obligations (such as balance sheet audit, disclosure by designated employees),
- secrecy obligations (agreement not to use acquired information to one's own or to a third party's advantage),
- obligations pertaining to liability for omissions and reimbursement for expenses (including expert opinions, attorney fees, etc.)
- and obligations regarding dispute resolution (choice-of-law clause for the preliminary contract negotiations and arbitration agreements)

It is very important that the negotiation contract state whether these obligations are to remain in effect after the execution of the acquisition contract or whether they are to be extinguished by or integrated into the provisions of the acquisition contract.

It should be mentioned that the involvement of a broker (in practice often banks) can serve the secrecy requirements of the seller as well as the purchaser. A broker's professional expertise can furthermore be of great advantage to the prospective purchaser.

3. Preliminary contracts

When the basic terms regarding the acquisition contract are settled, a preliminary contract can be entered into even if certain issues still require further clarification. Such a preliminary agreement will impose an obligation on the parties to enter into a final acquisition contract.

B. Requirements of form

As a general rule, a contract for the sale of a partnership (other than a GmbH & Co. KG) which does not involve the transfer of real property need not conform to a specific form or meet specific legal requirements other than those pertaining to the enforceability of contracts in general. Contracts regulating the sale of all the assets and equity holdings of a GmbH, however, must conform to specific legal requirements.

The GmbH law (GmbHG) requires that the sale and transfer of equity holdings of such a company be effected by a German notary public ("Notar"). A "Notar" is a person who has the same training as an attorney but who acts impartially in a quasi-governmental function. A "Notar" must be involved in the transfer of the holdings of a GmbH regardless of whether their sale amounts to a partial or whole transfer of ownership.

If the contract is void because the special notarization requirements of the GmbH law have not been met, the purchaser has the right to be reimbursed in an amount equal to the sales price already paid. That right stems from the principle of unjust enrichment. The purchaser, however, will have to refund any profits obtained from the company if he or she knew or was grossly negligent in failing to realize that the contract was void.

Merger agreements through which an AG or GmbH transfers its assets as a whole to another corporation (merger by amalgamation) or by which several corporations or closely held companies such as a GmbH transfer their assets to a new corporation (merger by consolidation), need to be notarized and require compliance with the applicable statutes. Among other requirements, both companies must have their principal place of business within the Federal Republic of Germany. In practice, however, mergers are extremely rare.

IV. Specific Sale Considerations

A. Pending litigation

Upon the acquisition of the equity holdings of a GmbH, the company remains party to all on-going litigation and liable for any judgment. In order to avoid conflicts, key points such as the following should be settled in an acquisition agreement:

- the seller should disclose whether any and what kind of suits are pending (and what type of litigation is to be expected according to the best of his or her knowledge),
- the seller and purchaser should jointly defend on-going suits, subject to their agreement concerning the nature and extent of each of their obligations,
- the parties should determine whether, depending on the outcome of pending litigation, the object of dispute will be re-transferred to the seller and, taking that prospect into account, make the necessary adjustments in the purchase price
- and the parties should reach an agreement concerning the right of either of them to appeal, recognize, settle, or dismiss actions and determine which one of them will be liable for the legal costs involved.

B. Legal liability of the purchaser for obligations

When the purchaser acquires the equity holdings of a GmbH, the GmbH as a legal entity remains liable for its existing obligations. Personal liabilities of either the seller or purchaser or both can nevertheless arise. Sellers are liable, for instance, if they have fallen into arrears in their payments of the original capital investment or in their fulfillment of additional service obligations.

Seller and purchaser will be jointly liable, according to their proportionate share holdings, for any overdue obligations to the GmbH which were not satisfied by other owners.

Needless to say, in any case the purchaser must have full knowledge of and access to the GmbH documents ("Gesellschaftsverträge") which clearly define the rights of the owners and their financial obligations.

C. Labor law requirements

The complexity and impact of German labor law on business operations tends to cause potential foreign investors serious concerns and may in fact prevent a successful acquisition.

Purchasers typically desire to retain those employees needed for a successful perpetuation of the company's business activities, and it is important that they take the proper steps in doing so. If a previously independent company is incorporated into a larger business structure, the loss of autonomous decision-making power often encourages management and executive personnel to resign.

On the other hand, there are cases in which company purchasers have the legal obligation to assume existing employee relationships, although they may have no interest in doing so or may wish to change the relationships. This might occur, for instance, when someone acquires stock or equity holdings in a company. Employee relationships remain unchanged in that case as there was no actual change of employer. Since German labor laws have such an enormous impact on business operations, it is essential that potential foreign purchasers familiarize themselves with the laws and their implications.

Germany has very clearly spelled out employee-dismissal regulations, and there is only a limited number of legally recognized conditions under which employment can be terminated. Its labor laws also include special protection measures for employees based on age, seniority, maternity or the presence of a handicap. These employee-friendly laws may seem as unusual and surprising to foreign purchasers as the obligations employers have under certain circumstances to continue making wage payments to employees on leaves of absence. The high degree of German employee protection, insurance, vacation and other benefits tends to cause initial astonishment, as does the fact that German labor laws grant employees the right to participate in company management and co-determine its policies. These issues will be dealt with in Chapter 5.

Upon becoming the new owner of an enterprise, a purchaser automatically assumes from a legal perspective all the employment relationships that currently exist in the enterprise. It should also be noted that employees have the right to object to a transfer of their employment agreement to the new owner. If their objections are sustained, the seller will remain the employer. The purchaser is liable for all of the overdue wages owed to employees who are still in the company's retention at the time of acquisition. The seller and purchaser are jointly liable for all obligations which accrued prior to the acquisition and are due within a year after the transfer. Thus, the seller and purchaser have to regulate such liability between themselves in the form of a contract. For the most part, however, only the seller is liable for the claims of any employees who resigned prior to the acquisition. The purchaser needs to be aware of potential exceptions to that rule. Following a successful acquisition, the purchaser also becomes liable for vested interests in retirement payments and the pension commitments the company has made to its employees.

German labor laws grant employees special protection rights in the event of an acquisition. Their employment cannot be terminated as a direct result of it, which is to say that terminations stemming from the transfer of a company from one owner to another are legally prohibited. The termination of personnel following an acquisition is allowed only within restriction; for example, if restructuring plans were already in place at the time of the sale and there are objective reasons why the personnel affected by them cannot continue to be employed. The law also provides that upon acquisition the existing terms of collective-bargaining agreements and the existing wage-and-salary structures continue to be valid and binding. They cannot be changed if that would have an adverse effect on the employees, whose interests, by law, cannot be limited or abridged as the consequence of an acquisition.

Furthermore, it is important to note that as the result of an acquisition or merger a company's employees might gain the right to be represented on certain of its administrative boards. If, as a result of the sale, the company now employs more than 2,000 people, the right of employee participation in management comes into effect. The company must provide for employee representation on the supervisory board ("Aufsichtsrat").

In summary, the necessity of pre-sale legal review of all the labor-law issues and implications involved in an acquisition cannot be underscored too strongly. A potential purchaser should be well informed about the legal situation and take the necessary measures of protection in advance of purchase in order to avoid costly, never-ending future litigation (see Chapter 5).

D. Breach of contract

It is of particular importance to a purchaser to know what the legal outcome will be if the actual assets of a business enterprise were incorrectly represented in the purchase agreement or if the enterprise does not develop as projected and described in the agreement. If no contract provisions address these issues, then the following prevails.

Because the sale of stock or equity holdings is an effective legal transaction, sellers are liable only for the legality of the ownership interests. That is to say, they are not responsible for the conditions of whatever it is the ownership interests entitle their holders to (the assets of a company). The purchasers of stock or equity holdings are protected by law only when they in effect acquire the entire enterprise. Yet even in that case, the seller can be held liable only for the lack of those assets whose absence would undermine the very existence of the enterprise as whole. For example, a seller would be liable for a material deficiency that might exist in discrepancy to the capital asset account. The seller, however, is not generally liable for any incorrect statements concerning sales, profits and profitability or the total amount of the existing liabilities. Prospective purchasers are therefore well advised to demand specific warranties from the seller of a business, and this in writing, as their chances of holding the seller liable for any statements, indications or promises would otherwise be very weak indeed. A written warranty, however, would serve as a court-recognized basis for proving deception and/or damage and make it possible to tag an appropriate monetary figure to it. This warranty should be an integral part of the attorney-prepared purchase contract if it is to have the full potential to stand up in court.

Since purchasers of closely held companies are at a relative disadvantage to the sellers and since there is a great deal of ambiguity concerning their rights and obligations in general, it is highly recommended that all unclear and open issues be resolved in writing. In how much detail the various issues ought to be treated depends largely on the negotiating parties. However, the minimum to be obtained from the seller should be a guarantee concerning the net assets and profits of the enterprise. It should include attests to past business performance and to existing or non-existing transactions as well as to realistically projected future developments. In conjunction with such an agreement, the form and extent of the seller's liability should be agreed upon.

The seller should also guarantee that the balance sheet is complete and accurate, was prepared in accordance with the proper, legally proscribed accounting principles, and will be updated by way of supplement if necessary. The parties should also make an agreement as to what independent certified public accountants will verify the balance sheet. Procedures for any necessary adjustments of the purchase price should also be clearly laid out. The seller should be asked to provide warranties regarding the firm's inventory, hidden reserves, high-risk transactions and sale restrictions as well as warranties pertaining to the validity of any operating permits and licenses. The statement procured from the seller should also contain mention of any provisions governing the transfer of know-how and any restrictions, geographical and otherwise, on competition. Such restrictions may also apply to the prior owner's right to use his or her name in another business. The seller's obligations to disclose pending litigation and other liabilities can be supported by a guarantee that the information was provided to the best of the seller's ability and knowledge.

A mechanism should also be in place for establishing the liability of the seller and determining the type and extent of damage for which the seller is responsible. It is to the advantage of both parties to agree to a purchase price reduction rather than to the purchaser's right to rescind a sale in the event that the seller becomes liable for certain damage. Provisions for the right to rescind a sale should be made only in the most extreme cases.

E. Expenses

Expenses incurred through the acquisition of an enterprise should be covered in the agreement. Attorney and notary public fees are legally fixed in Germany. The amount is determined according to the value of the matter in question. In the case of a whole-company acquisition, the value of the company determines the amount of the legal fees. When stock or equity holdings are being transferred, the legal fees are based on either the total nominal capital or the purchase price of the holdings. If individual assets such as real estate are being sold, the fees are based on the assets' current market value. For example, if the acquisition price of the equity holdings of a closely held corporation such as a GmbH is € 250,000.--, the attorney will be entitled to up to € 7,500.--, and the notary public who certifies the sales contract and the assignment of the equity holdings will be entitled to € 1,250.---. Variation in these fees is allowed in individual cases; usually attorneys charge in acquisition cases hourly fees, ranging from € 200.-- to € 400.--. Further expenses include the costs for the registration of the equity holdings in the commercial register or, in the case of the transfer of real estate, in the real-estate register. Those fees are comparatively lower.

V. Restrictions

A. Restrictions on sale

Prospective purchasers should make themselves aware of any restrictions the seller might have on the rights to sell the object in question. If any restrictions exist, the sales contract could be void or ineffective until the necessary approvals have been granted. Special areas such as family (domestic relations) and inheritance law, will not be considered here, although they may be of high impact and should not be overlooked when considering a purchase.

The purchaser of an enterprise has to know who is authorized to effect its sale. The sale or merger of an AG cannot be agreed to by the board of management or supervisory board alone, but requires the consent of a qualified majority of the stockholders at a general meeting. Such consent can be dispensed with only if a part of the enterprise is being sold and the corporation can continue its activities in conformity with its existing articles of corporation. In the case of the sale of a GmbH or other closely held corporation, it is not clear whether the power of a managing director is sufficient to effect the transfer of the company or whether a meeting of owners must be called and a resolution authorizing the transfer adopted by a qualified majority. Thus, it is advisable to insist on such a resolution. It should be noted that the transfer of ownership interests of a closely held corporation can be restricted by the articles of incorporation, and the transfer can be made subject to the consent of the other owners.

B. Antitrust regulations

A prospective purchaser must be aware of the applicable antitrust regulations. These can apply to the acquisition of an entire enterprise or to the acquisition of only a partial interest in one. There is either a notification or a registration requirement. The acquisition of all of the assets of the enterprise or of an essential part of them is subject at least to compliance with the applicable notification provisions. The acquisition of shares of stock or equity holdings of a company is subject to such notification compliance if the ownership interests in question together with any interests already owned constitute a prescribed percentage of the voting stock or holdings. It can be as low as 25%. However, the duty of notification is triggered only if the combined firms have at least a 20% market share, €

250 million in yearly sales or 10,000 employees. The duty of registration is triggered if one of the firms participating in the sale of ownership interest or assets has at least € 1,000 million in world-wide yearly sales or if two or more of the participating firms had at least € 500 million each in world-wide sales in the last complete business year.

In satisfying the notification requirements, the Federal Cartel Authority ("Bundeskartellamt") must be notified immediately after the sale. If the Federal Cartel Authority subsequently determines that the sale violates market control provisions (and determines that the acquisition does not qualify for an exception), it can prohibit the transaction within one year after the sale, and in such a case it will allow the parties an appropriate period of time to undo the transaction. If a sale of ownership interests or assets must comply with the more burdensome registration requirements of the Federal Cartel Authority, registration must occur prior to the closing of the sale. The Federal Cartel authority then has a period of four months in which to prohibit the transfer. The antitrust regulations must be examined closely on a case-by-case basis.

C. European Community regulations

The non-European purchaser must realize that the European Economic Community Treaty contains its own antitrust regulations and that ordinances and decisions of the Council and the Commission can be directly binding on individual parties within the Member States (see Chapter 9).

VI. Special Considerations for Foreign Purchasers

A. No basic restrictions

Basically, there are no restrictions on the acquisition of German companies by foreign purchasers. The transfer of assets or the acquisition of ownership interests by foreign investors can be prohibited only when this is necessary to protect the national interest, which is, for example, the case when armament control is involved. An acquisition can also be prohibited if an attempt is made to use it as a means of circumventing restrictions on the employment of foreigners not holding German residence permits.

B. Transfer of shares and assets

German international property law does not permit a choice of law as to the actual transfer of property, whether it is personal property or real estate. The transfer of a German company through the sale of assets or ownership interests must, therefore, take place in accordance with German law. The acquisition of ownership rights in German companies by foreigners is furthermore subject to the company's own articles of incorporation, which are governed by local laws. Thus, it is necessary to ascertain whether a stockholder or owner agreement or the corporate charter imposes any prohibitions.

IX. Conclusion

The German civil-law system offers potential business purchasers considerably more protection than the Anglo-American common-law system. They are, nonetheless, well advised to seek a well thought out written agreement, which will enable them to make more informed business decisions and help them avoid future conflicts. This chapter does not contain a complete description of all the legal issues that might arise in the acquisition of a company. Prospective purchasers are emphatically advised to rely on their own attorneys and tax consultants when preparing to make such a complicated transaction. Although as a general rule it is always highly advisable to seek professional, individual help before acting on any decisions that could be of considerable economic impact, this is particularly true in any issues involving taxes. German tax laws are constantly being revised. It is therefore essential that the current validity of the information presented here be verified, modified or adapted to a particular case by professionals who are abreast of the developments in the German tax-law arena before any binding commitments are made on the basis of it.

Acquisition-Agreement Checklist

Below, in the form of a checklist, are the essential issues which should be negotiated and included in an acquisition contract:

1) Parties

- including authorized representatives and persons with full powers of attorney

2) Preamble

- Motives and basis of the transaction

3) Object of sale

- acquisition of shares or assets
- Purchase of shares: special clause for the transition of loan accounts
- Sole proprietorships / partnerships: special clause for the transition of special equities. Reference to balance sheet and/or itemized listing of assets (indispensable when the object of sale is a part of the business)
- due diligence
- Special consideration: seller's right to withdraw capital to the date of closure
- Special consideration: seller's obligation to balance losses shown in the cash accounts or special accounts

4) Assumption of liabilities

- Acquisition of shares in the business: no specifications
- Acquisition of an enterprise: regulation of liabilities to the date of closure
- Acquisition of part of an enterprise: categorized itemization of assets
- Right of indemnity for non-assumed liabilities

5) Transition of employee relationships

- Enterprise as a whole: no specification required. Automatic regulation by Par. 613a BGB. Right of recision potentially possible in the event of employee objections
- Part of an enterprise: itemized categorization of employee relationships

6) Pension obligations

- Internal division of the pension obligations (no effect on employees)
- Transfer of support obligations to an independent relief fund
- Seller's termination obligation prior to transition
- Any hiring of new employees prior to closure requires purchaser approval

7) Current Contracts

- Purchaser approval
- Rights of indemnity

8) Personal securities

9) Unanticipated liabilities

- Warranty that all liabilities are included in the balance sheet
- Division of risk: obligation to indemnify, reduction of purchase price, set-off claims

10) Further declarations and regulations regarding:

- Contracts with advisors
- Division of sales and profits
- Security rights
- Long- term delivery contracts
- Pending transactions (division of future profits and losses)
- Approved cartels
- Currently existing non-competition agreements
- Currently existing powers of attorney
- Legal disputes

11) Permits under public law

- Warranty that the assets of the firm are unencumbered and its operations unendangered

12) Prohibition of competition

- Scope in terms of content, time and place

13) Determination of purchase price

- Determination criteria
- Basis for the determination of book values
- Quota-share regulation in the case of partial purchases
- Differences based on increase / reduction of current assets or short-term accounts receivable/accounts payable up to closure
- Right of indemnity for later payments decreasing the value of the firm, e.g., taxes
- Balance at transition: cooperation duties, valuation criteria, choice of CPAs including arbitrator

14) Warranties

- Completeness of all information provided
- Correctness of statements according to the best of knowledge
- Balance: continuation of current practices, no incurring of new liabilities
- Sales and profits: express assurance is necessary to hold the seller liable
- Exclusion of any rights to recision
- Reversal of transaction: maximum liability, secrecy obligations

15) Actual transition

- Exact point in time
- Method of transition (physical, assignment, transfer of trademarks, obtaining of records, etc.)
- Assurance that no essential changes have taken place between the time of contract and sale
- Methods of payment of the purchase price
- Purchaser's obligation to close (provided no essential changes have occurred and all pre-agreed conditions have been fulfilled)

16) General Regulations

- Duties of disclosure after sale
- Assurance that no illegal antitrust agreements exist
- Right to purchase further stock or equity holdings in the enterprise
- Choice of law
- Assumption of expenses (attorney, notary, commercial register, real-estate register)
- Division of taxes
- Jurisdiction
- Rescue clause

17) In the case of antitrust notification requirements:
- receipt of permission as a condition for suspension

18) Statute of Limitations
- for warranty claims
- for tax indemnity claims

19) Arbitration clause

Valuation of Business Enterprises

Bernd Tremml

I. General Information

The purchase of a business enterprise or shares of stock in one generally does not occur until the value of the business has been appraised. The question as to what method should be used in determining the value of a business enterprise was vehemently disputed in Germany for a long time.

The method that had traditionally been employed for years and is now generally known as the "Stuttgart Procedure" ("Stuttgarter Verfahren") has fallen out of use except for specific tax purposes, primarily in the sectors of property and inheritance tax law. This method basically consists of determining the capitalized value of potential yield (productive or earning value) and the tangible value. The development of this procedure was heavily influenced by the post World War II economic climate, which led to an over-emphasis of the tangible value or, in other words, of the value of the (undamaged) business enterprise just as it stood. The productive value of the enterprise, on the other hand, was figured solely on the basis of past results. On the whole, the Stuttgart Procedure, which ordinarily provides very low valuations of commercial enterprises, is now no longer an acceptable method of valuation for any purpose other than tax purposes; outside this sector it generally provides inaccurate results.

Due to the unsuitability of the Stuttgart Procedure, multifarious valuation procedures were developed that ostensibly took operational economic considerations better into account. The controversy over which method of valuation engendered by these so-called "practical procedures" was the best now seems at last to have come to an end in the Federal Republic of Germany. The most substantial contribution in this direction was provided by the publication of the opinion of the Institution of Certified Public Accountants in 1983 regarding the basic means of conducting a valuation of business enterprises. This led to the solid establishment of the premise that the productive value of a business enterprise is the sole relevant value. Of decisive importance, therefore, is the recognition that a business enterprise is worth only as much as the future withdrawable profits. In determining this productive value, the tangible value now has nothing more than a supportive function.

In the valuation procedure, the local statutory and tax law framework play an important role, and the purchaser or prospective purchaser should turn the valuation over to a consultant who is well versed in these specific domestic regulations. However, before entering into a valuation contract the potential purchaser absolutely has to take the following points into consideration.

The value of the commercial enterprise is always founded upon the individual perceptions of the prospective purchaser; it is impossible to appraise the value of a "business" as an object without clarification of such subjective value perceptions. Furthermore, the final price for the purchase of the business is not completely determined by rational factors. Prospective purchasers and their consultants or appraisers must, therefore, specifically define and determine the type of "business value" that is to be applied. Purchasers could be interested in finding out the decisive value, which provides only the top or bottom price limits and, thus, represents a neutral objective value that can be ascertained by using strictly non-subjective, verifiable value arguments. However, they could be primarily concerned with the determination of the so-called "fair settlement price," which consists of a compromise that also takes a certain number of the prospective purchaser's value perceptions into account. This function of the business valuation process should be made completely clear in order to prevent misinterpretation or misuse.

II. The Productive Value of the Business Enterprise

A. Problems and principles of appraising productive value

1. The value of a business enterprise is equal to the cash value of all its future net profits. In theory, that value is comprised only of the surplus earnings that can be permanently withdrawn without causing harm to the yield-bringing substance of the business organization. In actual practice, however, this pure theory has to be considerably modified.

    For example, commercial law restricts the formal premises upon which a profit-distribution decision can be made and allows distribution only of those profits that have been judged to be in compliance with commercial law regulations and on the basis of properly kept books. Due to such restrictions, a situation can arise where surplus profits do exist but, due to a lack of simultaneously distributable profits, are not available to investors. It is therefore essential to make additional assumptions concerning the future profit-distribution performance of the business.

2. When the distributable profit is used as a guideline, however, this immediately gives rise to the problem of the time placement of future yields. Such yields should be properly assigned to the periods of time for which they are anticipated. Of course, the further into the future the appraiser's projections are made, the less accurate they become. The appraiser should, therefore, weigh out the ascertained and projected yields for each future period of time in such a manner that their value on the key date will progressively diminish the further away from this key date the projections are made.

3. The same problem applies to the accuracy of predictions in general. Since the uncertainty of expected profit flow leads to various predictions, it is

necessary to weigh each of the projections individually in terms of its overall probability.

4. The amount of future distributable profits for each of the future time phases of valuation must include a deduction of the accrued interest that could have accrued as of the key date, had the funds been invested differently. The internal interest rate (profitability) of an investment alternative is used to establish the rate of interest that ought to be deducted from all future yields. In other words, the future business profits are compared with the expected surpluses of an investment alternative. In determining this interest rate, the appraiser will ordinarily refer to the on-going domestic interest rate for long-term investments in the capital market. In the Federal Republic of Germany, it is common practice to use, as an orientation, the reports on investment returns on fixed, interest-bearing securities ("Umlaufrenditen") publicized by the Federal Reserve Bank of Germany ("Deutsche Bundesbank").

   In some cases, depending on the purpose of the valuation (see the above delineation as to how careful the projected earnings are to be figured), it will be necessary to add a risk figure to the affixed interest rate. It is a matter of controversy whether the interest rate should be "inflation purified" as well. Normally, however, the inflation situation and inflation expectations have already influenced the capital market interest rate, and further inflation purification would therefore be superfluous. If the interest is "inflation purified", however, this should have occurred before any risk factor was added, since the result would otherwise include an "inflated risk."

5. The business enterprise must be valued in terms of its *total* function. This aspect is of particular importance to the mixed and affiliated enterprises frequently found in the Federal Republic of Germany ("GmbH & Co. KG," divided enterprises, joint-stock companies and silent partnerships), which are generally formed predominately for tax purposes. Experience has proven that it is extremely difficult to trace such divided enterprises back to a uniform object of appraisal. Furthermore, because such mixed businesses so frequently fail due to collisions with commercial or tax laws, statements concerning their valuation can be made only on a single-case basis.

6. The complaint is frequently made that the net worth of German enterprises is too low. If the total net worth is outside the currently common range, the appraiser should use empirical values (such as the common net worth of other enterprises within the same branch of business or the reasonable and proportionate amount of borrowed capital) to figure the total value of the corporation on the basis of normalized finance structures.

7. The possibilities of alteration to the enterprise which are open to the purchaser are generally not to be taken into consideration. Whether or not the valuation includes the future measures contained in the seller's plans depends on the purpose of the evaluation. In general, such proposals are taken into consideration only insofar as preparatory measures have already been initiated and implemented (e.g., the results of research and development projects or investments in equipment).

8. A past analysis should always provide the basis for appraising the future earning capacity, but not, in the sense of determining a "yield sequence" that can be extrapolated into the future. Instead, the past results should be purified for extraordinary fluctuations or any infringements of accounting and valuation principles (including infringement of the principle of determining results properly according to time periods). Only then will it be possible for the appraiser to recognize the course of development and, proceeding on the basis of past development, to predict future turnover, draw up an investment plan, estimate the depreciation requirements and make a projection of the interest burden.

9. As already mentioned above, the tangible value of the enterprise is relevant only as the intermediate value of the business transformation process. In this regard, it simply represents previous expenditures and has merely an auxiliary function in figuring the productive or earning value of the business enterprise. As such, it is the essential object of reference in determining the amount of operating capital and the financial resources that will be required in the future in regard to all productive-value items that depend upon the tangible value. It is also indispensable as a foundation for investment planning (reinvestments!).

10. Personnel related value factors (for example, the personal qualifications of the management staff) definitely play an important role for the purchaser. It is questionable whether such factors should be included in a computed business appraisal since, in such a case, it is not possible to arrive at anything more than very rough estimates. In the case of unincorporated firms or enterprises that are owned, operated and driven by individuals on the equity of their own names, it is both possible and necessary to affix a value to that equity and to do so irrespective of whether or not the investor plans to continue the business in its previous legal form.

B. Guidelines for determining productive value

1. Purification of past values:

The last three to five fiscal years should be considered and any nonessential operational assets should be eliminated. Expenditures and earnings should be assigned to the time periods in which they occurred. There will be some necessary modifications such as depreciation on the basis of repurchasing costs, purification of extraordinary influencing factors and the ensuing changes (especially any changes relating to interest and tax expenditures).

2. Analysis of earning capacity

Once the purified past results are available, a quantity framework should be made on the basis of them. If it is to be successfully used for future planning, it must include the following elements:

- Prediction of sales
- Investment plan and projection of write-off requirements (age structure of production equipment, any repurchasing costs)
- Calculation of financing needs and projection of interest burden (non-operational expenditures)
- Projection of results within the sector of essential operational assets
- Consideration of personnel factors
- Separate valuation of nonessential operational assets

Prediction of tax expenditures: this requires a supplementary calculation for determining the expected tax advantages.

PART II

SPECIALIZED LAWS IMPACTING THE FORMATION, ACQUISITION AND OPERATION OF A BUSINESS IN GERMANY

Key Aspects of German Tax Law

Hans J. Goriss

I. General Considerations

Investors and Traders who want to enter the German market are well advised to present their investment scheme and their marketing plan to a German tax consultant bureau before they enter the market. An experienced tax adviser can optimize the measures to promote investment and marketing in Germany before the final form is committed.

The financial and fiscal impact of German law concerning the subsidies and the taxations has such great effect on investment schemes and marketing plans that it can alter the desired result transforming a positive outcome into one that is negative or vice-versa.

The impact of the incentives and the taxation has been of such import that in German Universites of high reputation, new courses of study entitled "Steuergestaltungslehre" have been developed and disseminated.

Investments and business decisions designed to promote investment and marketing which are implemented without the advice of a tax expert may be subject to limited corrections with such advice post implementation and of course the results may be less than optimal in this case.

II. The influence from incentives to the investment decisions in Germany

One should assume that an investor has a comprehensive know-how concerning the production and sale of his products, and that he wants to exert this know-how in Germany. In order to realize his plans, he should know:

- If there are investments in Germany, then there is a great variety of possibilities for subventions which are granted by the Commission of the European Communities, the Federal Government Department of Economics, the Ministries of the Lands within the Federal Republic of Germany, and by those institutions which are commissioned. The common authorities also regulate with respect to certain financial means, ie. they provide for entrepreneurial investments;
- There are certain political goals which are connected with subventions, goals which are often compatible with those of an enterprise. This is why the authorities can support the development and the marketing of new technology, and the development of neglected regions. They can also

support efforts to insure that jobs are preserved if, for example, there is an operation that is faced with the threat of closure because the entrepreneur is too old;
- In principle, incentives are equally available to German and foreign investors;
- Government incentives, accelerated tax depreciations or investment *grants can* be received for investments in special regions and/or for other special purposes;
- Subventions and financial grants can be awarded as an allowance or as a favorable credit. They can total to more than 20 % of the sum of the investments;
- Investment schemes, financial plans and marketing schemes have to be presented to proper authority for approval before the measures are enacted. There is no legal claim to these financial aids. The questions of if and in what amounts these supports are granted depend on the experience and know-how of the adviser.

Within the framework of the investment schemes, the investment aids (allowances, credits, contracts of guarantee) together with the estimated impact of the taxes should be taken into consideration and integrated.

III. Overview of Tax Laws

A. The international incorporation of the German tax law

First, taxation in Germany is guided by whether or not the person liable to pay the tax (taxpayer in terms of the current tax law) is eligible for relief under the international Double Taxation Agreement. International intergovernmental tax conventions take precedence over German tax law.

Therefore, one must first address the following questions before entering the market:

- Which country develops the activities that directly relate to the taxes?
- Did this country conclude a legally valid agreement to avoid double taxation?

Because there are several countries that did not ratify the agreement to avoid double taxation with Germany, activities should be organized from a country that has the legal protection of such an agreement.

The regulations of these agreements precede any corresponding national regulations (international law supersedes national law).

If there is indirect participation of low - tax countries thru taxable persons that are *resident* in Germany, then "to prevent international fiscal evasion", Germany enforces several regulations requiring that taxes on the profits of the subsidiary companies in the low-tax countries be paid for in Germany.

Given that Germany is a member of the European Union, there are several legal statutes in the EU which supersede the German tax and subvention laws. These regulations are primarily concerned with the granting of subventions and the Value-Added Tax Law.

B.   Overview of the German tax law

There are cases where German tax law joins tax liability. For a foreign investor, the following types of taxes are important:

- Personal Income Tax = Einkommenssteuer
- Corporate Income Tax = Koerperschaftsteuer
- Capital Yield Tax = Kapitalertragssteuer
- Business Tax = Gewerbesteuer
- Value-Added Tax = Umsatzsteuer
- Real Estate Tax = Grundsteuer
- Real Property Acquisition Tax = Grunderwerbssteuer
- Wage Tax = Lohnsteuer

The following table gives an overview of the regulations governing these taxes. The government and the parliaments have the power to change these fiscal regulations. This overview highlights the law as found in January 2002:

Type of Tax	Tax-payer	Taxable Object = AssessmentBasis	Tax-free Amount	Rates
Personal Income Tax	unlimited taxable natural persons	world-income with sum of their taxable income = income from: 1. agriculture and forestry, 2. business, 3. self-employment, 4. employment 5. investments 6. rent 7. other incomes	Basic relief 2001: DM 14.093,- (single) DM 28.187,- (married) 2002: € 7.235,- (single) € 14.471,- (married) 2003/04: € 7.426 (single) € 14.853,- (married)	Basic rate: BR Top Margin Rate: TR 2001: BR: 19,9 % TR: 48,5 % 2003: BR: 17 % TR: 47 % 2005: BR: 15 % TR: 42 %
Personal Income Tax	limited taxable natural persons	taxable income reached in Germany income		see above

		1.-7. (from above)		
Corporate Income Tax	Legal persons	fiscal income = corporation tax profit		from 2001: 25 % and „Halbeinkünfteverfahren"
Capital-Yield Tax				20 % to 35 %
Business Tax (City-tax)	Business enterprises	Business profits		about 13 % to 20 %
Value-Added Tax	Entrepreneur	Taxable turnover		16 %; 7 %
Real Estate Tax	proprietor of the real estate	Taxable value of the real estate		about 0,4 % to 1,5 %
Real Property Acquisition Tax	Buyer and seller of real estate	Value of the purchase of the real estate		3,5 %
Wage Tax	employer	Taxable wage		see Pesonal income tax

1. Personal Income Tax

A person must reside in Germany for longer than 183 days of the calendar year, to be liable for unlimited personal income tax. Failure to meet this precondition can be advantageous in some respects because the taxpayer can appeal to an array of special arrangements; for instance, he can opt to pay the German personal income tax.

Taxable income is only one form of income found in the preceding table. For members of large Christian churches, church taxes are collected based on agreement with the respective church. These taxes are usually 9% of personal income tax.

Currently, there are solidarity surcharges added to the personal income-tax that are used to help redistribute the financial burdens between Eastern and Western Germany. At present, these amount to 5.5 % of the personal income tax.

Some profits from selling stocks or other shares of corporations can be tax free if certain conditions are met (no essential holdings or shares ownership exceeding two years; remaining of the profit of selling stocks in the business capital).

Tax exemptions for profits generated from the selling of real estate have experienced substantial limitations. The most important of these limiting provisions requires that the real estate in question be the seller's property for more than 10 years, and the seller not have the intention of trading real estate as a business (for example, the three objects rule, etc...).

In Germany there are no property increment taxes as there are in Spain.

First of all, the different incomes have to be determined separately and then added together. With regard to the offset of positive and negative incomes, there are some restrictions to the types and amounts of income.

We have to expect some modifications to these rules because they are controversial. One should be well informed if he wishes to make investments in commercial income, or investments in an income received from rentals or leasings, or in an income derived from "closed funds".

The tax burden found in the tabular overview can be influenced by a participation in limited partnerships or similar investments.

Because of the income tax burden, there is a large market in Germany that is occupied with private capital investments in closed funds. It is often said that increases in capital are created by optimum model constructions built from tax savings.

If you have an offer, an auditor's report of the respective funds that is written according to the guidelines of the institute of the auditors of Germany should be submitted; and if you have this report, you should not make your decisions without the advice of a tax adviser.

The personal income tax is levied only by the federal authorities, which is to say that there is no regional or local taxation of personal income.

2. Corporate Income Tax

Juristic persons who pursue their industrial interests and who are not discharged in the consequence of specific exemptions of the corporate income tax, they fail with their profits to the corporate income tax. This is likewise a Federal Tax, which is levied by the same principles all over Germany.

To make special agreements, as is permissible in Switzerland or in the Netherlands, is not usual in Germany.

The determination of the taxable income is derived from the trade balance, taking into account specific provisions regarding certain operational expenses or nondeductable valuations provisions (donations, corporate income tax, specific provisions for pension, valuation for inventories, etc...).

Beginning from 2001-01-01 there is layed down the "Halbeinkünfte-Verfahren" that rules that the profit of juristic persons is taxable with 25 % tax. In case the profit distributed to the shareholders, 50 % of the distribution is taxable by the individual income tax of the shareholder. In case there is a conglomeration of companies the structure of the companies ought to be optimised by a tax lawyer.

For the international comparison, it is important to recognise that the treatment of certain operational expenses, e.g. cars, is addressed more boldly in Germany than in other countries, i.e. France. The acknowledgment of tangential operational expenses, e.g. nannies because of operational appointments, entertainment, formal requirements of the receipts and of the allocation to an account, is substantially reduced in the international comparison.

In Germany, the legal institution of the hidden profit distribution to the members of a partnership or to closely affiliated persons is of great importance. This concerns the transfer price for the delivery of services of affiliated companies of taxable persons that are located in foreign countries. In this case one should always consider if he can and/or should take advantage of such a transfer price with third foreign persons.

If one wishes to sell a taxable enterprise, the seller often identifies a usable lost carryover; accordingly, there are some limitations which are unsettling, and in every case this should be taken into consideration with a tax adviser.

Under certain conditions agreements to transfer profits and control agreements can be concluded between legal partnerships. In this way an individual can give up his legal independence and become a non-independent organ of a taxable controlling company. Under these conditions, the start-loss of a new company can be offset by the profits of an existing company and can thus result in a reduced payment of corporate income tax.

3. Business Tax

The regulations concerning the special agreement establishing a relationship between two companies are almost identical in the areas of the business tax and the corporate income tax; therefore, the effects of tax savings relative to the corporate income tax and the business tax can be concurrently optimized.

The business tax is a local tax that is fixed and levied by local authorities. Juristic and natural persons as well as the associations of persons that realize a commercial income within the meaning of paragraphs 15 ff. EStG are liable to the business tax. Several years ago, aside from the trade income, trade capital was subject to taxation. Today, only the trade income is taxed.

The ascertainment of this is first guided by the determination of the taxable income from trade for the business tax and for the corporate income tax. When this is identified, a conversion factor that applies a multiple to the local rate of assessment is employed. Generally, the amount of the business tax varies between 14 % and 20 % of the profit. The business tax reduces the basis of assessment for both the corporate income tax and the personal income tax, and this follows because it is defined as an operational expense. The business tax, while it is politically controversial, is debated and fixed on an annual basis. Very often it is considered one of the essential criteria when deciding on the choice of location for a business.

4. Value Added Tax

Value added tax is imposed on the supply of goods and services within Germany, on the importation of goods into Germany, and on the withdrawal of goods for the entrepreneur's own use.

There following cases provide exemptions from the VAT:

- the export of goods;
- the granting of loans;
- the assumption liabilities and guarantees;
- the deposit of securities and similar banking and insurance transactions;
- the transfer of securities;
- the import of special commodities (f.e. aurum utalium);
- the transfer of shares in closely held corporations and partnerships; and the transactions covered by the real estate transfer tax.

Normally, the VAT is levied at 16 % of the net sales price. A reduced rate of 7% exists for food, agricultural products and some professional services.

The primary economic objective of the VAT is to tax the domestic consumption of goods and services without distorting competitive relationships. Foreign business enterprises can recover the VAT at home, subject to reciprocity.

With the event of the Single European Market in 1993, movements of goods between EU countries are no longer classified as imports and exports. Also, these movements are not subject to border controls, which means that there is no mechanism for levying the VAT on imports. The German business purchasing goods from a supplier in another EU country makes an INTRA - UNION ACQUISITION and an INTRA-UNION SUPPLY for a corresponding delivery. The German buyer (acquirer) calculates the "acquisition tax" according to the VAT rate that would have been assessed had the products been purchased from a German supplier. It is this amount that is reported in the monthly VAT return.

This amount also qualifies as a deductible input tax so that, with the exception of banks and insurance companies, it is effectively an 'in' and 'out' item for entrepreneurs.

It is important to know that there are many formal accounting rules that must be adhered to, so that the value-added tax which is paid to the supplier, can be reduced as a value added tax (VAT), on input by the monthly application of the turnover tax to the administration of the finances.

In cases where an enterprise is established abroad, the following types of transactions are always viewed as having occured in the country of the recipient enterprise:
- transfer of patents, copyrights;
- licenses for royalties, licenses for sales know-how;
- advertising;
- services of lawyers, engineers, and accountants; and
- electronic data processing services.

Transactions in connection with trade fairs are generally performed in the country in which the trade fair takes place.

5. Real Estate Acquisition Tax

Real Estate Acquisition tax is levied at 3.5 % of the purchase price on the transfer of land and buildings. Both, seller and buyer, are jointly liable with respect to the tax authorities, even if the original contract designates the buyer as solely responsible.

Exemptions from real estate acquisition taxes are given for transfers by gift or inheritance, transactions between parents and their children, and, to a certain extent, reorganizations within the context of a jointly owned estate.

6. Real Estate Tax (Land Tax)

Proprietors of land and buildings are subject to the real estate tax. This tax is a local tax that varies between 0.6 % and 1.0 % of the value, which is determinated by law. It is important to know that the "defined value" amounts to about 40.0 % of the current actual market value. The tax is fixed at the beginning of each calendar year and paid to the local municipality in which the property exists.

7. Wage Tax

The enterprise is responsible for the income tax which is withheld from the salaries of employees by the employer. Generally, the employer pays the withholdings on a monthly basis to the tax authorities.

Furthermore, the enterprise is responsible for the German social security and the health insurance taxes. In the German social security system, the enterprise, if it is a domestic employer, will pay social security tax and health insurance for all salaried employees.

If the entrepreneur selects the legal form of a company for his commercial activities, his remuneration is relegated to the income category "unselbstaendige Taetigkeit" (employment). This means that his salary is considered an operational expense, thus reducing both the business tax and the corporate income tax.

However, if the entrepreneur chooses a partnership as the legal form for his commercial activities, his remuneration is *profit*, in which case the trade tax is not reduced.

IV. Key Aspects for the Purchase of Corporations in Germany

A. Optimization Possibilities in German Tax Law

In the last few years, it has been a declared goal of the German government to make Germany a more attractive location for internal and foreign investors. This is reflected in the new regulations for the transformation and consolidation of companies and the new statutory income tax and corporate tax regulations. In part, these new regulations have already been presented above.

These special laws make it possible to optimize the purchase of corporations. In this connection, the regulations vary from total or temporary tax exemptions for certain procedures to the usage of more favorable tax rates. Hence, the regulations of the 'Umwandlungssteuergesetz' (*conversion tax law*) make it possible for companies to merge to new units, without having to uncover hidden reserves in the corporations and thereby producing tax burdens.

According to the changed regulations of the income tax law, profits made from the sale of shares in limited liability corporations have to be "half taxed" only as of 2002 (cf. Reorganization of Par. 16, 17 EStG (income tax statute) as well as the explanation to the half- income- procedure mentioned above). This applies to the investment in business assets and in private means equally. Indeed, the sale of capital shares of business assets is only benefited if the shares are part of the working capital for at least a year.

If a limited liability corporation makes the sale, the profits arising from the sale of shares as of 2002 are normally totally exempt from corporate taxation. Here as well, the precondition is that the shares belonged to the limited liability corporation for at least a year at the time of the sale.

The tax aspects should not narrow the view for other main aspects concerning the purchase of corporations, which will be discussed subsequently.

B. On Time Integration of Fiscal and Legal Aspects in Corporation Purchases

Normally, tax aspects are not the decisive factor in corporation purchases, but marketing reasons are relevant for the purchase: Capturing or securing a market segment, creation and usage of synergy effects for an improved price - and service - policy with respect to the customers, as well as obtaining and securing financial resources, of technical know-how or secured supplier's service are examples of relevant items in such a purchase. Thus, the marketing strategies for the takeover of corporations should be first developed

On such an occasion, it is important to timely work the legal and fiscal aspects into the marketing model while elaborating a marketing and capital spending plan. The classic theory of the oriented division of business economics into the sectors marketing, finance, production and purchase has, unfortunately, left many corporation with the habit that marketing accountants integrate tax or legal aspects too late or not at all.

The following example may illustrate this:

The corporation which comes into consideration for purchase has a strong position in the market and pursues its marketing in a traditional form. The marketing plans provide that the strategy will be changed after the takeover. In such a case, the following questions have to be taken into consideration:

1. Should the previous marketing be supplemented via Internet- or Network Marketing, perhaps in combination with a franchise system?
2. In which federal state and at which location should workstations emerge?
3. Will the direct marketing (possibly with telephone- marketing) be performed from a foreign location into Germany?
4. Are the produced parts going to be homemade or manufactured abroad?

For fiscal and financial reasons, it is important to decide if the marketing work will be transacted by independent business enterprises, commercial agents, employees or part- time workers.

Correspondingly, the corporations have different legal and/or financial obligations such as the employer's duty to withhold or pay wage taxes, various social obligations or the duty to provide for compensation claims of the commercial agent, for which duly provisions must be composed. The situation in the sector of purchase/ production is similar.

This example makes it easy to recognize what a great impact legal and fiscal implications have. They could lead to significant additional expenses or to an ultimate loss of subsidies, if the purposeful form of organization is not timely prearranged with the responsible expert advisor, or if the right motions have not been timely filed.

Again, we refer hereby to the devastating effect of the disqualifying time periods.

Inter alia, the effects of these lead to the complete loss of benefits, if the application for benefits is not timely filed. This may cause damages of several million dollars.

C. Exclusion of Obligations in Corporation Purchases

Basically, the purchase of a corporation results from the acquisition of the company's assets or through an asset deal, i.e. through the purchase of company assets, which are of interest to the buyer. For example, the customer base, machinery, patent rights, know-how etc.

Through the use of these asset deals, one attempts to avoid the negative aspects such as bad assets, obligations, contingent liabilities, floating liabilities from employment contracts, confirmations of pension entitlements, guarantees, risks resulting from tax audits etc. Since this means the takeover of single economic goods, it is called singular succession in tax law. Singular succession means basically that the purchaser of corporations acquires only several economic goods and stays clear of obligations towards the vender, if he does not make any legal mistakes in the purchase.

In contrast, the purchase of company shares is called universal succession. Universal succession generally means that the buyer takes over all rights and obligations of the vender, all liabilities resulting from employment contracts, and all responsibilities towards the financial management.

As a general rule two aspects support the takeover of a corporation via the asset deal procedure:

1. The purchase price is tax deductible. With this reduction of the tax burden a significant part of the purchase prize can be financed.

2. The takeover of incalculable risks can be widely avoided by an asset deal.

If the asset deal is not possible, the purchaser should consider the transformation of the corporation into a partnership after the transaction, to keep the advantage of deducting the tax on the purchase price.

If a corporation is burdened with such economic problems that only continuation via singular succession makes sense, many important steps have to be taken into consideration, so that through unforeseeable legal mistakes, economic problems do not arise in the course of the succession. Some of the corporation purchases fail because lawyers or tax consultants were not duly assigned to solve these problems.

D. Optimization of the Corporation - Structure

Another substantial aspect of the purchase and / or the new foundation of a company in Germany is to support the acceleration of property growth via strategic performance. This can be achieved due to an optimization of the corporate structure. In this way, remarkable liquidity effects can be produced, which the German legislator has recognized and desires through its legislation.

The transformation law with its extended possibilities to split, merge, outsource, and the associated option to set book values, current values and interim values, provide a wide range of opportunities. Because of the limited scope herein, only several possibilities can be discussed here. Such optimization opportunities are often ignored in practice, since bigger companies commonly employ younger tax consultants to save costs, who handle the current tax declarations. They frequently lack training in tax law concerning company tax law, respectively in "tax balance politics" for the formation of corporate - structures.

V. Conclusion

When making the efforts to avoid tax burdens, one may not oversee that it is impossible to avoid all taxes. In considering investing in Germany, one must realize that the available infrastructure with respect to traffic, health care, professional knowledge, cultural recreation possibilities for employees, and a secured constitutional state which concerns itself with research, subsidies and other supporting measures to create and safeguard jobs, can not be provided without a certain amount of tax revenue. Accordingly, good tax politics can only add up to a reasonable tax optimization, not to the avoidance of all taxes.

Aspects of German Labor Law

Wolf D. Schenk

I. Generals Aspects

Labor law regulates contracted relationships between employers and employees. The liberal concept of contractual freedom is based upon the economic equality of the contracting parties. During the industrial revolution it became clear that there was no such equality between workers and employers, so a movement evolved to construct the legal corpus thought necessary for the protection of employees. These early developments became the springboard for current German labor law and their incipient ideas can still be found in the administration of justice. This becomes especially clear in the fact that an employee cannot waive the right that the contracting parties cannot decide whether a contractual relationship has to be understood as an employment relationship which is subject to the labor law or not.

It cannot be underestimated that labor law has become an important instrument in shaping the modern German corporation and its economic constitution. The state, therefore, demonstrates its interest in forming the underlying concepts and principles of the employment relationship through juridical means.

Social law is closely related to labor law despite the fact that in Germany, the courts representing these entities have exclusive jurisdiction ("Arbeitsgerichte" and "Sozialgerichte"); social law, for instance, regulates social insurances (pension insurance, health insurance, accident insurance, care insurance), unemployment relief and work permits.

In the past employees ("Angestellte") and workers ("Arbeiter") were treated by law as distinct entities, but due to Federal Constitution Court decisions it is no longer acceptable to consider this distinction binding in all cases. Today it is only of importance in the organization of social insurances. For the remainder of this chapter the term "employee" shall denote both employees and workers.

II. Sources

Labor law is influenced by the Civil Code (contracts of service law), the Commercial Code (commercial employees) and numerous special acts such as the Vacation Act, the Continued Payment of Wages Act (during illness of employee), the Working Mothers Protection Act, and others. It should be noted that because regulations in the Civil and Commercial Codes are rather short, it is difficult to extract existing labor law from them. Labor law is case law more so in Germany than in other countries. The European Community also influences German labor law through their so-called guideline competence and through the decisions of the

Court of Justice of the European Community; for instance, there are decisions and guidelines banning discrimination within employment relationships on the basis of gender.

Also, it should be noted that collective labor agreements belong to the sources of labor law.

III. Classes of Employment Relationships

Typically, an employment relationship lasts for an indeterminable period and the law states that there must be well defined reasons to delimit their duration. Practically speaking, this regulation provides only limited application because of the passage of the Employment Promotion Act ("Beschaeftigungsfoerderungsgesetz") which permits short-term employment contracts for periods of up to two years. This law was originally planned for a limited enforcement period but has since been prolonged. Under this law, short-term employees are given the same rights and protections as any other employee; yet some additional regulations apply: salaries cannot exceed the amount of € 325,-- a month; income tax payments are not required; also contributions for social insurances must be paid.

Another class of relationship is the trial period employment relationship. These relationships are permitted but the trial period is not allowed to exceed six months. As these arrangements sanction shorter periods of dismissal notice, an employee who has not completed the six month trial period cannot benefit from protections against dismissal.

Apprentices are considered employees and there are special regulations governing these relationships. Apprentices must have the opportunity to attend vocational school.

A category of "employee" that is growing at a significant rate is constituted of those who work at home. This type of employment is increasing primarily because modern computer technology has made it possible to perform work in geographic locations different from those of traditional firms (so called "tele work / Telearbeit"). According to the above criteria, home workers and "tele" workers are not employees, but through a special act they have attained the same status as employees. Accordingly, one can infer that "tele" work can be regarded as a true employment relationship if the employee has the responsibility of being available online at a pre-specified time.

IV. Who is an employee ?

German law acknowledges relationships described as "free-lance", such as contracts between doctors and patients, lawyers and clients, craftsmen and customers, and so on; but such contracts are not within the aegis of labor law. Whether or not these relationships are subsumed under labor law is dependent upon: their integration into the organization of an employer; whether or not they are bound by instructions; if they have to work within certain hours; whether or not they have to work at a fixed location within the company, and so on.

The employer who offers work on a free-lance basis often has an interest in his employee not being legally defined as an employee. In this way certain tax and expense advantages can be accrued. These approaches to labor contracts are often considered as means of avoiding applicable labor law.

In many cases the labor courts have hindered such free-lance employer/employee schemes. Many contracts that originally qualified as free-lance based have been transformed into employment contracts via arguments of employer integration; even contracts like partnership agreements, contracts for work and services, and franchise contracts have been forcibly transformed (catch word: sham free-lance based / "Scheinselbstaendigkeit"). The state demonstrates its interest in such relationships in response to tax and insurance policy; that is, the state seeks to ensure that salary taxes and social insurance contributions in every work relationship are properly addressed. In fact, the employer has been made liable for such payments; therefore an employer is at great risk should he compensate a worker on a free-lance basis when in reality a true employer/employee relationship exists. Payment "spot-checks" are often used by the state as an instrument in enforcing these matters.

By law a representative of a legal entity is not subject to labor law (this is the case for a manager of a limited liability company, a member of the managing board of a stock corporation, of a registered association or of a registered foundation) and the reasoning for this is clear: because these individuals execute the will of the legal entity they represent, they cannot be subject to its will.

Indeed, so-called executive officers ("leitende Angestellte") are bound by regulations, but because they work in the decision-making centers of institutions and execute their will, they are subject to special treatment by law. In fact, there is no clear definition for an executive officer; it depends on the case at hand. One indication that may help in discerning this takes place at the point in time when the employer decides which of his staff members will work with him. Executive officers are employees; functionally, however, they belong on the employer's side which is why the law grants them a special position. As such, they are not entitled to vote for the shops council; instead they have their own speaker committee. Additionally, they are not subject to regulations concerning working time, so they do not receive payment for overtime. Another feature, though less desirable, includes the fact that their employment contracts can be terminated more easily; but as a higher threshold of good faith towards their employer is generally a precondition for employment, there are no stringent requirements for dismissals due to questionable behavior. The employer can also terminate the relationship without citing reasons as long as appropriate compensations can be accounted for.

V. Employment Contracts

The basis for an employment relationship is an employment contract. It is possible for parties to enter into such contracts orally or even by implication, which of course can create difficult circumstances regarding proof of contract; therefore it is always advisable to enter into written contracts. Apart from this, at least one month after the confirmation of the relationship, the employer is obligated to write down the essential terms of the contract, endorse the document and then transfer it to the employee.

Should the employer fail to fulfill this obligation, the employment relationship will still be in effect. The employee thus retains the right to receive a written and signed document which has to include all the terms as required by law.

In principle the partners of a contract are free to agree upon the terms they wish; but in fact this freedom is restricted. Already the law includes certain restrictions on periods of notice, working time and so on; furthermore, the parties are bound to the regulations of existing union agreements; and finally, there are the arrangements between the employer and the shop council that must be respected.

The most important responsibility of the employee is his commitment to work. The employee must be at the employer's disposal during the designated working time and the employee must refrain from any activity that could prejudice his work. This could range from excessive drinking to the participation in such activities as sporting events that could result in injury. Violating any of these provisions can provide grounds for dismissal.

An employee has the right to practice other occupations while working for any given employer as long as his work performance for that employer is not compromised.

The employee has certain duties of good faith to his employer. During the existence of the employment relationship the employee is not allowed to work for a competitor and consequently to transfer company secrets. This regulation, however, is not applicable once the relationship is terminated. Should the employer wish to obstruct his former employee from working for a competitor, the employer and the employee must enter into a written contract which is enforceable for at most two years and which guarantees that the employee receive at least 50% of the salary he received at termination.

An employment contract is not void because one of its provisions is in violation of law. In fact, only the specific provision in question is invalid until it is replaced.

VI. Conflict of Laws

In principle the partners of the employment contract are free to apply a law different than German law for the employment relationship. It is possible, for instance, to implement American labor law in the case of an American sent to Germany;

however, an important limitation exists: the relationship is not allowed to deprive the employee of specific protections regarded by German law as binding in all cases. This can only be determined by comparing and contrasting the corresponding regulations of German law with those of the alternate law. Protections against dismissal, the regulations addressing the continuation of the employment relationship in cases where businesses are sold, the regulations concerning juvenile work protection, the regulations addressing protective legislation for working mothers and the regulations pertaining to the protection of severely disabled persons are regarded as binding by the administration of justice. Also, compliance with union agreements is required by law.

VII. Dismissal

In principle every employment relationship can be terminated; the employee is free to do so, however the employer is more confined and must adhere to certain rules. Certain union agreements such as collective bargaining agreements mandate that after a specified duration of time, the employee is "non-dismissable". This, however, does not exclude the so called "exceptional dismissal", see below. Public services, in particular, conform to this format, but it is also found in other areas of employment and occasionally in individual employment contracts. German labor law does not go as far; the duration of an employment relationship is only of importance with respect to periods of notice. Periods of notice expand depending upon the duration of the relationship: if the employment relationship has lasted between two and twenty years, the period of notice extends to one month beginning with the end of the calendar month; and after twenty years, seven months beginning with the end of the calendar month.

The employer is not entirely free to dissolve the employment contract: the Termination Protection Act defines certain parameters restricting his rights to do so. Its provisions, however, are applicable only to companies with more than five permanent employees and only to "dismissed" employees whose employment relationship has continued for more than six months beyond the point in time of the dismissal notice.

Under the Termination Protection Act, dismissals are considered under various circumstances. They depend upon the behavior of employee, upon reasons existing in the person of the employee, and upon urgent business needs.

The Act stipulates that every dismissal which is not socially justified is invalid. Dismissals are socially justified by reasons existing in the person of the employee (for instance, long absences due to illness) or by reasons existing in the behavior of the employee (lack of collegialism, cantankerous behavior, etc.).

Dismissals dependent upon urgent business requirements are problematic. Indeed, dismissals due to technical business requirements, economic reasons, or other legitimate business needs are in principle justified, but other circumstances must be considered. The following paragraphs address some of these particulars.

In principle the employer is free to organize his business in any way he deems necessary. If jobs are abolished, the court has no recourse for review except in cases where some form of abuse is evident; but before an employer dissolves a contract, it is his responsibility to determine if the affected employee can be transferred to another department within the business. When this occurs, the employer is in reality offering another contract while terminating the current one. The employee can challenge the initial termination at court with the reservation that should he lose, he can accept the offer for the new contract. In instances where sections of businesses are relocated, the employer has to make an offer of work to the affected employee at the new location. Should he fail to do so, then any employer-initiated termination occurring as a result of the relocation is invalid.

Again, for dismissals dependent upon urgent business requirements, the principle of "social selection" must be considered. The employer is not allowed to terminate the contracts of employees he doesn't want; instead, he is required to consider which employees are most adversely affected by the dismissals. Relevant criteria for this is the length of service with the firm, age, family obligations, and possibly the consideration of other circumstances. As a rule, younger employees are least affected, and are therefore most likely to be released.

A precondition for "social selection" is that the circumstances of the work possessed by the affected employees must be comparable, that is, in reference to the rank of the affected employees and the type of work performed. This constitutes a difficulty for the employee who desires to challenge a dismissal; for instance, some years ago, the Labor Court in Munich ruled on the occasion of a dismissal wave at the Siemens AG that different groups of engineers were not entirely comparable with one other.

In every case the so-called "exceptional dismissal" with or without notice is possible if the continuation of the employment relationship is deemed unreasonable. As a rule, valid reasons for the discontinuation of a relationship are limited to severe violations of the contract by the employee. If the violations are severe, as in cases of embezzlement where even small amounts of money are considered severe, such exceptional circumstances render dismissal without notice justified *ipso jure*. If the violations are not severe, then a repeat incident may lead to an exceptional dismissal, however, this is contingent upon the employee having received prior warning. Of course these rules also apply to the previously mentioned "non-dismissable" employee. And furthermore, the non-dismissable employee can be dismissed if the employer decides that their work facility is to be removed in which case the affected employees have recourse to their common rights as outlined in the Termination Protection Act.

If an employee wishes to challenge a dismissal, he must file his appeal at the appropriate Labor Court within three weeks after dismissal. Should he fail to observe this, the dismissal will become effective. The employee can file an application for belated admission if he can prove that extenuating circumstances prevented him from taking action in a more timely manner (for instance, receipt of the dismissal during a planned vacation).

In principle, only the Labor Court has the power to decide if a dismissal is lawful or not. If one of the parties files an application for termination of an employment relationship because its continuation is deemed unreasonable, the Court can terminate the relationship and order a compensation for the dismissal (as mentioned earlier, this provision does not apply to executive personnel). As a rule this compensation is based upon the following: for each year of the employment period, half of the monthly salary is estimated and rewarded. As long as compensation does not exceed the amount of € 8.181,--, no social insurance contributions are required to be paid. Higher ceilings exist for older employees. It should be noted that frequently, a regular salary in addition to that determined by the above calculation is embedded within the compensation plan. In this case, taxes and social insurance contributions must be paid.

In practice, about 80 % of all the dismissal trials end with the parties agreeing to the termination of the contract and to the payment of compensation, and as a rule one begins with the above formula when deriving the compensation. Occasionally, however, there are cases where more extravagant amounts of money are assessed, but this depends on the particular circumstances of the case and on the negotiating skills of the concerned lawyers.

Certain groups of employees are protected from "routine" dismissals. To these belong representatives of employees (works council etc.), pregnant women, mothers until the expiration of the fourth month after delivery, and severely disabled persons with the approval of competent authority.

Special rules apply to mass dismissals. Definitions for this category include: when within one month, in a smaller firm (20 to 60 employees), more than 5 employees are terminated; in medium sized firms (60 to 500 employees) 10 % or more than 25 employees are terminated; and in firms with more than 500 employees at least 30 employees are terminated.

The president of the employment office must receive notification of such mass dismissals who then reviews and justifies them. One month after this notification, no dismissal can be reversed. Under special circumstances, however, the notification period can be extended to two months. The dismissals become effective only with the concurrence of the president of the employment office. He also can order certain facilitations for the employees to be terminated, for instance, the admission of short-time work.

VIII. Transfer of a business

A special protection against unlawful dismissal exists in cases where a whole firm or sections of it are transferred to a new owner. According to Par. 613a of the German Civil Code, dismissals which result from the transfer are invalid. This means that all employment relationships are transferred by law to the new owner.

If, as is often encountered in practice, the available work has to be reduced due to changes in the organization of the business, any dismissal restrictions resulting from the provisions of Par. 613a of the German Civil Code become inapplicable.

It is often disputed whether or not a transfer of business exists; for example, the European Court ruled in a 1995 case that a sole janitor employed by a firm in Hamburg, Germany constituted a part of the business establishment. Based upon the decision of the employer to contract an independent cleaning firm, the court ruled that the janitor automatically became an employee of the new cleaning firm. Although this judgment has been challenged by most of the German Labor Courts, it demonstrates the types of difficulties encountered in this area of law.

Collective bargaining agreements are not immediately influenced by transfers. Generally they cannot be changed for at least one year following a transfer, that is, unless the new employer is prebound to a different agreement.

IX. Collective Bargaining Agreements

The conditions of employment for most of the larger firms are subject to collective bargaining agreements. Collective bargaining agreements are arrangements between labor unions and either employer's associations or single employers.

Collective bargaining agreements contain regulations that may cover a wide range of issues such as the fixing of minimum salary levels, the fixing of periods of notice that may exceed legal limits, industrial safety regulations, etc..

As a rule, collective bargaining agreements apply only to the parties entering into the agreements, or as stated earlier, between the labor unions and either the respective employer's associations or single employers. It should be noted that an employer can apply the same provisions to employees not bound by these agreements, although there exists no obligation to do so .

The government can declare collective bargaining agreements generally binding which has the effect of extending their coverage to all concerned employment relationships.

Collective bargaining agreements can be restricted both locally and chronologically. Additionally, they can be terminated. The right to terminate is often used when labor unions wish to secure better terms, however it should be kept in mind that a collective bargaining agreement remains in effect despite termination until a new agreement is concluded.

X. Co-Determination

German law acknowledges two forms of worker participation in management : the works council and "co-determination". Co-deternimation is defined as the participation of employees in the supervisory boards of large firms.

A. Works Councils

The legal foundation for the formation and the activity of the works councils is the Works Constitution Act.

There is no obligation to form a works council; however, should employees choose to establish one, the employer is required to support that decision. This applies only to firms with more than 5 employees.

Organizations receiving exemption to this requirement include religious communities including their charitable and educational institutions.

Special provisions apply to specific institutions such as those serving ideological purposes such as political parties, the administrations of labor unions and employer's associations, health care and health assistance enterprises, the Red Cross, boarding schools, scientific libraries, etc.. Very important are the special provisions for businesses that depend upon the rights of free speech, the freedom of the press and the freedom of reporting; thus, press firms, publishing houses, private television and radio enterprises are included in this category. Other restrictions in the powers of the works council can apply to businesses and institutions only so far as certain characteristics of these enterprises conflict with the provisions of the Works Constitution Act. Some employers, for instance, are not required to keep works councils apprised of the current economic developments of their respective businesses. A reconciliation of interest and/or social compensation is mandated only in cases where fundamental changes in the conduct of a business occur. More discussion of this matter follows.

Works councils are associated with single business entities (the business unit). If an enterprise has several businesses, a central works council is formed, and in the case of a group of companies (organized combinations of several independent companies) a central works council of affiliated companies is established. The members of the latter two forums consist of members of the respective single works councils. They concern themselves with matters that are so encroaching that they cannot be resolved at the level of the single works council.

The individual members of the works councils are elected every four years by company staff. The expenses for the elections and the work of the councils are compensated for by the employer.

The operational duties of the councils are exercised in a co-operational manner. To these duties belong social, personnel and economic issues. Social matters constitute concerns such as the social climate of the business, the behavior of the employees, determining work hours, statements of vacation plans, operational wage arrangements, etc. .

Works councils can only block the decisions of employers. This tends to foster an environment conducive to agreement which itself is reinforced by a special committee called the conciliation committee. This committee consists of equal numbers representing the employer's side and the works council. Also present is an independent chairman whose selection both parties must agree to. Customarily, the vote of this chairman decides the issues at hand, but, as a rule, he initially attempts to design conciliatory solutions all parties can agree to. This latter approach has the advantage that such agreements cannot be challenged in the courts, whereas arbitration awards formed through the conciliation committee can, to a certain extent, come under judicial review.

The most important right of co-operation in personnel matters is exercised with respect to employments, transfers, arrangements in groups and dismissals; for instance, the works council can refuse consent to the employment of a new worker not only if the employment violates hiring guidelines, but also if another employee is made redundant as a result of the hiring.

Another important right is the right of the council to co-operation at dismissals. The council has the power to protest dismissals, which may not necessarily reverse them, but which can result in lengthy drawn-out lawsuits. Should a lawsuit result over a dismissal, the affected employee (or employees) retains the right to continue work and receive compensation beyond the established period of notice.

In economic matters the rights of the council are restricted to the receipt of comprehensive information about the economic conditions of the business, and this applies only to companies with more than 100 employees. An exception to the restricion is enforced when a fundamental change in the conduct of the business occurs. Activities such as company closures, transfers, merges, changes in the organization of the business, changes in the purpose of the business or the introduction of new work methods and production processes, require the consent of the works council to be effective. If agreements can't be reached, conciliation committees are established through which either arrangements are negotiated or arbitration awards are granted. These proceedings are termed "reconciliations of interests" and "social compensation plans".

The successful co-operation of the employer with the works council finds its expression in work agreements which have direct application and are binding. An employee can waive a right granted him by a work agreement but only with the consent of the works council. Agreements can be terminated within a period of three months as long as no replacement agreements are concluded.

B. Co-determination Law

The co-operation of employees within the parameters of Co-determination Law is very different. This law only applies to corporations with more than 2000 employees. Religious communities, enterprises serving ideological purposes, and media concerns are exempt.

Co-determination requires that the supervisory board be staffed on a basis of equality with representatives of the shareholders and the employees. The representatives of the shareholders are nominated by the shareholders whereas the representatives of the employees are elected either in a direct election or by delegates. Often, officials of the works councils are on the supervisory board.

The supervisory board has considerable authority, especially during a business crisis. It can exercise powers to nominate or dismiss boards of management. In this respect, employees directly influence the operations of the corporation.

Naturally, the varying interests of the shareholders and the employees can lead to voter deadlock over controversial matters. In such cases, new votes are conducted whereby the respective chairmen of the supervisory boards claim two votes and thereby determine the respective outcomes.

Residence and Work Permits

Michael Wendler

I. Work permit laws

A. General points

The legal sources of work permit laws until now have been Par. 19 Promotion of Labour Act (AFG) and the Regulation concerning Work Permits for Non-German Workers (AEVO), which was introduced on the basis of Par. 19 section 4 AFG and which regulates the conditions that must be satisfied in each case before a work permit can be granted.

By introducing the Law for the Reform of Promotion of Labour dated 1997-03-24, the legislator abrogated the Promotion of Labour Act (AFG) as per 1998-01-01, excepting Par. 221 and 244 AFG, and transferred the laws on promotion of labour to a newly created 3rd book in the Code of Social Law (SGB III). In passing the Regulation for Granting Work Permits to Foreign Workers (ArGV) dated 1998-09-17, the regulating body has made use of its right to pass regulations in accordance with Par. 288 SGB III. ArGV regulates the conditions and exceptions in which work permits can be granted. Accordingly, ArGV corresponds in terms of regulatory contents with AEVO.[1]

The main principles of work permit laws will remain unchanged, even after the new law has been introduced. Accordingly, it is still fair to draw on the judicial rulings made on the basis of Par. 19 AFG and AEVO.

The law now makes no distinction between general and special work permits. A work permit in the meaning of Par. 285 SGB III has now replaced the general work permit. The privileged form of the special work permit has now been replaced by the work permit in the meaning of Par. 286 SGB III.

---

[1] The explanations under items 1 to 3 refer to the current legal provisions. At the start of 2003, the "Law for the Control and Limitation of Residency and the Integration of Citizens of the Union and Foreign nationals (Immigration Act)" will transform the whole system of work permit and residency laws. This law is currently being put to the legislators in the Federal Republic of Germany. In view of the fact that sweeping changes in this legal subject matter are imminent, item 4 will already deal with the main elements of the "Immigration Act".

B. Compulsory work permits

In order to engage independent employment in the Federal Republic of Germany, foreign nationals require a permit from the Federal Employment Office in accordance with Par. 284 section 1 SGB III; in most cases, these permits are issued by the local employment office. This ban on working also constitutes a ban on employment for employers.

C. Legal sources

The legal basis for the current work permit laws is mainly found in Par. 284 ff. SGB III and in the Regulation for Granting Work Permits to Foreign Workers (ArGV), which was passed on the basis of the authorisation to pass regulations specified by Par. 288 SGB III and which regulates the conditions for granting work permits to foreign nationals.

Work permit laws have strong ties to residency laws. For example, a work permit may be granted only if the foreign national is in possession of a residency permit (Par. 284 section 5 SGB III); conversely, withdrawal of the residency permit also constitutes withdrawal of the work permit in accordance with Par. 8 section 1 no. 1 sentence 2 ArGV.

Par. 285 section 3 SGB III regulates that foreign nationals whose place of residence is abroad or normally reside abroad, but who are in gainful employment in the Federal Republic of Germany, may only be granted a work permit if this is specifically dictated by the ordinance.

The corresponding regulation in residency laws is Par. 10 section 1 Foreign Citizen Law (AuslG), according to which a residency permit may only be granted for periods of work lasting in excess of three months according to the provisions of the ordinance passed on the basis of Par. 10 section 2 AuslG. The Regulation concerning Residency Permits for the Pursuit of Dependent Employment (AAV) does grant the regulatory body certain exceptional cases for granting work permits to certain groups of people or for certain types of profession. The regulation also contains effectively identical provisions for granting work permits to recently immigrated foreign workers in exceptional cases, the so-called Regulation for Exceptional Cases Despite a Freeze on Work Permits.

Finally, priority-ranking union laws and numerous bilateral and multilateral agreements also take effect on national work permit laws. Par. 284 section 1 no. 1 SGB III has only a declaratory significance for EU citizens who are entitled to live where they please and are therefore exempted from the need to have a work permit; the same has applied accordingly since 01.01.1994 for citizens of EFTA states, excepting Switzerland, as agreed in the European Economic Community Agreement (EEC Agreement dated 1992-05-02, BGBl. II 1993, P. 266, 1294).

II. Residency laws

A work permit according to Par. 285 SGB III in connection with Par. 1 ff. ArGV is the normal, unprivileged form of work permits. They can be restricted to a certain job or business and are granted in accordance with the situation and development of the job market. In the first instance of employment, the issue of a general work permit may be made dependent on the waiting period and the fixed day, as specified by Par. 285 section 4 SGB III in connection with Par. 3 ArGV. The factual characteristic of the situation and development of the job market guarantees the principle of prioritisation. The work permit must only be granted as long as it does not pose an obstacle to the chances of prioritised workers finding employment. This means that the applicant cannot take the place of any prioritised worker. However, a work permit can only be granted if a residence permit has already been issued. In accordance with Par. 5 AuslG, the residence permit is granted as permission to remain resident (Par. 15, 17 AuslG), entitlement to remain resident (Par. 27 AuslG), approval of residency (Par. 28, 29 AuslG) or authorisation to remain resident (Par. 39 AuslG). The version that is granted is dependent primarily on the purpose of residency.

The prioritised workers include German nationals, foreign workers who are in possession of an entitlement to remain resident or who are entitled to go and work where they please on the basis of being EU members or citizens of a country within the EEC Treaty, workers who do not require a work permit and finally workers in possession of a work permit in accordance with Par. 286 SGB III.

The work permit (Par. 286 SGB III) is generally granted for all of Germany, regardless of the situation or development of the job market and without any restriction to a certain line of work or a certain business (Par. 286 section 3 SGB III).

A. Material area of application

In essence, each form of dependent employment that may limit the chances of German workers or foreign workers who have been placed on a par with German workers should be regarded as requiring a work permit in the meaning of Par. 284 section 1 SGB III. Self-employed gainful employment does not cover this area. Apart from this, it would be fair to draw on the definition in Par. 12 section1 DVAuslG (Implementation Regulation for the Foreign Citizen Law) in order to define the terms.

B. Personal area of application

In effect, all workers that are not German nationals as defined by section 116 of the German Constitution (GG) must be in possession of a work permit.

At the moment there are no bi- or multilateral agreements with other countries that exempt workers from the obligation to obtain a work permit (Par. 284

sentence 1 no. 3 SGB III), if one disregards the exceptional regulations for the employees of international organisations, e.g. the European Patent Office or the deployed NATO armed forces.

The following persons do not require a work permit: foreigners without own nationality (Par. 17 section 1 HAG), holders of an unrestricted work permit or residence permit (Par. 284 section 1 no. 2 SGB III) and members of EU states who may live and work where they please (Par. 284 section 1 no. 1 SGB III). The latter group in this list derive their rights from overriding community law (section 48 ff EGV, VO 1612/68).

In accordance with Par. 19 section 4 sentence 2 AFG, the regulatory body can approve exceptions to Par. 19 section 1 sentences 1 and 3 AFG for individual professional groups and persons. The regulatory body has made use of this with a comprehensive catalogue of exemptions in Par. 9 AEVO. It is important to draw particular attention to Par. 9 no. 15 and 16 AEVO, which dictate that people born in Germany and in possession of an unrestricted work permit and foreign nationals in possession of an entitlement to remain resident are exempted from the requirement to hold a work permit. With these exceptions, the regulatory body has recognised that these groups of persons are essentially integrated within German society. The other facts specified to Par. 9 AEVO that lead to exemption are characterised by the fact that certain groups of persons and forms of employment on the domestic job market neither affect the domestic job market nor the principle of prioritisation.

III. Immediate programme to satisfy demand for IT specialists

A. Overview

The IT-ArGV dated 2000-07-11 was introduced by the Federal Ministry of Employment and Social Order to regulate the manner in which work permits are issued to highly qualified specialists in information and communication technology. The IT-ArGV permits applications for work permits in a period of three years after coming into force. This is intended to help satisfy a current, temporary demand for highly qualified specialists with a university or polytechnic education focussing on information or communication technology or whose qualification is confirmed by a minimum annual gross salary of € 50,000.

The local employment offices offer employers support in the recruitment of highly qualified, foreign IT specialists. The work permits are granted exclusively by the local employment offices.

B. Details

The work permit remains valid for the duration of the employment, but for no longer than three years. However, it can be extended to five years. A residence permit will be granted once a work permit has been granted. The remaining details were published in the Internal Instruction/Official Circular from the BMA and the IT-ArGV.

IV. Law for the Control and Limitation on Residency and the Integration of Union Citizens and Foreign nationals (Immigration Act)

A. New structures

The centrepiece of the "Immigration Act" is a comprehensive re-regulation of laws governing foreign nationals. The current legislation governing foreign nationals will be replaced by a law concerning the residency, the gainful employment and the integration of foreign nationals in Germany (Residency Law). It appears likely that this new legislation will come into force on January 1, 2003. This new law will also incorporate the most important provisions of work permit laws. Accordingly, this will be the first time that the main provisions of residency laws and those of work permit laws for foreign nationals will be united in one law.

The number of residency titles will be reduced to two. In place of the authorisation to remain resident, the approval of residency, the restricted and unrestricted residence permit and entitlement to remain resident, there will now only be two residency titles: a (restricted) residence permit and a (unrestricted) settlement permit.

In order to make it easier to understand, the new residency law is no longer bound to the purpose of residency (education, gainful employment, joining family members, humanitarian reasons).

A new Federal Office for Migration and Refugees will look after a series of important tasks previously dealt with by the former Federal Office for the Recognition of Foreign Refugees. The main tasks are:

- coordination of the information between the government agencies dealing with foreign nationals, the labour market administration bodies and the German representations abroad concerning the migration of labour
- implementation of an optional selection procedure on the basis of a points system
- development of a national integration program and information concerning programmes on offer designed to integrate foreign nationals
- maintenance of a central register of foreign nationals
- implementation of measures to promote voluntary repatriation

In addition, the new Federal Office will be linked in organisational terms with the Federal Institute for Population Research as an independent academic research institution.

Furthermore, an independent committee of experts for immigration and integration will be installed within the new Federal Office. It has the task of carrying out regular assessments of the absorption and integration capacities within the country as well as the definition of the current developments in migration. It is intended to submit an annual report on the migratory situation. The report should also make statements on the necessity of immigration in a selection procedure and if necessary also recommendations on the maximum number.

B. Work migration

The forms of immigration will be possible within the field of work migration:

Immigration in a regular procedure is kept open and flexible in order to give work administration bodies room for manoeuvre and control. The examination of prioritisation by the work administration bodies is simplified. In addition, access to the job market will in future be regulated by regional circumstances. A proposal has been voiced in this context to give the administrative committees that already exist within the local employment offices greater competency. The current double authorisation procedure (application for residence permit and application for work permit) will be replaced by an internal approval procedure. The work permit will be granted in one act with the residence permit once the work administration bodies have granted approval internally. The residence title is granted by the foreign nationals agency, thus meaning that the persons concerned are no longer required to make several applications and visits to the local government agencies (one-stop government).

There is the option of offering **highly qualified applicants** (e.g. engineers, IT engineers, mathematicians and executives in science and research) permanent residence from the start.

In addition to this, a new option will enable the recruitment of a limited number of specifically qualified foreign nationals in a **selection procedure**. This is an additional, optional instrument of control, which will most likely be open to a very small number of immigrants only at the start.

This will require a careful selection of applicants. The minimum terms are that the costs of living should be covered and the persons concerned should have professional qualifications. Additional criteria include age, qualification, language skills, relationship with Germany and the country of origin. This makes it possible to give special consideration to countries applying to join the EU. The selection procedure will be carried out centrally by the Federal Office for Migration and Refugees. However, this requires first of all that the Federal Office and the Federal Agency for Employment define a maximum number of immigrants for the selection procedure once the expert committee for immigration and integration has been consulted.

Foreign **university graduates** will be granted permission to seek employment once the work administrative bodies have approved. In addition, they will be given a one-year residence permit in order to seek employment. This is to prevent well-trained specialists who are urgently required in Germany going elsewhere to find employment. Up until now, they have regularly been required to leave Germany after finishing their studies.

A legal foundation will be created for self-employed persons from whom one can reasonably expect positive influences on the economy and employment. The condition is that there should be an economic interest or a particular regional demand.

Distribution Agreements

Michael Bihler

I. The Law Pertaining to Commercial Agents

A. Source of Laws

The primary source of German commercial agent law is contained in the Commercial Code (Par. 84 - 92c HGB). This law is nearly identical with the commercial agent law in effect in the other states of the European Community. The reason for this standardization is the 1986 enactment of a European Community directive (EC Directive of Dec. 18, 1986 ABlEG Dec. 12 1986 No. L328/17). This directive, which to a large extent was based on the German model, required the Member States to incorporate the commercial agent law contained in the directive into their own national law. All of the States of the European Community have now done so.

Most of the provisions contained in the HGB pertaining to commercial agents are mandatory; this means that such provisions are deemed to be binding on all principal-commercial agent relationships and any contractual terms to the contrary are void. In addition, even in those areas where the HGB does allow contractual deviations, a part of the German Civil Code (BGB) about the Regulation of Standard Business Terms allows such deviations, only if the commercial agent is not unreasonably disadvantaged.

This regulation applies to commercial agent contracts because, as a rule, such contracts are standard form contracts which have been drafted by a business enterprise for use by all its commercial agents. This rules serve to compensate for the relatively weaker bargaining position of a party faced with a standard form contract drafted by another through providing the party with certain legal protections. This is not to say, however, that no room exists for the tailoring of commercial agent contracts to the special needs of the parties. The following sections will discuss key aspects of the law pertaining to commercial agents and the extent to which deviations therefrom are allowed.

B. Commercial agent versus employee

A commercial agent is an independent contractor whose permanent business is either to act as an intermediary in bringing about direct legal relations between his principal and the third party or to enter into contracts with the third party on behalf of the principal (Par. 84, sec. 1, sentence 1 HGB). Whether a principal-commercial agent relationship has been created or whether the "agent" is in fact an employee is primarily a question of whether the "agent" possesses important distinguishing characteristics of independent activity. If this independence is not present, the commercial agent will be viewed as an employee (Par. 84, sec. 2 HGB).

Case law holds that the individual circumstances as a whole determine whether the requisite independence is present in any particular case. Criteria for such independence are that the commercial agent (1) is only to a limited extent subject to instructions and (2) bears personal business risk. These criteria are easily met, for example, when commercial agents are free to decide whether they will engage employees or contract workers and if so whom, and if all of the agents' business costs are paid out of their earned commission. Additional indications that agents work independently include the existence of their own place of business and/or organization. On the other hand, contract terms which limit agents' choice of employees or impose such a strict reporting duty on the agents that an air-tight control system is maintained raise considerable doubt whether a principal-commercial agent relationship is present.

C. Contract obligations

1. Commercial agent

According to Par. 86, sec. 1 HGB, the primary obligation of the commercial agent is to act as a middleman in bringing about direct legal relations between the principal and third parties or to enter into contracts with third parties on behalf of the principal. This obligation must be fulfilled with the diligence of a "prudent businessperson."

A commercial agent also has a duty to review the financial soundness of new customers. Although not expressly stated in the law, this duty is implied from the HGB's general requirement that an agent represent the interests of the principal in his arranging and procuring of customers and/or contracts (Par. 86, sec. 1 HGB). If the agent failed to screen the economic background of new customers, a principal's interests could be placed in jeopardy. Agents have a duty to ascertain the financial soundness of a former customer, however, only if aware of a delay in payment or other circumstances which impact the customer's credit worthiness.

This duty to review the financial soundness of customers is satisfied by the agent's use of informal methods of inquiry. In fact, a provision in a standard form contract which requires commercial agents to procure credit information at their own costs is invalid. However, if, the agent is reimbursed for the costs incurred, the parties may stipulate in the commercial agent contract that official credit reports be obtained and/or credit research be conducted.

Another important duty imposed on the commercial agent is to provide the principal with all necessary information. This duty includes in particular the obligation to promptly inform the principal of all successful arrangements or procurements of business. The exact type of information the commercial agent must transmit is determined by the application of an objective standard. The duty to report should not be so extensive and detailed that it collides with the independence of the commercial agent. On the other hand, the parties may establish a reporting system.

Another duty which is implied from the law's requirement that the agent protect the interests of the principal is the duty not to simultaneously work for the principal and for a third person who is involved in the same sphere or scope of business activity as the principal. The issue here is not whether or not the commercial agent's breach of this duty has actually caused the principal damage. Rather, activity which is in competition with the principal's business is prohibited because it disturbs the important relationship of trust which should exist between a commercial agent and a principal. While this duty flows from the law itself, generally a competition prohibition will be contractually agreed to by the parties in writing. In the event of a breach of the agent's duty not to work for a competitor, the principal has the right to terminate the commercial agent contract without prior notice. The principal may also seek contract penalties if they have been agreed to in the commercial agent contract ["Entscheidungen des Bundesgerichtshofs in Zivilsachen" (BGHZ 42, 59)].

Sometimes the commercial agent may also be charged with duties which are atypical for commercial agent activities and which extend beyond what is normally expected of an agent. The imposition of such additional obligations (for example, the duty to stock goods) raises the issue of whether or not the commission is adequate to compensate the agent for the extra duties or whether or not additional claims for remuneration exist.

2. Principal

Among other duties, the principal must provide the commercial agent with all that an agent reasonably needs from a principal in order to fulfill his responsibilities. This duty includes, in particular, the responsibility to keep the agent thoroughly informed (Par. 86a, sec. 2, sentence 1 HGB).

Principals remain free, however, to independently manage their businesses and are, therefore, under no obligation to involve commercial agents in this process. Decisions regarding production, marketing and sales, quality and price of goods are exclusively the province of the principal.

The only limitation to the principal's exclusive management right is the arbitrariness prohibition. If the principal, for example, arbitrarily and without a valid reason, discontinues or suspends production, commercial agents must be advised in advance. If the principal fails to provide such advance notice, then the agents may be entitled to damages.

D. Commercial agents' commissions

1. General, regional and sole agents

According to Par. 87, sec. 1 HGB, the commercial agent is entitled to a commission on all contracts entered into during the time that a commercial agent contract is in effect and which are either (1) the result of the activity of the agent or (2) entered into with a third party who the agent had previously contacted regarding the same type of goods. Under this standard, the agent's activity need not be the sole or the primary cause of the contract between the principal (or the dealer on the principal's behalf) and customer. It is sufficient if the agent's action is only one of the reasons for the contract. In addition, the agent is entitled to a commission on all reorders or subsequent contracts unless the commercial agent contract specifically and expressly provides otherwise.

Often a type of commercial agent known as a regional agent will be assigned a specific area and/or circle of customers. In this case, the agent is not only entitled to a commission on contracts he or she has helped to secure, but rather on all contracts with customers from this geographic area or customer circle which are entered into during the time that the commercial agent contract is in effect. In addition, regional agents can require that the principal ensure that their territory is respected by other agents.

Another common type of commercial agent is the "sole" agent ("exclusive agent"), who, as the name suggests, possesses the sole right to represent the principal in an assigned geographic area. Like the regional agent, the sole agent is entitled to a commission on all contracts with customers from his or her assigned territory. Unlike regional agents, however, sole agents enjoy the additional right that even the sales and marketing activity of the principal in the agents designated territories is excluded unless the commercial agent contract specifically provides otherwise.

2. Overhang commission

Under the law, the commercial agent is entitled to a commission on sales which occur after the expiration or termination of the commercial agent contract if the agent has arranged or procured the sale or taken such preparatory steps that the sale can be said to be primarily the result of the agent's activities; or, if before the agent-principal relationship came to an end, the principal had received an offer to buy from a third person (Par. 87, sec. 3 HGB).

This right of agents to a payment of commission on sales occurring after the expiration of their commercial agent contract ("overhang commission") can, however, be contractually modified or eliminated if a factually justifiable reason for it exists. According to a precedent case ruling, a justifiable reason exists if, at the beginning of the contract term, the commercial agent receives commissions on sales that his or her predecessor initiated, and the agent's successor likewise receives commissions on any sales occurring after the agent's contract expires.

3. Unilateral changes to contract terms

As a rule, contract provisions which allow the principal to make unilateral changes during the duration of the commercial agent contract, such as unilaterally altering the agent's rate of commission, the borders of the assigned geographical area or the products which said agent handles on behalf of the principal, are unenforceable. The only options for a principal who wishes to make a unilateral change are: (1) in the case of a commercial agent contract with an unspecified duration, to make use of a special type of termination known as a "Änderungskündigung," which is a termination of the contract with the simultaneous option of renewal under altered conditions or (2) to connect the reservation of right to make unilateral changes to a specific reasonable set of circumstances; such as for example, the reduction of the assigned geographical area if sales are reduced.

4. Manifestation of the agent's right to a commission

Under Par. 87a HGB, the commercial agent has a right to a commission at the time the sales transaction is carried out. This means that the agent's entitlement occurs as soon as the principal has delivered the goods, regardless of whether or not the customer has paid for them. The parties can, however, contractually deviate or modify this rule (Par. 87a, sec. 1 HGB). One typical modification is for the parties to agree that the agent is not entitled to a commission until the third person has acted on the sales contract, that is, until the customer has actually made payment. This particular modification, which is generally regarded as enforceable, results in the commercial agent bearing the full risk for the execution of the contract.

5. Miscellaneous mandatory rights impacting agent's commission

If commercial agents agree to guarantee the payment of the procured customers ("del credere agent"), they are entitled to an additional commission (Par. 86b HGB). Another mandatory provision regarding the commission is contained in Par. 87a, sec. 3 HGB. According to this provision, commercial agents are entitled to a full commission on any contract they have entered into with the customer, even if the contract terms are subsequently partly or completely not fulfilled; provided that the partial or total lack of fulfillment is due to circumstances for which the principal is responsible.

Par. 87 of the HGB ensures that commercial agents are remunerated for their efforts when, based on reasons that have to do with the relationship between the principal and the third party, the contract is not executed. Contract terms which attempt to deviate from this law are unenforceable. Examples of this are a stipulation that the agent is not entitled to a commission in the event the principal would suffer a loss if the contract was executed, or a clause which requires the agent to bear the costs in the event of a legal dispute with the third party.

On the other hand, agents are not entitled to a commission if the contract is not carried out due to reasons for which the principal is not responsible. Such a situation may arise, for example, if a customer's default in payment results in the principal being legally entitled to refuse performance.

If the principal has reserved the right of "Selbstbelieferung," then the customer has the right to demand delivery of the goods contracted for only if the principal is able to acquire them. While such a reservation excuses the principal's performance vis à vis the customer, the agent nevertheless remains entitled to a full commission on the contract despite the principal's inability to perform. Because the agent has a right to rely on the principal's ability to deliver the goods which the agent has marketed in good faith, the fact that a supplier fails to provide the goods to the principal is deemed to be a circumstance for which the principal is responsible.

6. Amount of commission

The amount of the commission is usually agreed to by the parties in their commercial agent contract. In the event that the contract fails to address this issue, the customary rate must be paid (Par. 87b, sec. 1 HGB).

Ancillary costs for freight, packaging, duties and taxes which the principal incurs and separately lists in the customer's invoice are not considered a part of the customer's payment for the goods themselves and, therefore, have no influence on the amount of the agent's commission. On the other hand, ancillary costs which are passed on to the customer but not separately listed in the invoice are considered a part of the contract price upon which the agent's commission is based.

One exception to these general rules regarding the impact of ancillary costs on the commission is the value-added tax. Even though VAT is separately identified in the invoice, it is deemed a part of the customer's payment for the goods and thus influences the amount of the agent's commission (Par. 87b, sec. 2 HGB). However, the parties may (and usually do) contractually deviate from this law and instead agree not to consider the amount of value-added tax in determining the agent's commission.

A discount or other type of price reduction granted the customer has no impact on the amount of the commission. A provision in the commercial agent contract to the contrary is unenforceable. Finally, even if the parties agree to a reduction in the commission in the event the principal helps the agent to secure a contract, a Federal Court ruling holds that such an agreement is likewise of no force and effect.

The agent's commission must be calculated and paid on a monthly basis; however, the parties may agree instead to a three-month payment period. The actual payment to the agent must be made no later than the end of the month which follows the relevant accounting period (Par. 87c, sec. 1 HGB).

Agents have a right to all information contained in the principal's books or ledgers which are relevant to the calculation of their commission; for example, the names and addresses of all customers who placed an order, the type, amount and price of the sold goods, and information pertaining to returns and failures to carry through with transactions (but not, however, the reason for such returns or failures). Providing the agent with copies of customers' invoices alone is not sufficient. Because the agent's right to information is only extinguished when both parties are in agreement regarding the commission, it is recommended that the principal collect the necessary information at the time the agent's commission is calculated and then send such information to the agent along with the commission payment.

These laws regarding the settlement of the commercial agent's account are obligatory, and any agreement by the parties which limits the agent's legal protections in this regard are unenforceable. Monetary claims of either party arising out of the principle-agent relationship are subject to a four-year statute of limitations. The period begins to run with the end of the year in which the claim becomes due. It is usually not possible for the parties to bind themselves to a shorter limitations period, and at least in an AGB ("Allgemeine Geschäftsbedingungen") contract (standard form commercial agent contract subject to the rules for the Regulation of Standard Business Terms), even if the shortened limitation period applies to both parties.

E.   Termination of the commercial agent contract

A commercial agent contract with an unspecified duration or term may be terminated without cause by a one-month advance notice in the first year of the contract, a two-month advance notice in the second year, a three-month advance notice in the third to fifth year, and a six-month advance notice after the fifth year. The termination's effective date is the last day of the calendar month, unless the parties have provided otherwise in their contract (Par. 89, sec. 1 HGB). The length of the notice period can be extended by contract but not shortened. Even if the commercial contract provides for a probationary period, the above stated notice periods must be provided.

The Federal Court has ruled that it is not possible to terminate only a part of the commercial agent contract, unless the parties have agreed otherwise and such termination is limited to a part of the agent's activity that is capable of being separated from his or her other activities. A termination of the commercial agent contract for an important reason (due cause) can be immediately effected by either party without the necessity of providing advance notice (Par. 89a HGB). This termination right can neither be excluded nor limited by contract.

Important reasons for termination are facts which result in it being unreasonable to expect a party to keep the contract in force until the advance notice period has expired. Advance agreements stating which specific types of factual situations constitute important reasons are somewhat problematical. Basically, an important reason is a situation which has resulted in a shock to the relationship of trust between the principal and agent. For example, important reasons for the agent to terminate without notice could be an arbitrary, significant reduction of the commission rate by the principal or exploitation of the agent's efforts by a firm in which the principal has an ownership interest. Important reasons for the principal to terminate without notice could be, for example, the agent's definitive, unauthorized refusal to work, an agent's attempt to entice the principal's other commercial agents away from the principal in order to advantage a third party, or placing fictitious customer orders. In addition, acts by the agent which involve breaches of trust are particularly susceptible of forming an important reason for termination. Insulting, libeling or slandering the principal; criminal activity; intoxication on the job as well as the failure to notify the principal of transactions or of certain facts which could be of particular importance to a principal are examples of acts which can form the basis for a termination of the agent without notice.

If an important reason for a termination exists, then the termination must take place within a "reasonable" amount of time. Although the two-week time limit set by Par. 626 of the BGB is not applicable to commercial agent law, it is advisable to observe the two week limit in order to avoid legal difficulties later..

A party who terminates the commercial agent contract without notice, may be liable for damages, although it would not have been unreasonable for such party to keep the contract in force until the expiration of the notice period. For this reason, a commercial agent contract should not be terminated without notice without careful examination of the cause for termination. The trend in the case law is to limit the grounds which render it unreasonable to keep the contract in force until the advance notice period has expired.

Finally, if the principal wishes to implement a termination without notice based on the agent's performance (as opposed, for example, to conduct which involves a breach of trust), then, prior to the termination, the agent is first entitled to a warning. This warning must be in writing and describe the conduct which the principal finds contrary to their agreement, as well as contain a statement that in the event such conduct is continued, the contract will be terminated.

F. Compensatory claim of agent for loss of clientele

A commercial agent's work results in the development of a regular group of customers or clientele. This valuable service to the principal is not only remunerated through commissions, but also through compensation to the agent for his loss of clientele, at the time the commercial agent contract is terminated (Par. 89b HGB). Because the amount of this compensatory payment very often leads to a disagreement between the parties at the time the contract is terminated, it will be discussed here in detail.

First of all, this compensatory claim is not required upon the termination of all commercial agent contracts. According to Par. 89b, sec. 3 HGB, the payment is not required when it is the agent who terminates the contract, unless said termination is justified by an important reason for which the principal is responsible. It is important to note that agents are always entitled to compensation if they are terminated for age. Likewise, if the principal justifiably terminates the contract based on important reasons for which the agent is responsible, the agent's compensatory right is forfeited.

Terminations where no compensatory payment is required are the exception. Usually, when a commercial agent contract is terminated, it is a termination initiated by the principal with notice and without a reason for termination without notice. In such a typical termination, agents are entitled to a compensatory payment upon request if: (1) during the contract term they have made contacts with new customers and (2) such contacts could lead to considerable advantage for the principal following termination of the principal-agent relationship (Par. 89b, sec. 1 HGB).

The first requirement listed above (contact with new customers) is also deemed to be met if, as a result of the agent's activities, the business relationship with a former customer who had not been originally secured by the agent is significantly intensified. Generally, a significant intensification of a business relationship can be shown if, during the duration of the commercial agent contract, the sales figures corresponding to such previously secured customer are doubled.

If the principal demands that a new agent pay an "admission fee" for the right of assuming representation of the existing customers of an agent who is leaving, this fee has no impact on the question of whether or not the departing agent had initially contacted and/or intensified relations with these customers. Also, the new agent is not entitled to have the amount of the "admission fee" returned in the form of a compensatory payment, in the event his or her contract is subsequently terminated. It is, however, possible for the parties to specifically agree that upon termination, the agent is entitled to a minimum compensatory payment equal to the amount originally paid by the agent as an "admission fee." Such an agreement is sometimes included in the parties' contract in order to protect the agent who has paid an admission fee from an unexpected early termination of the commercial agent contract.

The second requirement listed above (provision of considerable advantage to the principal) is met upon a showing that, as a result of the termination of the commercial agent contract, the agent will lose commissions on existing or future contracts with new customers originally secured by the agent, and/or with former customers for whom the agent has been successful in significantly increasing the business relations with the principal. The amount of the agent's loss of commissions is generally equivalent to the advantage the principal would enjoy if no compensatory payment was required. Therefore, a forecast must be made of the future development of the business relationships between the principal and such customers and how much commission the agent would have earned if the contract with the agent had not been terminated. The question of whether or not and to what extent changes in the established clientele can be expected are particularly important in making this forecast.

The determination of the amount of this compensatory payment must also take into account all circumstances which bear on the fairness of the payment. In this connection, the reasons for termination, the agent's family situation and support obligations as well as the question of what extent the product has developed a strong market appeal due to the principal's advertising outlays should be considered.

The first step in calculating the amount of the agent's compensatory payment is to determine the agent's total annual commissions earned in the last year of the principal-agent relationship on contracts with new customers or with existing customers whose business relations with the principal the agent succeeded in considerably intensifying. The second step is to determine how many years in the future the principal can expect to do business with this particular customer pool. It is generally assumed that such relationships will continue for two to five years beyond the termination date of the commercial agent contract. The number of years or forecast period chosen depends on and corresponds to the overall rate of customer fluctuation one can expect in the particular situation. For example, if the parties choose a four-year period, they assume that the principal will annually lose 25% of the new or intensified customer relationships which are attributable to the agent's efforts.

The third step is to take the figure derived from step one and project it over the forecast period in order to determine the agent's gross compensatory payment. The sum determined in this way represents the gross compensatory payment. The fourth step is to reduce this gross sum by the amount of interest advantage which will accrue to the agent, due to receiving future commissions on a lump-sum basis. The fifth step is to consider if further reductions should be made based on reasons of fairness and, if so, to make such reductions.

Finally, the sum which results from the fifth step must be compared to the highest amount of compensatory payment allowed by law. This comparison is necessary because according to Par. 89b, sec. 2 HGB, the compensatory payment may not exceed the average yearly commissions or other income earned by the agent in the last five years.

The laws pertaining to this compensatory payment are mandatory. Any attempt by the parties to avoid the compensatory payment or to provide for a reduced payment *ahead of time* are strictly without legal effect. The only way that the parties may contractually impact this compensatory payment is through an agreement entered into after the commercial agent relationship has been terminated.

In such a post termination agreement, it is customary for the agent and principal to determine the amount of the compensatory payment. The parties may also extinguish the agent's right to a compensatory payment altogether, if they agree that a third person shall take the place of the former commercial agent and this substitution occurs. Again, it is important to emphasize that such agreements are only possible after the commercial agent contract has been terminated.

Commercial agents must assert their claims to compensatory payments within one year following termination of the commercial agent contract or they lose them. It is also possible for the agent to assert his claim prior to the termination of the contract. The law neither prescribes a particular form for the assertion of this right, nor requires that it be asserted through the courts.

G. Non-competition agreements

The principal and agent may legally enter into an agreement that the latter shall be restricted in his or her business activities for up to but not exceeding two years from the termination of the commercial agent contract. Any such restriction on competition must be limited to the territory or the clientele of the agent as well as to the product or other matter that was regularly sold on behalf of the principal.

If a competition agreement is reached, however, the principal is required to pay the agent a reasonable compensation which corresponds to the length of time the agent's activities are restricted (Par. 90, sec. 1 HGB). This compensation serves the purpose of ensuring that the agent is provided with the necessities of life during the time the restriction is in place and represents consideration for the agent's promise not to compete.

The law does not address the amount of compensation the principal must pay. A reasonable amount is determined by considering the disadvantages that the agent incurs through the competition restriction and as well as the corresponding advantages for the principal. Other earnings of the agent are not deducted from the compensation; the fact that the agent has other earnings is considered in determining whether the compensation is reasonable.

Up until the time the commercial agent contract expires or is terminated, the principal may give written notice relinquishing his right to a non-competition agreement. Six months following the written notice, the principal is relieved of the duty to pay. Further, the agent forfeits his right to compensation if the principal terminates the contract with or without notice based on important reasons for which the agent is responsible. To ensure that the agent complies with a non-competition agreement, it is possible for the parties to agree to the imposition of contractual penalties.

H. International commercial agent law

If the principal's main place of business is in a foreign country and the agent represents the principal in Germany, the parties may contractually determine which country's law will apply. According to the Introductory Act to the Civil Code ("Einführungsgesetz zum BGB"), however, their contract may not violate the fundamental principles of German law designed to protect the rights of employees (Art. 30 EGBGB). This provision is applicable to commercial agent contracts despite the clear recognition under German law that commercial agents are independent contractors and not employees.

If this conflict-of-law issue has not been resolved by the parties in their agreement, the law of the place which has the most significant relationship to the contractual relationship applies. Generally, this question is resolved in favor of the main place of business of the agent and not of the principal (BGHZ 53, 332). This issue is nevertheless subject to debate.

In situations in which agents, regardless of where they actually reside, operate outside of the European Community, the parties may include terms in their contract which are contrary to all of the requirements of the German commercial agent law. In other words, the mandatory provisions of German commercial agent law (including Art. 30 EGBGB) are not applicable. The parties are free to agree to subject their agreement and the resolutions of disputes arising from it to the law of a foreign, non-European country.

II. The Law Pertaining to Authorized Distributors

Authorized distributors are individuals or entities who, on the basis of a long-term business relationship, buy and resell goods in their own name and on their own account. Because of the existence of a long-term contract between authorized distributors and manufacturers (or importers), the former acquire duties which result in their position resembling that of commercial agents. In many particular respects, the interests of authorized distributors and commercial agents are frequently similar. The courts have taken this similarity between the two types of independent contractors into account and in certain cases applied the laws pertaining to commercial agents to authorized distributors.

In particular, the case law holds that according to Par. 89b HGB, authorized distributors are entitled to compensatory payments for the loss of clientele at the termination of the manufacturer-distributor relationship if the following two requirements are met:

- the legal relationship between the authorized distributor and the manufacturer is more than a mere buyer-seller relationship. This is the case when authorized distributors have become so integrated in the marketing organization of the manufacturers that their rights and duties resemble those of commercial agents

- and -
- the authorized distributors are required to turn their customers over to the manufacturers at the time the distributor-manufacturer relationship comes to an end and the manufacturers are immediately able to make use of the customer accounts to their own business advantage should they so desire.

The contract between the parties is the starting point for determining whether authorized distributors are integrated in the marketing organization of the manufacturers. If authorized distributors are made responsible for certain marketing areas and if they are ascribed certain duties such as sales promotion or fostering the good reputation of the brand, this sufficiently indicates that an integration has occurred. The same applies if authorized distributors are required to pay advertising costs, maintain a stock or are induced to sell products at the manufacturer's or importer's recommended price. Moreover, in each case a careful examination should be made to determine if the actual day-to-day dealings of the parties deviate from their contract and whether the actual practices have, in effect, supplemented or altered the formal contract.

According to case law, it is quite easy for authorized distributors to prove that they are contractually bound to turn over their customers upon termination of their contracts. It is enough, for example, to show that they regularly turned their customer addresses over to the manufacturer during the time the contract was in effect, even if the manufacturer did not insist on being given the addresses or have any intention of using them. Case decisions have also shown that it is enough if invoices or their supporting documents, sales reports (daily or otherwise prepared), weekly status reports or customer questionnaires are transmitted per distributor contract to a marketing firm retained by the manufacturer or importer.

Manufacturers and importers who wish to avoid the very negative consequences of the analogous application of Par. 89b HGB requiring a compensatory payment for the loss of customers must pay very strict attention to the drafting of the distributor contract. In particular, the contract must expressly state that the manufacturer (or importer) has no interest in the transmission of customers and the reasons why this is so.

If, however, the authorized distributor is contractually bound to transmit customers, the authorized-distributor law provides that the distributor's right to a compensatory payment cannot be contractually excluded. In order to preserve this claim, the authorized distributor must raise it within one year following the termination of the distributor contract. Moreover, as with commercial agents, authorized distributors who terminate their contract due to age or sickness and for whom the continuation of their sales work would be unreasonable are entitled to compensatory payments for the loss of customers. If the manufacturer terminates the distributor contract, the compensatory payment is excluded only if the termination was based on serious cause.

The calculation of the amount of the compensatory payment for the loss of customers is made in essentially the same manner as described above in connection with commercial agents. In the case of authorized distributors, however, it is especially important to reduce the compensatory amount based on fairness reasons in order to account for that portion of the product's market appeal which is attributable to the manufacturer's (or importer's) advertising expenses. As a rule, this will result in the compensatory amount being reduced by 25%.

Computer Law

Michael Karger

I. Protection of Computer Software

A. Applicable German laws

As in the United States, the question of how computer software rights can best be protected has long been the subject of debate in Germany. Instead of enacting a specific law designed for software, Germany has followed the lead of the U.S. to a large extent and determined that software rights are to be protected by copyright laws. Assuming certain requirements are met, software is also protected by patent and antitrust laws. Protection of the product name is provided by trademark law, which was amended by the Trademark Act of 1996 ("Markengesetz").

Although the provisions of these individual areas of law work together to provide quite extensive protection for software, this protection is not without some gaps. The legal interplay of copyright, patent, antitrust and trademark law is complicated and not always easy to understand.

1. Copyright law

The most important protection for software is afforded by the German Copyright Act ("Urhebergesetz"). This law was amended in 1993 in order to conform to the European Council Directive of 1991 regarding the legal protection of computer programs. In its amended form, the law ensures that nearly all computer programs that demonstrate a minimum of intellectual creativity are protected. Prior to this amendment, the Federal Court ("Bundesgerichtshof") had required that software meet stringent criteria before it was entitled to protection. It ruled that only programs demonstrating an especially high degree of creativity were capable of being protected.

Similar to U.S. law, German copyright law protects only the "manifestations" (referred to in German as the "Ausdrucksformen") of a computer program. The ideas and principles upon which it is based are not protected.

A copyright originates with the creation of the software and expires seventy years after the death of its author. Registration of the copyright is neither necessary for its creation nor its enforcement.

Also, as under U.S. copyright law, owners of copyrights under German law are said to possess a "bundle of rights." They have the right to copy, revise and distribute the software. Nevertheless, it should be noted that by law there are certain uses that a copyright owner cannot prevent authorized users from making of the program. For example, the authorized user is entitled to make a back-up copy of the program, to test the functions of the program in order to understand the ideas and principles upon which it is based and to undertake measures to correct any mistakes in the program. If certain requirements are met, the user may also perform a decompilation of the program (separate it into its distinct parts). The rights granted by law to the authorized users of the program may not be altered by contract, provisions in licensing contracts which attempt to strip users of their legal rights are void.

The rightholder in terms of the German Copyright Act has the exclusive right to authorize or to do

- any form of distribution of the software itself or of copies,
- as well the permanent as the temporary reproduction of the software in any form,
- any alteration of the software, as translation.

Databases are protected under Par. 87a - 87e and Par. 4 German Copyright Act.

2. Patent law

The criteria which must be met in order for software to be protected under patent law are substantially more difficult to meet than under copyright law. Therefore, relatively few persons or companies apply for the issuance of a patent for their software-related inventions.

Under German law, programs for data-processing systems are clearly not viewed as patentable inventions. However, an invention, which otherwise meets the requirements of the patent law is not rendered unpatentable just because one of its parts is a computer program. In this case, the entire invention, including the program, is entitled to a patent. In order to receive a patent, the invention must involve a technology which meets the criterion of originality, be based on inventive activity and be commercially useful.

For instance, patentable are:

- inventions related to computer programs which change the composition or use of a data-processing system
- or -
- inventions which relate to the data-processing system's ability to function and, in doing so, direct the way in which the technical elements of the data-processing program work together.

Therefore, the types of computer program-related inventions capable of being patented include operation-system programs, programs which concern measuring and norm technology and programs for the processing of digital pictures or signals.

On the other hand, programs for such tasks as inventory administration, accounting, calculation or word processing are not patentable under German law because they do not demonstrate the requisite technical characteristics.

The right to the invention and the right to be granted a patent belong to the inventor. In order to be granted a patent, the inventor must register the invention with the Patent Office ("Patentamt"): The rights which derive from the patent end with the patent's expiration date which, as a rule, is twenty years from the date of it issuance. The owner of a patent has an exclusive right to it and can, for example, prohibit any other person from using the process or the results derived by using the patent.

3. Trade Secret Protection

Practice has shown that after copyright law, antitrust law is the next most important source of protection for computer software. According to the Unfair Competition Act ["Gesetz gegen den unlauteren Wettbewerb" (UWG)], it is illegal to expropriate the achievement of another

- when that achievement has significant impact on competition,
- when it involved considerable costs
- and -
- when such expropriation or take-over amounts to depriving the owner (for example, a software writer) of the fruits of personal labor.

Therefore, it is illegal to make copies of computer programs and offer them on the market.The Unfair Competition Act prohibits the unauthorized exploitation of business and trade secrets. Computer software can represent a protected business secret when the information in the program is not information which is otherwise readily available. This means that the secret contained in the software must be such that other persons do not have access to it or can achieve access to it only with considerable difficulty. In particular, "programming secrets" are protected. Antitrust law thus protects the entire spectrum of confidential technical know-how including the ideas that form the foundation of such know-how. However, to the extent and at the point where the secrets are publicly known, trade secret protection is lost.

4. Trademark law

According to the new trademark law, which was enacted in 1996, all marks, which are designed to distinguish one product or service from another are capable of being protected. This includes but is not limited to words, pictures, word-and-picture combinations and sounds. In order to be protected, the distinguishing mark must be registered in the trademark register and actually used in the marketplace.

If the trademark is not used for a period of five years, it can be challenged. The owner of the trademark has the right to its exclusive use and can, therefore, prevent others from using it. The protection afforded by a trademark registered in Germany extends throughout the entire country and is valid for ten years from the date of the application filing. The term of protection can be extended for another ten years by paying an additional fee, and this process can be repeated as often as the owner wishes.

B. Applicable European Community laws

The European Community strives for standardization of the national laws of the Member States that provide protection for computer software rights. In the long run, this standardization will occur in all the areas of law discussed above. Presently, more progress has been made in some areas than in others.

1. Copyright law

Although considerable differences exist between the general copyright laws of the Member States, much progress has been made in the specific area of computer software and data-bank protection. A 1991 European Council directive concerning the legal protection of computer programs requires all Member States to bring their laws into compliance with its provisions. Germany incorporated the directive's provisions into its national law in 1993. This directive requires that the Member States adopt certain minimum rules in order that a similar level of computer software protection be achieved throughout the Community. Such minimum rules ensure that the exclusive right of the copyright owner includes the right to prohibit others from copying or revising the software and distributing it to the public. On the other hand, the directive also requires that Member States adopt provisions which ensure that an authorized user has the right to make a back-up copy of the program. It is important to note that certain of the owner's rights arising from the copyright are exhausted upon the sale of the software program within the European Community.

2. Patent law

The European Patent Agreement of 1977 forms the authoritative basis for the European Community patent law. As a result of this agreement, the European Patent Office ("Europäisches Patentamt") was established in Munich. This office serves as the central administrative agency responsible for conducting the research and investigation necessary for the issuance of a European patent. The patents issued by the European Patent Office are valid throughout Europe from the date of their issuance, but are simultaneously subject to the differing patent laws of the individual Member States. For this reason, one can say that no standard European Community patent currently exists.

The requirements for the granting of a patent according to the European Patent Agreement of 1977 are essentially the same as the requirements for the issuance of a patent under German law. It is expected that the European Patent Agreement will be replaced sometime in the future with an agreement that establishes unified protection throughout the entire Community, although no exact time has as yet been specified.

3. Trademark law

In 1988, the European Council enacted a regulation pertaining to trademarks which resulted in an important change. It established uniform European-wide trademark protection which is effective in all the Member States. European Trademark Law is administered by the European Trademark Office in Alicante, Spain. One can apply for and receive a trademark only for the entire European Community. If issued, the trademark is effective throughout the Community; if declared invalid, it is likewise invalid throughout the Community. The regulations provide a protection time period of ten years and require that the trademark must be used to remain protected.

II. Procedures in the Event of an Infringement of Software Rights

The owners of computer software are entitled to seek judicial relief if their rights are violated. As in the U.S., it is possible for the owners of software rights in Germany to receive speedy interim relief in the form of a judicial order enjoining an infringement. The application for such a temporary injunction ("einstweilige Verfügung") does not require the payment of a bond. In the main action, the plaintiff may sue for a final order prohibiting the infringement as well as for damages and the surrender of any property of the defendant that constitutes the infringement.

In many respects, the infringement proceeding in Germany is subject to different civil rules of procedure than those applicable in U.S. legal proceedings. For example, under the German rules of civil procedure, no right to pretrial discovery (as that term is understood in U.S. jurisprudence) exists. The owners of software rights cannot compel defendants to give them evidence of the documents in their possession. As a result, proving an infringement is often difficult, especially in cases in which the plaintiff needs the source code of the other party in order to prove that the original program is identical with the program of the defendant.

Since, in contrast to the U.S. civil process, there is no trial by jury in Germany, all the evidence is reviewed and the legal issues decided by the judge. And, whereas the parties' experts play an important role in the U.S., they are of limited importance in determining the outcome of a German court case. If judges are unable to answer technical questions themselves, they call in an independent court expert ("Sachverständiger"), whose opinion, as a rule, is accepted by the Court.

The testimony of the parties' own experts is usually given very little weight. Another important difference from the U.S. judicial system is the possibility of conducting two fact-finding procedures (trials) in Germany, since in an appeal evidence can once again be presented.

In summary, it can be said that the protection of software rights in Germany is essentially the same as the protection afforded under U.S. law. Nevertheless, many considerable differences exist concerning procedural details. Not all of the well-known principles of U.S. law will be automatically recognized in Germany.

Electronic Commerce

Raimund E. Walch

I. Applicable German Laws

There was no special legislation on Electronic Commerce transactions in Germany until recently. An "E-Commerce law" did not exist and the adjudication in this field was sketchy and unsystematic. Although commercial transactions in open data nets (as E-Commerce could be plainly described) have never been conducted in a law-free zone it seemed for long that the tried and tested contract law of the German Civil Code (BGB) could provide the answers to all emerging problems and the Federal Information and Communication Service Act of 1998 (IuKDG) was apt to fill the legal loopholes in the field of individual electronic communication. Triggered by several European Directives related to consumer protection the German Federal legislator enacted two special laws, the Act on Distant Sale Contracts (FernAbsG) and the Act on Electronic Business Transactions (EEG) together with an Ordinance on the Duty to provide Information to consumers (InfoV). As part of the recent reform of the German contract law these Acts were incorporated into the system of the German Civil Code and can now be seen as the legal framework for all commercial transactions in open data nets.

In E-Commerce practice it is of vital importance for both seller and buyer that their respective acts have legal validity and that closed contracts are legally binding. In this respect the knowledge of the respective applicable German laws and regulations is decisive for both business-to-business (B2B) and business-to-consumer (B2C) online distributors.

II. German Civil Code (BGB) - law pertaining to contracts

A. Closing of Contracts in open nets

Under German Civil Law a contract is closed when two corresponding willful acts are exchanged - the offer and its acceptance. This basic rule for any contract is also applicable for those commercial transactions, which rely on the exchange of electronically transmitted acts by E-Mail or mouseclick.

The blank order form on a homepage (business-to-business or business-to-consumer) can be seen as the general invitation of the seller to the buyer to accept this offer. By filling out the order form or by simply clicking on the OK-button the consumer accepts this offer and the contract is entered into. In most cases, however, order procedures are organized in a different way. If the seller only generally describes his products on the homepage and expects the customer to place the order then the contract is entered into when the order is finally accepted and confirmed by the seller.

Accordingly, it is also part of each businesses' E-Commerce strategy to ensure the legal validity of business transactions by efficiently designing and organizing such order procedures.

The acceptance of an offer can be either explicit - the order confirmation is sent by mail or E-mail - or implicit by simply delivering the product to the customer.

Both willful acts (offer and acceptance) are binding and can only be revoked before they reach their destination.

The acceptance of the offer can be expected in 2 to 3 days - failure to do so would mean that the contract is not concluded. There is no rule that silence to an offer would mean acceptance except for B2B transactions where there is no need for consumer protection.

B. General Terms of Business

For business-to-consumer transactions in open nets General Terms of Business ("Allgemeine Geschäftsbedingungen") are not automatically binding for the consumer but have to be incorporated, which obligates the seller to explicitly refer to his General Terms of Business and allow the consumer to have access to them. The possibility to access them not the actual knowledge is sufficient. On the other hand electronic General Terms of Business must be clearly structured and should not be too long because otherwise the detailed adjudication protecting consumers may apply.

Electronic commercial transactions which are finalized with the use of tele-services and media-services follow different rules since the enactment of an European Directive on E-Commerce. General Terms of Business in B2B and B2C must be accessible to customer and consumers at the latest when closing the contract and the technical means to save them on disc, CDs or hard drive must be ensured.

C. Distant Sale Contracts and Electronic Business Transactions

Unlike traditional sale transactions, buyer and seller do not necessarily have physical contact when buying via the internet. As the buyer cannot see and touch the product before buying he or she can easily be deceived about its quality.

The lack of personal knowledge of each other as well as the product in the virtual world caused the E.U. and - consequently - the German legislator to enact the Act on Distant Sale Contracts of 30th of June 2000, now incorporated into the German Civil Code. By granting a right of revocation and increasing the seller's obligation to inform the buyer before and after the deal, consumer protection has been maximised.

If applicable, the law protects private consumers insofar as they have - under certain conditions - the right to step back from the contract and ship the product already bought back to the seller.

Such consumer protection is threefold:

- the seller has to fully inform the buyer about the key details of the contract including his right to return the product within 14 working days
- the seller has to give a written confirmation of all those key information given before closing of the deal
- the buyer has the right to fully and unconditionally return the product with money back guarantee within 14 working days.

However, the consumer is only entitled to these benefits if a so-called "Distant Sale of Goods and Services" between consumer and non-consumer (tradesman) can be identified. Following the legal definition a contract must be prepared and finally closed with the exlusive use of such means of communication which lack simultaneous physical contact: letters, catalogues, telphone calls, telefaxes, E-mails and broadcast-services, tele-services and media-services are examples for such means of communication.

The law does not apply to those tradesmen who have no distant sale distribution structure but only use telephone, telefax or E-mail from time to time for selling their products. It is the seller, however, who has to prove that he does not have such an organised distribution structure.

There are a variety of exemptions for a number of services offered on the online marketplace such as financial services, home delivery services, distant learning offers and the sale of real estate. For these services the law does not apply by definition.

The obligation to inform the consumer is detailed in an Ordinance on the Duty to provide Information to the consumer (InfoV). It obligates the seller to reveal the following core details of the contract before the contract is closed (list not complete):

- name and address of the seller
- all steps which lead to the closing of the contract
- net price (tax and other costs included)
- payment and delivery
- delivery and shipping costs
- cancellation of the contract and right to send back the product
- the commercial purpose of the deal

These details can be electronically transmitted but need to be clear and understandable for the average consumer.

Not yet clear is whether these pieces of information can be presented on a linked page, which may or may not be read by the consumer, or whether the seller has to ensure that the buyer must read the information before the contract is closed.

Once the customer knows all the above details before closing of the contract the same has to be effectively handed out to the customer in written form or confirmed in an E-mail plus additional information as follows:

- conditions and legal consequences of the cancellation of the contract (including shipment back to the seller)
- address of the complaint department and the legal address of the seller with name of one legal representative
- information on customer service, legal warranties and given guarantees
- conditions of cancellation of the contract for long-time contracts

The written form ("textual form") requires that there is a signature (scanned but no digital signature necessary) on the confirmation sent to the customer, which must reach him once but at the latest when the product is shipped. It is no longer sufficient to present the prescribed (compulsory) information on a website before the contract is closed without written confirmation of the same after closing.

The sanctions for not informing the consumer in the described way are considerable:

Infraction of pre-contractual obligations to inform the consumer may lead to damage claims but also to a prolongation of the 14 day revocation period to a maximum of 6 months. This means that the seller may be exposed to the buyers' change of minds for as long as six months.

Also, consumer protection agencies can sue the seller for omission of wrong or insufficient information.

The scope of required disclosures has been considerably extended by the European Directive on Electronic Commerce. With its transfer into the German Civil Code not only contracts between tradesmen and consumers but also B2B contracts with "customers" have to follow specific rules on the disclosure of information. Only if B2B or B2C contracts for the delivery of goods or services are closed using tele- or media-services (which includes all online shops) the law applies and the seller (tradesman) has to

1. establish effective technical means which allow the customer to discern operational errors and to correct them before the offer is placed
2. electronically confirm the receipt of the customer's order without delay

3. inform the customer beforehand
    - about the technical steps which proceed and finally lead to the closing of the contract,
    - whether the contractual document is saved by the tradesman after closing and whether it is accessible for the customer,
    - about the establishment of effective technical means for the correction of operational errors,
    - about the languages which are available for the transaction,
    - about the code of conduct or practice which may be applicable or which accepts the tradesman as binding for himself.
4. establish technical means for the electronic access to the contract details including the seller's General Terms of Business and the possibility to save them.

The law does not apply if the contract has been closed by E-mail correspondence without the use of tele- or media-services (individual communication) or if customer and seller have agreed on the exclusion of these obligations (only for B2B contracts!). No such exclusion is allowed neither for B2B nor for B2C contracts for the latter of the above duties: The electronic access to the contract details including the seller's General Terms of Business must be ensured at any times.

Again, the violation of these obligations lead to the prolongation of the 14 day revocation period for B2C contract. Other sanctions - especially in the B2B sector - are waiting to be clarified by the courts.

Protection of Internet Domain Names

Wolfgang C. Leonti

This article will first provide an overview of the German domain name registration process. It will then discuss potential legal claims and arbitration procedures against domain name-grabbers. The author tries to find answers for the following questions: What considerations must be taken into account in the German registration process of a domain name? How can a company proceed against someone who has grabbed the desired domain name before the company had a chance to register it? Are there government authorities or organizations providing support?

I. Introduction

Due to the rapid growth of commercial activities on the internet, many companies have rushed to set up their own web sites. First a company must register its own unique electronic address (technically called a "domain name") so that internet users can find and access the site. However, given the current first-come, first-serve principle for registration of domain names, a new problem has surfaced: when a company with a well-known trademark attempts to register its name or trademark as a domain name, it is told that someone else has already registered the domain name. Upon further investigation, the trademark's rightful owner learns that the registrant is not a bona-fide commercial user of the domain name, but rather is merely a domain name-grabber; that is a person who registers a domain name using a well-known trademark before the legitimate trademark owner has had an opportunity to do so in the hope of extracting a quick payoff from the company.

II. Overview of the German Registration System

The Internet has become the world's largest computer network connecting several million computers worldwide. Each computer can be accessed by an alphanumeric domain name. Domain names in Germany are registered with the DENIC e.G. on a first-come, first-serve basis. The top level domain for Germany is ".de" which is also called a country-code top level domain (ccTLD). The German registrar usually does not verify the legitimacy of the domain-name registration. Since each domain name may be assigned only once on a worldwide basis, disputes are inevitable on this front. In the last few years, this problem has been aggravated by the rapid slump in domain-registration prices. Whereas the price for the registration of a ".de" domain, for instance, was still in the order of 50 Euro as recently as 2 years ago, ".de" domains are now available for as little as 50 Cent a month – or even free of charge – from the major resellers. This situation has led to a veritable torrent of new domain names. Consequently, it is no surprise that it is becoming increasingly difficult to find a suitable domain name for a company's web site. Generic domain names, i.e. domain names consisting of a general single-word designation and the .de endings, are all but sold out. Even domain names consisting of three or four letters are virtually all taken today. Today, the question of whether a suitable domain name is still available is a key issue that must be resolved as early as upon establishment of a company.

A. Registration Guidelines

In principle, the prerequisites for domain registration differ from country to country. For the registration of ".de" domains, German case law has defined the following rules:

Rule 1: no brands, no names of other companies

Rule 2: no celebrity names

Rule 3: no titles of magazines, movies, software

Rule 4: no city names or car license-plate numbers

Rule 5: no names of government institutions

Rule 6: no typing-error domains.

B. Registration Process

Usually, a domain is registered via a internet service provider. The company applies for registration of the desired domain name with the provider, which, in turn, obtains protection of the name from the competent authorities such as DENIC e.G. in Germany, VeriSign (former Network Solutions) for the international top-level domains ".com", ".net". and ".org", and recently Afilias Inc. for the new TLD ".info". (Aside: at present, the new TLDs are ".info", ".biz", ".name" and ".pro"). On the internet, you can also search the "who is database" on the registrar's web site to check whether the desired domain name is still available. You can also apply for registration of your domain name directly with the registrar in your own name. The necessary steps in this process are explained on the registrars web site. In many cases, the costs of direct registration are considerably higher.

C. Domain Owner, Admin-c

Make sure that the domain name is secured only in your own name rather than in the provider's name. It frequently happens that providers refuse to release domain names in disputes with their customers because they want to use them as a means of exerting greater pressure on their customers. German case law has not yet found a uniform approach to the question of whether this is a violation of competition law or whether the provider has a rightful interest in retaining the domain. By registering a domain in your own name, however, you can avoid this problem. If the domain holder is a company, an individual with an address in Germany must be named as administrative contact (admin-c), at least for ".de" domains.

III. Domain Name-Grabbing

In principle, a company can take action against any party commercially using its brand name or longstanding business name on the internet. You can also take action against a party registering the company name as an internet domain without being authorized to do so. Operation of a homepage under this name is not necessary. Resourceful profiteers, in particular companies offering web-site design, often secure domains in their own name with a view to forcing companies to contact them under all circumstances. If the companies in question subsequently try to set up a web presence under this domain name, they find that it has already been registered by someone else.

You can initially respond to such behavior by sending the party in question an warning letter. As a rule, this should consist of a written statement in which you clearly state the domain name in question and request surrender of the domain. You should also indicate why you believe that you are lawfully entitled to this domain name. This written statement should be sent by certified mail, so that you have proof of receipt. Depending on the purpose and scope of utilization of such an Internet domain, the amount in dispute is in the range of 40,000 to 50,000 Euro. To ensure that the domain name is subsequently actually registered immediately in your name, you must also notify the registrar of your dispute with the current domain holder about the rights to the domain. You should submit proof that you have previous rights to this name, and as a precaution, you should ask the registrar to secure the domain in the event of release until the dispute has been resolved. This is called wait or dispute application.

IV. Legal Claims

A. Court Litigation

If an warning letter fails to have the desired success, German law offers the possibility of asserting claims to a domain name through litigation. The tricky aspect in this context is to find the right wording for the statement of claim. Although the German Federal Court of Justice recently ruled against the domain grabber in the action brought by Shell Oil AG for the "shell.de" domain name, he was only ordered to renounce the domain. The court did not uphold the claim for transfer of the domain. For this reason, it is absolute essential to submit the above-mentioned dispute or wait application prior to filing a statement of claim. In this context, a particularly devious instrument "SnapNames" exists for international TLD´s. This is an official service provided by VeriSign offering its customers to search the internet for certain domain names that are released and automatically register them on behalf of the customer.

From a legal perspective, victims of domain grabbing can usually assert claims based on their name-bearing rights, company law, trademark law and competition law.

Litigation is advisable for German .de domains, since an individual's German address for service is usually known. In the case of international domains such as .com, .net and .org, domain grabbers are usually located in a foreign country. In these cases, dispute resolution in accordance with UDRP seems advisable.

B. Arbitration Procedure, UDRP

To facilitate resolution of international disputes in particular, the "WIPO Arbitration and Mediation Center", a kind of international arbitration service provider, has created what is known as "Uniform Domain Name Dispute Resolution Policy" (UDRP). The rules laid down in this policy have been authorized by ICANN (Internet Assigned Names and Numbers Authority). So far, the responsibilities of this arbitration center are limited to international top-level domains (TLDs). Everyone can have recourse to this center. The complainant must state that the registered domain name is identical to the trademark owned by him and that the current domain owner does not have an independent right to or legitimate interest in the domain name in dispute. However, this procedure does not yet apply to Germany's ccTLD ".de".

The procedure, which was introduced only recently, has already proven its worth in a number of domain disputes, since it is relatively uncomplicated and relies as much as possible on electronic communications in the handling of the procedure. In the simplest cases, the fee amounts to at least 1,500 USD. If the Arbitration and Mediation Center finds that the domain holder is not entitled to a domain, it orders transfer of the domain to the complainant. The decision of the arbitration panel will then be binding for the respective NIC (Network Information Center).

V. Outlook

One potential approach to alleviating the problem of domain-name scarcity – at least to some extent – is known as "domain-name sharing". By adding an entry index page, several entitled parties can share a domain name; links will take visitors to their respective web sites. This approach is particularly useful in cases in which two companies from different sectors use identical or similar trademarks or company names.

Prior to domain registration, a company should conduct comprehensive analyses to verify that no other party has overriding rights to the domain name. There is usually a good chance of winning against a domain name-grabber if a company has not only an identical company name, but also a registered trademark. To save time and money, it is advisable to use the WIPO arbitration procedure for international TLDs.

Notaries in Germany

Christian R. Wolf

I. Legal Status of the Notary

A. Independent holder of public office

The German notary is an independent holder of public office responsible for recording legal transactions (Par. 1 of The National Rules and Regulations for German Notaries ["Bundesnotarordnung" (BNotO)]). As opposed to attorneys, notaries are not members of the free professions but rather the agents of state authority. On the other hand, notaries are not civil servants either, but are independent holders of public office not subject to any personal orders or subject-matter-related instructions.

The status of the notary as the holder of public office precludes the free right to set up practice. Instead, the German states appoint only as many notaries as are necessary to ensure the regulated cultivation of the law (Par. 4, Sentence 1 BNotO). Thus, even if candidates can prove professional qualification, they have no lawful claim to be endowed with the notary office.

B. Types of Notary Offices in Germany

In Germany there are basically two different types of notary offices. In the federal states of Bavaria, Hamburg, Mecklenburg-Western Pomerania, Saxony, Saxony-Anhalt, Saarland and Thuringia and in parts of the federal states of Baden-Württemberg and North Rhine-Westphalia notaries are appointed as notaries only (*"Nurnotare"*, or, "notaries only") who exercise their office full time. In the federal states of Berlin, Bremen, Hesse, Lower Saxony, Schleswig-Holstein and in parts of the federal states of Baden-Württemberg and North Rhine-Westphalia, lawyers are appointed to practice the profession of notary in addition to the profession of attorney (*"Anwaltsnotare"*, or, "attorney/notaries"). In the state of Baden-Württemberg there are - as an historical residue - still District Notaries ("Bezirksnotare"). In deviation from the usual system, these notaries are civil servants of the federal state.

C. The Professional Education and Training of the Notary

An eligible candidate for the office of notary is anyone who has completed his or her education as an attorney at law and achieved full qualification as such ("Volljurist"). The notary initially goes through the same training procedure as a German judge or attorney, but must upon completion of the undergraduate curriculum achieve further qualification through post-graduate studies. In order to ensure the retention of Germany's extraordinarily high standard of notarial services, the appointment to the office of notary generally requires that the candidate have an outstanding academic record.

D. The Chief Professional Responsibilities of the Notary

1. Impartiality

The notary is not the legal representative of a single party but rather the impartial counselor of all the parties involved in a given matter (Par. 14, Sec. 2 BNotO). Notaries, as opposed to attorneys, do not fight for the rights of their clients but rather stand above the interests of the parties by helping them to find a just way of balancing out their opposing objectives. In doing so, they cannot impose a binding decision with judicial authority, but can only influence the outcome of the legal process by advising and informing the parties. The impartiality required of notaries means that they cannot take sides with or against any of the parties by showing preference or prejudice. No bond to one of the parties, no favoritism or disfavoritism, no biases, no concern with their own personal advantages or disadvantages may influence notaries in the performance of their professional duties.

2. The Duty to Refuse Performance of Illegal and Unethical Transactions

Notaries must deny performance of any official functions that are not reconcilable with their official duties, particularly when their active support is requested in the pursuance of objectives that are obviously illegal or unethical (Par. 14, Sec. 2 BNotO). Furthermore, the German code of professional conduct ("Standesrecht") proscribes that notaries avoid even the slightest appearance of infringement of the law.

3. Dignified Behavior

Through their behavior both on and off the job, notaries are required to demonstrate that they are worthy of the respect and confidence that the public places in their profession (Par. 14, Sec. 3, Sentence 1 BNotO). Notaries thus have the duty to do honor to their profession at all times and in all places, regardless of whether their activities and behavior are job related or strictly private. For example, notaries are required to maintain order in their financial affairs. They may not live beyond their means, must pay their bills on time and are not permitted to demonstrate self-submission to boundless profit seeking by wagering in high-risk speculations. Furthermore, they are forbidden to display morally or conventionally reprehensible behavior and to transgress against the dictates of decent personal conduct and respectable standards of living through, for instance, immoderate drinking or fraternizing with immoral persons. Notaries are not even allowed to tolerate the involvement of a family member in unrespectable activity. (Par. 14 III, Sentence. 2 BNotO).

4. The Duty to Perform Professional Services

Notaries have the obligation of performing all the services associated with their office. They may not refuse their notarial services to anyone without valid reason. Legitimate reasons for refusal exist only when active involvement in forbidden activities is being solicited or when personal interests in the matter makes the legally proscribed impartiality next to impossible (Par. 3 of the German Notarial Recording Code ["Beurkundungsgesetz" (BeurkG)]).

5. Prohibition of Middleman Activities

Notaries are forbidden to engage in the brokering of loans and real-estate and to enter into obligations as loan guarantors or to offer any other form of security or any guarantee for one of the parties in conjunction with a transaction performed in the course of fulfilling their professional duties. They furthermore have the duty of making sure that none of the persons in their employ are involved in such commercial activity.

6. The Duties to Examine and Inform

Notaries have the obligation to examine the motives of the parties, clearly explain the facts of the matter to them, inform them of the legal ramifications of their desired transaction and, upon having done so, to protocol their statements clearly and unambiguously. During the course of this procedure they must pay special care to ensure the avoidance of mistakes and doubts and make sure that inexperienced and / or unsophisticated parties are not disadvantaged. If they have any suspicions that the transaction goes against the law or the true motive(s) of one or more of the parties, then they are obliged to share their second thoughts with all present. If, however, notaries have any doubt about the legal validity of the transaction, they cannot simply refuse to record it . In such a case they are obliged to inform the participants of the reasons for their doubts and to make note of those reasons as well as the statements the parties issued in response to them in the protocol.

Again, while informing and advising the parties, notaries must at the same time strictly adhere to their obligation of impartiality. They may not advise one party to its advantage while disadvantaging the other.

In informing the parties involved in a given transaction, notaries are obliged to adhere to the generally accepted rule that they must always chose the way that is most certain. Only if the parties insist on a divergent, less certain concept may a notary, after informing them of what that may entail, embark on their chosen uncertain path.

7. Selection of the Most Economical Alternative

If various alternative ways to conclude or perform a business transaction are available, the notary must select the alternative that is most economical. This fundamental principle is limited only by the principle discussed above that obliges notaries to take the most certain path.

8. No Financial or Tax Consulting

The law does not hold the notary responsible for providing information concerning the financial outcome of a business transaction. It is the sole responsibility of the parties to the contract to obtain such information for themselves by consulting advisory specialists (attorneys, tax consultants). The notary likewise has no obligation to inform the parties concerning the tax law consequences of a given contract.

In practice, however, it is hardly possible to adhere to these limiting principles. Notaries today are generally expected to provide financial advice and especially tax advice, particularly in questions concerning property-acquisition tax and inheritance tax. Should the notary be lacking sufficient knowledge in these areas, this should be explained to the parties and they should be encouraged to involve advisory specialists.

9. Obligation of Secrecy

Notaries have the obligation of strictly maintaining secrecy in all matters negotiated before them and in regard to the names of the parties involved. Any violation of the obligation of secrecy is threatened with penalty.

10. Obligation to Have Liability Insurance

Notaries are required to have professional liability insurance to cover any pecuniary losses resulting from the performance of their professional activities. The minimum policy amount is € 250,000.-- for each insurance case. In practice, most notaries, because of the back-up policies offered by the notary associations, are insured for at least € 500,000.--.

II. Duties of the Notary

The main duty of notaries is the recording of legal transactions as well as the certification of signatures and copies. The most important areas of their professional activity will be explained below.

A. Real-Estate Law

Notaries are responsible for the recording of all types of real-estate transactions, especially those involving purchase contracts and real-estate gifts. If such transactions are carried out in non-notarial form, they are invalid. The purchase contract and the statements to the real-estate registry office necessary to carry out the contract are usually prepared by the notaries themselves. However, it is also possible that the parties to the contract present their notary with a ready-made document, which the notary then reads aloud and the parties sign in his presence. The notary can document such ready-made drafts, however, only if their content is legally permissible and contains no disadvantage for one of the parties to the contract. Especially in the case of very complex real-estate transactions, it is common that the contracts have been drafted by the attorneys of the parties and already checked in terms of their legality.

In addition to documenting real-estate contracts, notaries are responsible for the official execution and registration of "limited property security rights," especially liens, mortgages, rights of passage of the property by pedestrians and motor vehicles and similar property encumbrances. The notarized form is here, also prerequisite to having the property registered in the real-estate registry, which is prerequisite to having the transaction become lawful.

In summary, it can be said that all legal transactions according to the German real-estate law require a notarized form, and can be conducted in an effective and valid way only through the involvement of a notary.

B. Company Law

German law requires that all companies involved in commercial trade ("Handelsgesellschaften") be registered in the commercial register ("Handelsregister"). The registration process requires the certified registration of the company shareholders ("Gesellschafter") and the managing director(s) ("Geschäftsführer"), which can be done only through a notary. The duty to register and the duty to obtain notarized certification of the entry application also exists for any and all changes in the company, especially for increases or decreases in its nominal capital or for changes in the shareholder body and / or the company management.

The articles of incorporation ("Gesellschaftsvertrag") themselves, however, do not always require notarization. The articles of incorporation of a general partnership ("Offene Handelsgesellschaft" [OHG]) or a limited partnership ("Kommanditgesellschaft" [KG]) are not subject to any specific form. Notarization in this case is possible but not absolutely necessary. On the other hand, the articles of incorporation of an investment company ("Kapitalgesellschaft"), a GmbH or AG require without exception notarization. The same applies to any changes in the articles of incorporation of an investment company, especially to measures for increasing and reducing the nominal capital value. In the case of the stock corporation ("Aktiengesellschaft" [AG]), every meeting of the stockholders must additionally be recorded by a notary.

The transfer of shares in a company must be notarized only in the case of the GmbH.

C. Inheritance Law

According to German law, a one-sided last testament (will) can be effectively executed by the testator in his or her own handwriting. Notarization is a further possible means of executing a testament. For people unable to write, it is the only possibility. An advantage of the notarized testament is the advice provided by the notary, which ensures that the last testament of the testator is expressed in a way perfectly in keeping with the law.

In addition to the one-sided testament, German law provides for the possibility of drawing up an inheritance contract. Whereas the one-sided testament is freely revocable at any time, an inheritance contract is binding insofar as the testator did not reserve the right to revocation. The form of an inheritance contract is chosen whenever there is a desire to provide a security for an intended heir that the promised inheritance will not be revoked before going into effect. An inheritance contract always requires notarization.

Within the domain of inheritance law, notaries are additionally responsible for certifying a number of further statements that must be presented to the court of probate ("Nachlaßgericht"). For instance, an application for issuance of an inheritance certificate must be certified by a notary. The same applies to a disclaimer of inheritance. Also requiring notarization are contracts for the renunciation of inheritance or of compulsory portions of an inheritance as well as any contracts made among the heirs-to-be. Inheritance purchase contracts and similar contracts that grant control of an estate in its entirety likewise require notarization.

D. Family Law

Family law comprises a further important area in which German notaries are active.

German matrimonial law provides, fundamentally, for a community of accrued gain among marriage partners ("Zugewinngemeinschaft"). This community is a marital regime of the separation of property ("Gütertrennung"), which is intended to keep the financial assets of both spouses separate. However, upon termination of the marriage through death or, particularly, through divorce, the financial gain accrued by both spouses during the duration of the marriage will be divided equally among them.

Any deviations from this basic regulation can be agreed to by the marriage partners in the form of a notarized matrimonial property agreement ("Ehevertrag"). First, an agreement defining the marital property regime as one based entirely on the separation of property can be entered into, which rules out the equal division of accrued gain upon termination of the marriage. On the other hand, it can also be agreed that the property brought into the marriage by each of the partners individually becomes common property ("Gütergemeinschaft"). Between these extreme poles of property separation and property pooling, there are many conceivable ways of modifying the statutory regulations governing the marital property regime and the way accrued gains are to be divided at the end of the marriage. It is possible, for instance, to limit the amount that can be laid claim to as a share in the accrued gain to a fixed sum of money or to keep certain financial assets, especially shares in a business venture, out of the division of accrued gain entirely.

Furthermore, it is possible by way of a notarized matrimonial property agreement, to regulate alimony payments upon divorce and the way in which the accrued pension expectancies shall be divided. In particular, it is possible that one or both spouses waive the claim to post-matrimonial alimony payments or the division of pension benefits. It is also possible to limit the claims in terms of their amount or duration.

A matrimonial property agreement can be made before or during the course of a marriage (pre-nuptial or post-nuptial agreement). If the marriage has already broken down and is to be dissolved by divorce, a divorce settlement can be made before a notary that includes the items of regulation mentioned, as well as further agreements, particularly those pertaining to the division of mutual financial assets and household property and those concerning child custody and visitation rights. In this manner it is often possible to achieve considerable cost savings in a divorce suit since, if the matter has been comprehensively regulated by a notary in advance, only one attorney needs to be hired for the divorce proceedings, whereas without a notarized agreement, two attorneys are an absolute must.

E. Other Responsibilities of the Notary

The notary is also responsible for the following transactions:

- the preparation of affidavits that are to be presented to government authorities,
- the keeping in safe custody or delivery of money, securities and other valuables,
- overseeing the drawing of lots,
- overseeing voluntary auction sales,
- the issuance of powers of attorney to persons authorized to represent companies, insofar as this authorization derives from an entry in the commercial register or similar register,
- the provision of professional services to the parties in all other undisputed proceedings, especially the preparation of documents and drafts and the advising of the parties together with their representa-

tives in court and in their dealings with administrative governmental authorities.

III. Validity of the Notarized Documents

Most of the cases in which the parties commission the services of a notary are cases in which the notarized form is required for the validity of the transaction.

The notarization of documents has yet further functions that make it advisable to chose this form, even when it is not proscribed by statute:

A.   Probative Force of Notarized Documents

A notarized document presented in a civil process provides full probative evidence that the statements contained in it were made by the parties (Par. 415, Sec. 1 Code of Civil Procedure ["Zivilprozeßordnung" (ZPO)]). It is not necessary to convince the court of the correctness of the documents. The only objection that can be raised against a notarized document is that of forgery, which is generally difficult to prove since notarized documents contain the assumption of genuineness within themselves (Par. 437 ZPO). Only if the document displays superficial flaws such as erasures or a broken seal is its probative force disturbed. In that event, it is up to the court's discretion to decide how great of an extent the probative value of the notarized document is influenced by the superficial flaws.

B.   Notarized Document as Writ of Execution

A prerequisite to the procuring of a writ of execution or enforceable instrument, is generally a non-appealable court decree according to German law. Such a decree often can be substituted through submission to immediate enforcement in a notarized document. In this case, the notarized document is itself the basis for the enforcement measure (Par. 794, Sec. 1, No. 5 ZPO). A purchaser of property, for example, can in this fashion subject himself in the real-estate purchase contract to an immediate enforcement of the claim against him in the amount of the purchase price, thereby enabling quick procurement of a court order in case of default. Instead, with an enforceable copy of the notarized document, which the notary provides without further examination, the seller can initiate enforcement measures. The notarized document can in such cases spare the parties lengthy trial proceedings.

Submission to immediate enforcement in a notarized document is, however, possible only when the content of the debt is the payment of a specific fixed sum of money. The German legislature is currently planning to widen the "submission to immediate enforcement" to include other performance obligations of a debtor as well. This will increase the significance of the notarized document in this area.

C. Enforceable Attorney Settlement

A further possible way of avoiding a time and cost intensive court trial is to have a notary declare a settlement agreement enforceable. In this case, the so-called "enforceable attorney settlement" ("vollstreckbarer Anwaltsvergleich") can replace a court decree as the basis for enforcement measures.

IV. The Fees of Notaries

A. Fee-Setting Principles

1. Identical Fees for All Notaries

The fees of notaries are regulated by statute ("Kostenordnung" [KostO]). The amount of the fee depends first of all on the object of transaction. A further determining factor is the value of the transaction. For two-sided statements, that is to say, for all contracts, the notary receives a double fee; for one-sided statements, a simple fee. Powers of attorney and applications to the land registry ("Grundbuchamt") and registry court ("Registergericht") are figured at half the regular fee. For enforcement and counseling services performed in the course of finalizing real-estate transactions notaries also receive one or more half fees, depending on the nature of the case at hand.

2. Prohibition of Fee Agreements

The fees charged by notaries are proscribed by statute and thus cannot be subjected to individual agreement. In particular, notaries are forbidden to waive a portion of their fees in cases involving high transaction values. The measures are very much tighter here than they are in the area of attorney fees because notaries are not members of a free profession but rather the holders of public office.

3. Digressive Scale

The notary fee scale is digressive, which is to say that the fee becomes progressively lower in proportion as the value of the transaction rises. The simple fee for a transaction with a value of € 5,000.-- is € 42.--; for a transaction with a value of € 100,000.-- it is only € 207.--.

4. Minimum Fees and Maximum Fees

The minimum fee for a notary service is € 10.--. There are, however, various maximum fees. For instance, the fee for the recording of the resolutions of shareholders can in no case exceed € 5,000.-- (Par. 47, Sentence 2 KostO). The maximum fee for the certification of signatures is € 130.--. In cases involving the recording of articles of incorporation and changes of corporate form, the maximum amount that can be assumed as representing the value of the transaction is five million Euro.

5. Fee Reductions in the New Federal States of Germany

Notary fees are reduced by ten percent in the territory once comprising the German Democratic Republic (GDR), that is, in the federal states of Saxony, Saxony-Anhalt, Thuringia, Mecklenburg-Western Pomerania, Brandenburg and the eastern portion of the City of Berlin. The reduction presupposes, however, that the cost debtor has his place of residence within the territory of the new federal states.

B. A Few Examples of Notary Fees

1. Real-Estate Purchase Contract

The recording of the purchase contract for a piece of real estate with a value of € 250,000.-- generates a notary fee in the amount of € 864.---. In addition to the recording fee the notary receives several side fees, amounting in total to about thirty percent of the recording fee, for the enforcement of the transaction at the land registry, for the procurement of the required permits and, in the event that encumbrances have to be discharged for the procurement of the discharging documents. Further costs are added for printing expenditures at the rate of € 0.50 per page, postage costs and sixteen percent value-added tax (VAT). The costs of a real-estate contract with a value of € 250,000.-- thus run somewhere in the range of € 1,500.-- and € 1,700.---.

2. The Formation of a GmbH

The formation of a limited liability company (GmbH) with a nominal capital value of € 25,000.-- generates, independent of whether the notary drafted the articles of incorporation himself or the shareholders and/or their attorneys did so themselves, a fee of € 168.---. There is an additional fee for registering the company and the name of the primary managing director in the commercial register, which, in the case of a company with a nominal capital value of € 25,000.--, amounts to € 84.---. The formation of a GmbH with the legally required minimum nominal capital value of € 25,000.-- generates, including printing and postage costs and VAT, notary fees in the range of about € 450.---.

3. Testament / Inheritance Contract

The basis for measuring the fee for a testament or an inheritance contract is the value of the testator's estate at the moment of recording minus debts. A simple fee is charged for a testament, a double fee for an inheritance contract. A mutual testament of a wedded couple likewise generates a double fee. The costs of a testament in the case of an estate valued at € 500,000.-- would, for instance, amount to

€ 807.-- plus out-of-pocket expenses for printing and postage, in addition to sixteen percent VAT. The fee for an inheritance contract involving a net estate value of five million Euro would be € 15,114.-- plus sixteen percent VAT.

Real-Estate Property Law in Germany

Christian R. Wolf

I. Real-Estate Property

A. The Concept of Real-Estate Property in German Law

The concept of real-estate property is not legally defined in German law. From the statutes concerning real-estate property, however, it can be determined that real estate in the legal sense is a spatially limited portion of the face of the earth which is recorded in the land register. It follows that every piece of real estate in Germany is recorded on a page of the land register. The land registers are maintained by the local courts. Several pieces of real estate belonging to the same owner can be contained on a single page (for more details concerning the land register see section IV. below).

In addition to the land register, a cadastral map illustrating the land-share divisions ("Liegenschaftskataster") is maintained. The entire surface of the earth within the state territory is surveyed and divided into local sub-districts, units and lots, which are recorded in the cadastral map. The land register and the cadastral map of land shares must be kept in such a way that they always match perfectly. This is ensured through the notification of the land registry of any changes in the status quo or in the definition of the cadastral units by the land-survey office ("Katasteramt"). The cadastral map of land shares thus contains detailed information about the actual proportions of a piece of property and the land register contains the details of its legal circumstances.

B. Principle of the Oneness of Real-Estate Property and any Buildings Located Thereupon

Under German law, any buildings firmly attached to the ground and soil upon which they stand are considered to be integral parts of the real-estate property. The ownership of the buildings always rightfully belongs to the owner of the real-estate property and cannot be separated from it. The sale of real-estate property thus always includes the building located on it; it is not possible to sell the building without the land.

The legal situation in the former GDR was fundamentally different. There it was both possible and widely common to procure ownership of a building only, whereas the property on which it was located was simply leased. This regulation was retained in the course of the reunification of the German states: in the new federal states of Thuringa, Saxony, Saxony-Anhalt, Brandenburg, Mecklenburg-

Pomerania and the eastern portion of the city-state of Berlin there is still today the concept of independent ownership of buildings. This regulation, however, is limited to property previously divided in such a manner; it is most definitely not the rule of thumb in the post-reunification, reconstruction efforts. In the already existent cases, the land and the building located on it are each registered on separate pages in the land register.

II. Real-Estate-Similar Rights

A. Condominiums and Part Ownerships

In addition to total ownership of real-estate property, there exists condominiums and part ownerships of property. In the latter cases the owner has a fixed partial ownership share in a jointly owned piece of real-estate property in addition to sole ownership of an apartment located on the property or a part of a building that is separate and complete in itself and not used for residential purposes.

Particularly large apartment buildings, some of which have several hundred residential units, are erected in the form of condominiums. The advantage of condominiums is that they can be sold and mortgaged, together with a percentage share of the jointly held property.

Condominiums are special forms of authentic ownership of pieces of real-estate property and in many cases are treated just the same way as regular real estate. Every condominium, for example, has its own page in the land register.

B. Inheritable Building Right

A further real-estate-similar right is the heritable building right ("Erbbaurecht"). This is a transferable and heritable right to erect a building on or under the ground surface of a piece of property. There is a special land register for such rights. This, in addition to the independent ownership of a building (without the ownership of the property it is built on) in the new federal states, is the second exception to the rule that the ownership of a building automatically belongs to the owner of the real estate. Here the building is an integral part of the heritable building right, which entitles its bearer to the ownership of the erected building. This right is in many ways comparable to a long-term lease and requires its bearer to pay an annual leasing fee. It continues to endure insofar as it can be independently charged with mortgages, liens and other real-estate encumbrances.

The heritable building right offers both the property owner and the entitled party advantages; it enables the owner to achieve ongoing yields from the property without having to sell it. The bearer of the heritable building right has the right the possibility of erecting a building without having to pay a high purchase price for the land. Heritable building rights are thus often issued by churches or communities to promote social welfare housing projects.

Heritable building rights are generally granted for a duration of time ranging from somewhere between thirty and ninety nine years. After the elapse of that fixed period, the right expires with the result that the owner of the land automatically becomes the owner of the building and must provide adequate compensation to the former bearer of the heritable building right. The land owner can avoid this compensation obligation by offering the bearer of the heritable building right the possibility of extending his title for a further period of time that would approximately correspond to the predicable lifetime of his building as it currently stands. If the bearer of the title declines such an extension proposal, he thereby loses his lawful compensation claim.

III. The Purchase and Sale of Real Estate

The purchase and sale of real estate requires notarization (see chapter Notaries in Germany, section II, point A.). The transferal of the property, however, does not occur solely through the finalization of the notarial contract but rather not before the new owner is noted in the land register. Before that registration occurs, the purchaser simply has a claim arising from the notarial contract that the seller turn the property over to him.

The change of ownership cannot be noted in the land register until the notary has procured all the required official permits necessary to enforce the contract, the community in whose jurisdictional influence the transaction lies has waived its pre-emptive rights to buy the property and the purchaser has paid the property tax at the rate of 3.5% of the purchase price. This procedure generally takes several weeks or months. In the meantime the purchaser's position is still not completely secure. There exists, however, the widely used possibility of securing the property rights of the purchaser in advance by way of a priority notice ("Vormerkung") in the land register. This priority notice basically amounts to a reservation for the purchaser, which protects him against any attempts of the seller, who is still the registered owner of the property, to dispose of it in another fashion as well as against interventions by any creditors of the seller.

Appendix:
Permit Requirements for the Purchase of Real Estate by Foreigners

The German External Trade Act ("Außenwirtschaftsgesetz") provides for the possibility of making real-estate transactions with foreigners subject to the issuance of permits. No use has yet been made of this state authority, however, which would apply to both natural persons and legal entities. Foreigners and foreign companies can thus currently purchase property in German with no restrictions whatsoever.

IV. The Land Register

A. The Five Parts of a Land Register Page

Every page in the land register consists of five parts: the inscription, the itemized description of the current features of the property and Sections I through III. The inscription contains the names of the municipal court, the land register district and the number of the land register page. If the page has been prepared for a condominium or a heritable building right, it contains the additional label "Wohnungsgrundbuch" ("Land Register for Condominiums") or "Erbbaugrundbuch" ("Land Register for Building Leases"). The itemized description of the property shows the current state of the property and any changes to it that have been made in the past. Every piece of property receives a successive number. Reference is made to this number whenever further entries are made. If any changes arise, for instance through a division of the property, the newly created pieces of property are registered under the successive numbers and the former piece of property is underlined in red. This "red penciling" makes it clear that the piece of property so marked no longer exits. The itemized list of the features of the property also contains the size dimensions of the property.

In Section I of the land register the owner or owners of the property are identified as are the legal grounds for their acquisition of it. In cases involving more than one owner, the nature of the joint relationship is also registered - for instance, "co-owners" or "GbR" ("civil-law partnership"). Sections II and III of the land register contain the registration of the encumbrances on the property, whereby mortgages (bank mortgages, land charges and annuity charges) are listed in Section III and all remaining encumbrances and restrictions are listed in Section II. The division into two sections here is merely an historical remnant - it would be just the same if all the property encumbrances were listed in one section (for more about each of the different types of property encumbrances see part V. below).

Since the content of a property encumbrance is often extensive and detailed, the right is merely registered in abbreviated form. For further information concerning the content of the right, reference is made to the files kept by the land registries, in which all of the documents pertaining to a given piece of property are archived. In order to find out what the right in total entails, it might thus be necessary to gain access to the land register files ("Grundakten").

A right is deleted through "red penciling" and the registration of a cancellation note. Any alternation of the right is likewise registered.

Plans exist to convert the land registers into electronic registers. Such pilot projects are already underway in the federal states of Bavaria and Saxony. Notaries are directly networked to the electronic land registers, which gives them on-line access to the files.

B. Access Rights to the Land Register

Anyone is granted permission to inspect the land register who can demonstrate a legitimate interest in the matter. The right to look into the land register also encompasses the right to inspect the land register files and any submitted but not yet registered applications as well as the right to demand simple or certified copies of pertinent entries in the land register or of documents contained in the land register files against reimbursement of the copying costs.

The question of what exactly constitutes a "legitimate interest" has been the object of various judicial decisions. From them it can be deducted that legitimate interest exists when enough facts can be presented to convince the land registry that access to the files is not desired for abusive purposes or out of pure curiosity. Here data protection has priority. A person with a legitimate reason for wanting to gain access to the records could be, for instance, a potential buyer in the process of concretely negotiating the purchase of the property with its owner, not however a prospective buyer who wants to get the name of the property owner by inspecting the books first.

Notaries are exempted from having to prove legitimate interest and thus have free access to all land registers.

C. Public Faith in the Land Register

The registration of a property right in the land register is prerequisite to its coming into existence. There is, therefore, a high degree of probability to back the assumption that any right registered in the land register actually does exist. Yet there are exceptional cases involving incorrectness of the land register, for instance, when the agreement that provided the basis for the entry never came into effect. Registration in the land register is indeed prerequisite to the coming into being of a right, yet it alone is not enough. Without a valid agreement between the property owner and the otherwise entitled person, no right has originated, not even if it has been entered in the land register.

Another way in which the land register can become inaccurate is through the death of a registered owner. Upon the death of a property owner his complete estate and therewith his ownership rights to any real-estate property are automatically transferred per force of the law to his heirs. In such cases the land register has to be updated.

Legal relations, however, should be able to assume even in such cases that the entries in the land register are correct. Par. 891 of the German Civil Code ("Bürgerliches Gesetzbuch" [BGB]) therefore establishes the legal premise for assuming that the land register correctly and completely reflects the rights to the property. This statute causes one of the oddest quirks in the entire German land registration system. And that's because the presumption of correctness gives way to yet a further legal effect entailing the protection of a purchaser who acted in good faith. A person who buys a piece of real-estate property from the person listed as its lawful owner in the land register, but who in fact is not the owner, lawfully acquires that property as long as he was fully unaware of the inaccuracy of the land register.

Just as legal relations may rely on the existence of registered rights, they may rely on the nonexistence of nonregistered rights. If, for example, a mortgage or a land charge has been improperly extinguished, it is not possible to assert to a later acquirer of the property that the right exists in fact. The only recourse of the actual holder of such a right, provided the property was acquired in good faith, is to sue the land registry for the compensation of losses stemming from its negligence.

Especially in cases in which a non-owner of a piece of property is still registered as its lawful owner in the land register, exploiting the good faith of an acquirer receives something in return, a purchase price. For instance, the non-entitled disposer of the property must turn the proceeds over to the actual owner. The actual owner, on the other hand, cannot demand reversal of the property ownership from the acquirer who acted in good faith.

The public faith in the German land register results in a very high degree of reliability in real-estate transactions. This holds particularly true for and is of prime importance to the lending against real-estate collateral, since the credit provider, who arranges to have a mortgage put on the property as security, can rely on the entries in the land register and risks no danger of not acquiring his right at all or only with a depreciated value due to such reasons as the lack of the legitimacy of the registered owner or because prior charges against the property were not registered.

D. Priority Ranking in the Land Register

1. The Priority Ranking Among Various Rights Listed in the Land Register

If real-estate property is encumbered by various rights against it, these rights are listed in the land register in terms of a specific priority ranking. The priority ranking of the rights listed in one and the same section of the land register is determined by the order of their registration. If the rights are listed in different sections, their priority ranking is determined by the dates on which they were registered. Rights that were registered earlier have priority over those that were listed later. If any rights were registered in different sections on the same day, they have identical priority among themselves. In the event that any rights in the same section have identical priority ranking, this is noted next to each of the rights effected.

The order in which the land registry must register various rights is determined by the dates on which the applications for registration were filed with the land registry. Every application for registration is precisely dated by the land registry in terms of the day and hour that it was received. The rules of procedure regulate that the land registry must enter the applications into the land register in precisely the order that is determined by the reception data contained in each of the applications. Of decisive importance here is not the date of registration but rather the date on which the application was filed. If several applications are filed at the same time, they have equal priority. Other rules apply only if a priority designation is affixed to the several applications that were filed together. The parties to a transaction involving several rights to be registered in the land register can thus agree in advance to their priority ranking during the notarial recording of the transaction or at the time when the rights are certified before the notary. The notary will then pass that priority ranking on to the land registry, which will register the rights according to the determined ranking.

It is also possible to change the priority ranking freely at any later date. This presupposes, however, that those entitled to the registered rights and the property owner are in accord concerning the priority ranking and agree to have the change made accordingly in the land register. Such a change in the priority ranking may not entail either an improvement or worsening of the status of any other rights contained in the land register.

2. Significance of the Priority Ranking

The ranking of a right contained in the land register is of prime significance for its value and security. It determines the consideration order and the chances of having the right satisfied in the event that the encumbered piece of property has to be put up for public auction. The priority rights of a creditor forcing the public auction cannot be impaired. After the fall of the hammer they still remain as an encumbrance upon the property. On the other hand, any rights that are lower in priority than the rights of the creditor enforcing satisfaction expire with the public auction. Therefore, when it comes to auctioning off the property, higher priority ranking results in higher justice. For that reason, credit institutions interested in securing a loan by having a land charge or mortgage noted in the land register tend to insist upon having top priority ranking. They are willing to accept a worse standing only if the market value of the property is so high that even in the event of a public auction the creditors registered in second place or even lower are guaranteed satisfaction of their claims.

Public faith in the accuracy of the land register (see point 3. above) also plays a role in the priority of a registered right. Should a right be noted in the wrong order in the land register, a third party acting in good faith acquires the right as it stands in the land register.

V. Rights to Real-Estate Property

A. Compulsory Form of Real-Estate Property Rights

Not just any kind of rights and limitations that the parties to a real-estate deal might agree to can be entered into the land register as encumbrances, but rather only those that the statues provide for. Due to the lack of statutory regulation it's not possible to enter, for example, any rights to rent or lease in the land register. Thus if an application for registration of a right not provided for by statute or for a right that is provided for but has been endowed with impermissible content by the parties is filed, the land registry must reject the application.

B. Rights of Section II (Selection)

1. Usufruct of Landed Property

Real-estate property, as well as condominiums and heritable building rights can be charged with a so-called usufruct ("Nießbrauch"). The usufruct grants the entitled party the right to take the property into his possession and make full use of it. The usufructuary is, other words, entitled to the personal use of the property as well as to any and all yields of the property such as renting and leasing yields.

The usufruct is frequently used in the form of a so-called proviso usufruct ("Vorbehaltsnießbrauch") if a piece of property in anticipation of succession to it by inheritance is to be transferred to the next generation by persons still living who, however, wish to reserve their rights to use the property themselves until they have deceased.

2. Easements ("Dienstbarkeiten")

Easements are limited in rem rights to a piece of property aimed at toleration or omission. For the most part, they serve the maintenance of good neighborly relations, the enforcement of building rights and now, particularly the securing of competitive interests. Examples of easements are the granting of the right to passage or the right to lay a water pipeline through the property, building restrictions on the property, tolerance of less than the normally required distance of a building on the neighboring lot or the tolerance of emissions from a neighboring lot.

There are two types of easements: the so-called "basic easement" ("Grunddienstbarkeit") is not a right belonging to the entitled person himself but merely in his capacity as the owner of the entitled piece of property. Not only the current owner of the property has a claim to this right: any other parties that might own the property in the future can likewise lay claim to it. The basic easement is thus passed on to the new owner as an integral part of the property when it is sold.

The so-called "limited personal easement" ("beschränkte persönliche Dienstbarkeit"), on the other hand, belongs to a specific natural person or legal entity. Such an easement is attached to the individual person who is entitled to it. It is neither heritable nor transferable. It is merely possible to let a third party exercise the right insofar as the owner permits. The limited personal easement is frequently ordered in the form of a right to tenancy ("Wohnungsrecht"), which guarantees the seller of the property the continued right to use it until his death.

3. Land Charges Conveying the Right to Recurrent Payments or Services ("Reallast")

The "Reallast" type of land charge is the method provided by law for the securing of legal debts and obligations through recurrent payments, payments in kind or services. The essential content of such a land charge is thus the obligation to give or a do a specific thing. The payments can be in money, in kind or in the form of services. The payments must, however, be recurrent. A one-time payment cannot be the object of such a land charge.

The payment obligations arising from such a land charge also have to be defined or definable, so that entitled persons with lower priority can, when ordering their right, already have the possibility of determining the capacity the higher ranking land charge based on recurrent payments would have in the event of a public auction. Accordingly, the content of such a land charge can be periodical payments of a certain amount of money ("Geldrente"), the maintenance of a grave or other care services such as personally tending to the person who has transferred the property. This right is mainly used by owners of property in order to secure their rights when transferring the property in anticipation of the succession to it by inheritance. Yet another important use of this right is to secure by way of entry into the land register leasing payments for heritable building rights ("Erbbauzins" [Compare section II. B. above]).

The payment obligations secured by such land charges can but must not necessarily be made through the fruits of the charged property. An obligation to make periodic monetary payments can be secured by way of a "Reallast" land charge even when the charged property produces no yields. The sole purpose of the land charge is to grant the entitled person the right to force a public auction of the property in the event that the promised recurrent payments are not made and to thereby satisfy his claims from the auction proceeds according to the value of the payments legitimately due to him.

C. Real-Estate Mortgages (Rights in Section III)

1. Definition and Types of Real-Estate Mortgages ("Grundpfandrechte")

Real-estate mortgages are liens ("Pfandrechte") against property. They serve to secure personal payment obligations, especially within the context of loan contracts. In most normal cases the debtor of the payment obligation and the liable owner of the property are one and the same person. It is, however, also possible to secure an obligation of a third party through a property mortgage, for instance, when a business loan of the husband is secured against a piece of property that is solely owned by the wife.

German law recognizes as mortgages the common mortgage ("Hypothek"), the land charge ("Grundschuld") and - as a subcategory of the land charge - the land charge conveying the right to periodic payments ("Rentenschuld"). The last form is of practically no significance. A common mortgage and a land charge both pursue the same objectives. The coexistence of the two forms can only be explained historically. Differences exist insofar as the common mortgage can by force of law originate and continue to exist only in the amount of the claim that is to be secured and only for as long as the claim continues to exist. On the other hand, the land charge is not dependent on the existence or the amount of the claim that is to be secured through it, as the land charge is abstract. For all practical purposes, this freedom of the land charge from the existence of the claim to be secured is virtually never asserted, since the land charge and the claim are always tied up together in the security agreement. In practice, the legal impacts of the common mortgage and the land charge hardly ever display any differences. Today the land charge is predominantly chosen and the common mortgage still shows up occasionally. The banking industry in particular exclusively uses the land charge to secure property loans.

The legal impact of the registration of a property mortgage is that the registered creditor is entitled to enforce public auction of the property in order to satisfy its claims in the event that the debtor's payments are overdue. The liability of the property owner is his risk of losing the property by way of public auction.

2. Economic Significance of Mortgages

The significance of mortgages in Germany in terms of the public economy is enormous. At the end of 1994, loans amounting to a total of 0.6 trillion Euro were secured through mortgaged loans on housing property alone.

The preference for securing loans through mortgages on real-estate property versus other types of collateral such as third-party endorsements or liens against moveable goods rests primarily on three factors: the long-term value continuity of property assets; the publicity of the land register in which it can immediately be seen who the property owner is, who the creditors are and what priority rankings the creditors have among themselves; the good-faith protection guaranteed by the land register.

3. Lending Principles

Before issuing credit against the registration of a mortgage the lending institution checks the credit worthiness ("Bonität") of the applicant as well as the hypothecary value ("Beleihungswert") of the real-estate property. The hypothecary value is not identical with the real market value of the object but is instead figured according to special internal regulations of the bank. The basis for the determination of the object's value are all the conditions that could influence the yield of the mortgaged object in the event that it might be necessary to forcibly turn it into cash. Such conditions include, particularly, the site value, the real value of the building and the utilization value of the land. The thus determined lending value may not be exploited by more than 60% (Par. 20, Sec. 2, No. 1 of the German Credit Law ["Kreditwesengesetz"]). The lending limit is justified by the fact that only in the rarest of cases is it possible to materialize the entire value of a piece of property should it have to be publicly auctioned. Rather, the average yield in a public real-estate auction is no more than fifty to seventy percent of the lending value.

4. Subjection to Immediate Enforcement

In the case of land charges to the benefit of commercial lending institutions, a declaration of subjection to immediate enforcement is generally made in the amount equal to the mortgage. This enables the creditor uncomplicated access to the assets of the debtor who has fallen behind in his payments without troublesome and drawn-out court proceedings (compare chapter Notaries in Germany section III. B.).

5. Personal Assumption of Liability

In addition to ordering mortgages, commercial lending institutions generally tend to demand that anyone they give a property loan to assume personal liability for the repayment of the loan with all their remaining personal assets. A subjection to immediate enforcement occurs here as well. The financing institution thus secures its interests not only through the mortgaged real-estate property, but through the entire personal assets of the debtor.

The Law of Bankruptcy and Security Interests

Reinhard Nacke

I. Introduction

Section 1 of the Insolvency Act defines the comprehensive goal of the insolvency procedure as the satisfaction of all the claims of a debtor's creditors jointly by, either realizing the assets of the debtor and dividing the proceeds or by reaching a divergent arrangement, whereby the business continues to exist. The debtor who acts in good faith is given the opportunity to be released from his remaining debts.

It is amazing that the exploitation of the enterprise has priority, as the purpose of the new insolvency law of 1999, among others, is maintaining the debtor. Through this, in one provision after another, the position of the involvence administration is strengthened over the suppliers and other contract partners.

On the other hand, characteristic of the insolvency law is the strength of the position of the creditors committee, which can have considerable influence over the direction of the proceedings.

The law further outlines the provisions concerning the discharge of remaining indebtedness. This provision allows natural persons who have been declared bankrupt to be released from their remaining liabilities if they agree for a definite time period to assign a substantial part of their future wages or salary to creditors. By this, the debtor who acts in good faith shall be given the opportunity to be released from his remaining debts.

Sections II - IV of this chapter describe the normal bankruptcy procedure, section V describes the composition proceedings, and section VI outlines the provision concerning the discharge of remaining indebtedness. This provision allows natural persons who have been declared bankrupt to be released from their remaining liabilities if they agree for a definite time period to assign a substantial part of their future wages or salary to creditors.

II. Steps Leading to the Institution of Insolvency Proceedings / Security Interests

A. Steps leading to insolvency proceedings

Insolvency proceedings may be instituted against the property of a natural or legal person through the granting of a court order issued in response to a petition filed either by one or more creditors or by the debtor himself.

As a rule, the pre-requisites for such a court order instituting insolvency proceedings include: (1) current insolvency (inability to pay one's debts) or (2) impending insolvency (the expected or existing lack of liquid resources). In the case of legal persons, the court may also grant an order initiating insolvency proceedings in the case of (3) excessive indebtedness. Excessive indebtedness exists if the liabilities of the business exceed the value of its assets. This excessive indebtedness is not shown by the normal financial statement. Rather, the determination is made with the help of the so-called "Überschuldungsbilanz" (excessive indebtedness financial statement). The basis of this special financial statement may, however, be the normal commercial balance sheet. **The primary difference between the commercial balance sheet and the excessive indebtedness financial statement is that, in the latter, it is very important to properly reflect the true value of the business's assets and liabilities.** In preparing the excessive indebtedness financial statement, a decision must be made whether property shall be valued according to its liquidation value or according to the "going concern" principle. Which method is used depends on whether a business analysis indicates a positive or a negative prognosis. If the business is not able to continue in existence, then the liquidation value will be used. Otherwise, the "going concern" method of valuation should be employed.

The manager of a legal person has a difficult task because he is required by law to file a bankruptcy petition as soon as the business has excessive indebtedness. In order to meet this legal obligation, he must, as a practical matter, begin to prepare an excessive indebtedness balance on a monthly basis as soon as the business finds itself in a financially critical phase. If the manager of the business fails to file a bankruptcy petition when required, he can be liable for civil damages as well as subject to criminal prosecution.

Prior to the official institution of insolvency proceedings, the Local Court with jurisdiction decides whether the petition for the institution of bankruptcy proceedings shall be initially accepted. Venue is not only determined by the official domicile (registered office) of the business, but also according to where the business conducts its economic activities. Therefore, efforts of a debtor to influence the choice of judicial forum by relocating the business's registered office or domicile are generally ineffective.

If the petition for the institution of insolvency proceedings is initially accepted, the Local Court will issue an order prohibiting the creditors from pursuing execution or enforcement actions in moveable assets, and will appoint a provisional insolvency administrator. Frequently, the debtor will be prohibited from managing his property. Such management rights will be transferred to the provisional administrator.

The provisional insolvency administrator has the following duties:

- to protect and preserve the property of the debtor;
- to carry on the business for the time being unless the court has ordered its closure;

- to determine if the assets of the debtor are sufficient to cover the costs of the insolvency proceedings.

B. Security Interests

In particular, this last duty means, that the provisional insolvency administrator must determine if the unencumbered assets are sufficient to cover his own expenses as well as his compensation. Still a uncountable number of applications (petitions) for the institution of insolvency proceedings are denied, and the basis for this denial is an insufficient amount of unencumbered assets. The reason that debtors often possess so few unencumbered assets is the extensive use of security interests in Germany. Hardly anywhere in the world do such far-reaching and commonly used possibilities exist for the supplier to secure the payment of an unpaid purchase price.

In most cases, the supplier does not retain ownership rights in the delivered product. In addition, it is common for the supplier to secure in advance a security interest in at least a part of the products that are to be produced with the help of the delivered product. Further, creditors typically require the debtor to assign to the supplier all accounts receivables which result either from the sale of the supplied product or from the product which the debtor has produced with such product. According to the standard business terms often found in contracts, the supplier does not lose his security rights with the payment of the purchase price. Rather, such rights are extinguished at the point when all claims against the buyer have been satisfied or when the value of the supplier's security greatly exceeds the value of his underlying claims.

Similar to the supplier, the bank which has provided financing also secures its loan by obtaining a transfer of ownership rights in business assets or assignment of the debtor's accounts receivables.

Unlike in most countries, the creation of security interests in personal property neither requires certification by a notary nor registration. Rather, sellers and buyers or banks and debtors create such interests through contracts which incorporate standard business terms. (Note: According to such standard business terms, the parties must comply with certain rules. Therefore, in order to avoid the possibility that the security interest is ineffective, it is very important to discuss such terms with an attorney.)

Notarization by a notary as well as registration is naturally required in order to obtain security in real property. A security interest in real property can arise through a land charge or mortgage.

The creditor who holds one of the above referenced security interests has the right to demand delivery of his property from the insolvency administrator (screening, e.g. in case of reservation of title), or in any event, the insolvency administrator is obliged to satisfy a secured creditor's claim before the satisfaction of other creditors' claims (preferential treatment). In case of goods delivered to the debtor under reservation of title, however, the administrator also can choose for fullfilment of the purchase contract and keep the products in order to – for example – continue with the business. Then he has to pay the full purchase price to the seller (see below IV. E.).

In case of preferential treatment, the insolvency administrator satisfies such preferred creditors' claims either out of the resulting proceeds of his sale of the secured property or out of the accounts receivables associated with such property which he collects. Above all this becomes practicable if the debtor in case of an extended reservation of title has sold the supplied product or if he has processed it.

C. Result of the preliminary investigation

When the insolvency administrator realizes such secured goods in the above described ways, hardly any value is left over for distribution to the remaining creditors or to cover the costs of the insolvency proceeding. One provision which helps to ensure that at least some remaining value exists, however, is the requirement that 9 % of realization proceeds from property obtained through the efforts of the insolvency administrator must be allocated to the insolvent's estate.

If the provisional insolvency administrator determines that the debtor does not possess sufficient unencumbered property to cover the costs of the proceedings, then he will recommend to the court that it deny the petition for the institution of bankruptcy, unless a creditor exists who is willing to provide an advance to cover the foreseeable costs. A creditor will only consider making such a payment if the insolvency administrator, given his economic expertise and his understanding of the debtor's circumstances, is in a position to at least recover and pay to the creditor a portion of the claim which such creditor stands to lose.

If the petition for institution of bankruptcy proceedings is denied, then a creditor may attempt to achieve payment of his claim by way of a separate execution/enforcement action. In conjunction with denying the petition to initiate bankruptcy, the court in the case of a bankrupt legal person (i.e., a business) will order it struck from the commercial register with the result that such business no longer exists.

III. Order of Events in the Insolvency Proceedings

A. Institution of the proceedings

If the court, based on the opinion of the provisional insolvency administrator, determines that the debtor has sufficient assets for the institution of bankruptcy proceedings, then it shall issue an order initiating such proceedings. The court appoints an insolvency administrator. If the debtor himself wishes to handle the liquidation, then the court shall appoint a person whose role it is to supervise the debtor's transactions during such winding up (liquidation). At the same time, all creditors are given a certain amount of time to present their claims to the insolvency administrator and reveal all of their security interests and rights in the property of the debtor. All persons with claims are required to seek relief from the insolvency administrator instead of the debtor.

In addition, the fact that bankruptcy proceedings have been instituted is publicized in the Official Gazette of the Federal Republic. This is a national publication which contains important information regarding businesses. Its primary subscribers are libraries and large firms.

B. Announcement of Claims, Surrender of Property

Typically, creditors announce their claims through use of a special form which the court provides for this purpose. Although a creditor can personally handle the announcement of a claim(s), most creditors secure an attorney to represent them in the announcement of their claim. In this way, the creditor ensures that he has an attorney who is familiar with the issues in case the insolvency administrator fails to recognize the claim(s), and it becomes necessary for the creditor to take legal steps to enforce such recognition.

Attorney representation is also advisable for those creditors with security interests in the debtor's property. Such a security interest can arise, for example, when the creditor deliveres property under a reservation of title or provided credit under the condition that he be granted a lien in the debtor's property (see above). If a creditor's claim is secured, it is not only necessary to correctly announce one's claim, but care must also be taken to ensure that the property which is owned by the creditor and not the debtor is surrendered by the insolvency administrator. Despite such security, voluntary delivery of the creditor's property is not always forthcoming. It can fairly be said that the insolvency administrator is interested in saving as much of such property as he can for all the creditors, thereby achieving the largest distributive share for each creditor as possible. The insolvency administrator who accomplishes this not only develops a good reputation, but can also command a higher compensation for his services rendered in the proceedings. Thus, the creditor's demand for recognition of his security right is quite often met with arguments by the insolvency administrator against the legal effectiveness of such right, rather than with a easily obtained recognition.

C. Committee of Inspection and Creditors' Meetings

In addition to the insolvency administrator, the court often appoints a Committee of Inspection consisting of representatives of creditor groups (i.e., creditors with claims of relatively greater value, creditors with claims of lower value, employees, etc.) The Committee of Inspection supports and oversees the actions of the insolvency administrator.

In addition, the creditors as a whole may decide important issues in a creditor's meeting to which all creditors are invited. Such decisions include discharge of the insolvency administrator, the appointment of his replacement, the closure of the business or its continued operation.

D. Distribution of Property to Creditors and Conclusion of the Proceedings

When the insolvency administrator has essentially brought the insolvency proceedings to an end, he presents the court with a recommended list of the amounts that each creditor shall receive. Upon receipt of the court's approval, the property of the debtor is distributed. Following this distribution, the court declares the proceedings to be concluded.

To the extent claims of creditors have not been satisfied, and assuming the debtor has any remaining property or income, creditors can file an execution or enforcement action against the debtor in an attempt to recover their claim. However, such execution or enforcement actions are not possible if the debtor has been granted a discharge of all his remaining liabilities (see I above and VI below). From a legal standpoint creditors can (and assuming their claims are not barred by the statute of limitations) always pursue their unsatisfied claims against a legal person because legal persons are not entitled to a discharge of remaining liability. All claims, which were recognized in the course of the bankruptcy proceeding remain enforceable for 30 years against any future property acquired by a legal entity. However, from a practical standpoint the possibility of property acquisition by a bankrupt business is not very large since as the result of the insolvency proceedings, the business has been struck from the commercial register and therefore is no longer permitted to operate as a business.

IV. Effect of the Institution of Insolvency Proceedings

A. Legal actions

The institution of insolvency proceedings results in a suspension of all lawsuits which have been brought by or against the debtor. In the insolvency administrator's discretion, however such actions can be pursued by the insolvency administrator. In addition, if the action involves certain rights of the creditor such as a claim for the debtor's surrender of secured property, the creditor also is entitled to continue the lawsuit.

B. Enforcement/execution

No individual creditor may execute upon the property of the debtor during the course of the proceedings. This does not apply to execution actions undertaken based on certain types of liability claims, which arose due to acts or omissions of the insolvency administrator.

C. Offsets

Creditors may not offset their claims against the debtor's claims during the insolvency proceedings unless the creditor would have been able to do so prior to the institution of such proceedings. This means, for example, that a creditor is not permitted to obtain a satisfaction of his claims against the debtor by purchasing goods from the insolvency administrator and then off-setting his claim against the purchase price he receives from the insolvency administrator. The offset ban also prevents a debtor of the insolvent business from buying up the claims of the insolvent business's creditors in order to offset them against the insolvent business's claims against him.

D. Contesting the debtor's prior transactions

Often creditors deal with the debtor in order to secure property in satisfaction of their claims prior to the institution of the bankruptcy proceedings. This can occur, for example, through the debtor's gift of money or property to individual creditors, through the debtor's satisfaction of the claims of individual creditors, or through the debtor's grant of security to individual creditors.

The law grants the insolvency administrator the right to contest such legal transactions i.e., the right to demand the return of such money or other property or rights therein. While the laws regarding such contests by the insolvency administrator are quite complicated, it can be said that all steps taken by the debtor for the benefit of a creditor will be critically examined if such steps took place within the 3 month period prior to the filing of the petition for the institution of bankruptcy proceedings. Such pre-insolvency petition transactions are suspect, even if the creditor is not given exceptional preferential treatment, but only receives what he is entitled to under his existing contract with the debtor. Moreover, even the receipt of security or a satisfaction of a creditor's claim pursuant to the outcome of regular judicial proceedings is subject to contest by the insolvency administrator.

E. Delivery of goods contracts

The insolvency administrator is not obligated to secure the complete performance of contracts, which, at the time of the institution of insolvency proceedings, have not yet been completely performed by the debtor or the other party. Rather, he has a choice whether or not to demand performance by the contract partner. If the insolvency administrator determines to demand full performance, then he must first ensure, that the debtor's obligations under the contract are performed by paying the full purchase price, for example. If the insolvency administrator decides to forego fulfillment of a contract, then the contract partner may only demand damages, and in so doing, such contract partner's claim shall be treated like those of a general creditor of the bankrupt person i.e., **such contract party receives payment only if all the other creditors also receive at least a partial satisfaction of their claims.**

The contract party has the right to a timely decision by the insolvency administrator regarding whether or not his contract shall be fully carried out. If the insolvency administrator does not reach a prompt decision in this regard, he loses his right to demand performance of the contract. An exception exists if the contract partner has sold property to the debtor under a reservation of title to such property. In this case, in order to prevent all property in possession of the debtor from being claimed for surrender, which is subject to reservation of title by creditors, a longer decision-making period is afforded the insolvency administrator (Par. 107 of the Insolvency Act).

F. Leases

If the debtor has leased immovable property, then such leases remain in effect after the institution of bankruptcy proceedings. The other party of the institution of the bankruptcy proceedings cannot terminate the lease for reasons which happens prior to the petition for bankruptcy. If the debtor has leased space himself, the insolvency administrator however has the right to terminate said lease. In so doing, he is entitled to take advantage of the shortest notice of termination period allowed by law even if a longer period had been agreed in the lease contract.

G. Employment Contracts

The earnings of employees for the last 3 months prior to the institution of the insolvency proceedings are guaranteed to be paid, because the law grants all employees the right to payment of these earnings from the government employment office, in the event of their employer's insolvency.

According to Par. 113 of the Insolvency Act, the insolvency administrator may discharge an employee upon giving a 3 month notice of termination. This is true even if the contractual or normal termination notice period provided by law is longer. This has practical significance primarily in the case of employees who have worked for the insolvent business for a long time, because such employees are often entitled to a much longer notice of termination. Termination of employees under the Insolvency Act are subject to challenge before the Labor Court just like any other termination. **The termination can be challenged on the basis that it is not justified in light of the fact that the business is to be continued in operation.** Such a complaint has a chance of success only if the debtor employs more than 5 persons. Only then are the provisions of the "Kundigungsschutzgesetz" (Termination Protection Act) applicable. (Note: See chapter Aspects of German Labor Law).

Despite the applicability of the Termination Protection Act, the insolvency administrator can reduce the number of employees in order to reorganize the business, provided that he is able to convince the Labor Court that the termination of a certain number of employees is absolutely necessary and that such terminations are fair. This latter condition can be shown to have been met by evidence that the insolvency administrator has taken the employees' length of service, age and support obligations into consideration in determining which employees to terminate.

V. The Insolvency Plan

A special variant on the outcome of the insolvency proceedings is the establishment of an insolvency plan. This plan, which can be presented by the debtor or by the insolvency administrator, enables the insolvency proceedings to be handled in more flexible ways.

While the outcome of insolvency proceedings often is liquidation of the business, the adoption of an insolvency plan can result in the business being continued in operation or continued in operation in a reorganized form rather than being liquidated.

An insolvency plan must be presented in a writing and contain a description of the stage reached in the insolvency proceedings, the measures which remain to be taken, the treatment of the creditors, etc.

The court can reject the insolvency plan under certain conditions, for example, if the debtor has presented a plan, which is obviously not feasible. If the court does not reject the plan, then it is presented to the creditors for their approval. For this purpose, the creditors with the most similar financial interests are grouped together. The insolvency plan is then deemed accepted by the creditors only if the following two conditions are met: (1) a majority of all creditors in each group agree to the plan and (2) the creditors in each group who have approved the plan represent a majority of the claims in such group.

If the plan is accepted, then its content determines whether claims shall be forgiven or deferred, or whether property of the debtor shall be sold etc. In other words, the insolvency plan determines how the insolvency proceedings shall be carried out.

VI. Discharge of Remaining Debt

In Germany the usual limitations period for the claims (i.e., period after which existing claims are barred) is 3 years. However, a debtor has the possibility of achieving a discharge of his liabilities if he can show that in the 6 years following the insolvency proceedings, actions taken vis à vis his creditors were taken in good faith.

As implied in the above sentence, a debtor is entitled to such a discharge only if he has been the subject of a bankruptcy proceeding, which has been concluded. Upon the debtor's application for discharge, the court releases the debtor from his remaining liabilities on the condition that he complies with certain duties, including:

- that he be reasonably gainfully employed or at least make a good faith effort to secure gainful employment;
- that to the extent not urgently required for his support or the support of his family, he makes half of all assets which he acquires through inheritance, the lottery, or earnings available to his creditors.
- that he provide notice of all changes of his address.

Enforcement of Rights and Claims through the Courts and Arbitration Tribunals/The German Attorney Fees

Reinhard Nacke

I. Judicial Resolution of Disputes

A. Overview of Germany's system of courts

In comparison to many other countries, the judicial system in Germany is characterized by a relatively large number and variety of courts. The reasons for this are the existence of several appeal levels for nearly every dispute, and the fact that specialized courts have been created to handle certain legal categories of disputes. Generally, plaintiffs may file a lawsuit in one of two courts. For civil actions, in which the matter in dispute is € 5.000,00 or less, the Local Court ("Amtsgericht") has jurisdiction in the first instance and all appeals must be filed in the Regional Court ("Landgericht"). In civil actions in which the matter in dispute exceeds € 5.000,00, original jurisdiction lies with the Regional court and appellate jurisdiction with the Regional Court of Appeals ("Oberlandesgericht") and possibly (particularly in cases involving large monetary disputes) in the Federal Supreme Court ("Bundesgerichtshof").

For certain legal actions, however, original jurisdiction lies with specialized courts; appeals from such courts decisions must then be filed in specialized appellate courts. Cases brought before the Commercial Division of the Regional Court and the Labour Courts are decided by a panel made up of professional judges and citizens known as "lay judges" ("Laienrichter"). In Labour Courts proceedings, these judges are recommended by employer and employee organizations. In matters before the Commercial Divisions of the Regional Court, the lay judges are citizens who have been recommended by the Chamber of Industry and Commerce ["Industrie- und Handelskammer" (IHK)]. The input of these lays judges often helps to ensure that the economic background of a case is considered in the decision-making process. A preference for arbitration over judicial resolution of a dispute on the basis the courts lack economic or commercial expertise is, therefore, unjustified (see II. below regarding arbitration tribunals).

The highest appellate court in Germany's judicial system is the Federal Constitutional Court ("Bundesverfassungsgericht"). This court is not only empowered to resolve issues submitted to it by one of Germany's states or by the Parliament ("Bundestag"), but also hears appeals from citizens who

- claim that their constitutional rights have been violated and

- can show that no other means of protecting those constitutional rights exist.

B. Length of time from filing of complaint to judgement

The time between the filing of complaint and final judgement can vary greatly from case to case. Often, in those lawsuits where one might even prefer a longer process, a final judgement is pronounced in two or three months, while in other cases in which the client strongly desires a speedy decision, the process can take years and involve at least two appellate levels.

Nevertheless, it can be generally said that if a lawsuit involves relatively clear facts, a final judgement can usually be obtained in less than six months. On the other hand, in legal disputes which are highly contested, complicated and involve large amounts of money, one cannot usually expect a trial court judgement until after more than one year. Experience has proven, however, that the time from initiations until conclusion of the judicial process is shorter in Germany than in other countries.

One reason for this could be the fact that the oral and documentary evidence submitted to the court is limited. While in many countries the parties must present the court with all documents and facts which have a relationship to their case, in Germany, each party determines which facts to provide the court and its opposing party. This means, as well, that there is no "pre-trial discovery" as that term is understood in the USA.

Moreover, in making its decision, the court must disregard facts which the parties themselves have agreed shall not be considered in resolving their dispute. The court must also accept the truth of any facts presented by one party which the other party has failed to challenge- even if the court has doubts about the correctness of such facts.

This limitation on the amount of oral and documentary information used during litigation leads to a simplification and reduction in time of the judicial process. In addition, it often results in the attorney's litigation strategy being a deciding factor in how the court resolves a dispute. On the other hand, however, if the attorney conducts the litigation in a careless or negligent manner, the court, being restricted in the information supplied by the attorney, the court often has no choice but to rule against the party represented by such an attorney. The attorney, therefore, shoulders a large responsibility for ensuring that the litigation is properly conducted. Furthermore, the attorney withholding key information which could be decisive on the outcome of the hearing, may be excluded from submitting such information at a later stage as the information could be rejected as belated submission.

C. Accelerated relief

Accelerated relief is possible, for example:

- in actions filed with the above mentioned Commercial Division of the Regional Court
- to enforce certain specified types of legal instruments (for example, checks, and promissory notes) or
- to initiate a special, largely automatic summary proceeding for debt recovery known as a "Mahnverfahren".

This last referenced summary proceeding is conducted primarily through the filing of forms and enables a plaintiff with a monetary claim which is uncontested to quickly and relatively inexpensively obtain a final judgement. The Local Court for Berlin-Schöneberg generally handles the "Mahnverfahren" brought by foreign claimants; for non foreign claims, the residence or domicile of the claims determines which Local Court has jurisdiction.

In addition, when a plaintiff can show that without such relief a danger of irreparable damage exists, accelerated relief is also possible to achieve either through the use of what is known as a "freeze order" ("Arrest") or through an application for a preliminary injunction. Through such proceedings, the plaintiff can- within days or even hours obtain accelerated relief in the form, for example, of a judicial order prohibiting the defendant from disposing of property or from engaging in certain conduct.

It is important to note, however, that accelerated relief through a freeze order or an application for a preliminary injunction will not be granted merely upon a showing that without such relief a defendant/debtor would be unable to pay a future judgement; rather, it must be shown that the debtor is attempting or has attempted to conceal property, or that as a result of a criminal offence, there is a suspicion that this could be the case. Finally, these procedures are not designed to conclusively determine the respective rights of the parties to a dispute. Only relief of a temporary nature which can, if necessary, be later rescinded- is available. Any seized money or property will not be turned over immediately to the creditor; rather, it will be held in safekeeping until the conclusion of the litigation.

Generally, it can be said, that the initiation of such an "Arrest" proceeding or the application or a preliminary injunction raises the legal costs considerably due to the possibility that the same dispute must be concurrently litigated in two proceedings- with each proceeding affording several levels of appellate review.

An additional way in which accelerated relief may be obtained is through a settlement arranged by the parties' attorneys in accordance with Par. 1042 of the Rules of Civil Procedure ["Zivilprozessordnung"(ZPO)]. When certain requirements are met, such a settlement is enforceable just like a judgement of a court. If the debtor fails to pay the amount agreed to in the settlement, then said settlement can be enforced in the way described below.

In addition, it is possible for a debtor to declare in an document which has been approved by a German notary that said document is acknowledged as executory title (Par. 794 sec. 1 No. 5 ZPO). This means that the debtor acknowledges that the document is one which justifies execution (see also the chapter "Notaries in Germany").

Naturally, these last two possibilities can only be used with the debtor's agreement. For this reason, their use is limited to situations where the parties' respective legal rights are very clear or where one party makes his entering into of a contract dependent on the providing of such a declaration by the other party. Particularly in transactions involving the sale of real property or ownership interests in a business, it is not unusual for the buyer to declare in a notarised sales contract that he acknowledges the document to be subject to enforcement proceedings.

D. Enforcement of judgments

The enforcement of monetary judgements is undertaken by a sheriff's officer ("Gerichtsvollzieher") when such enforcement involves the seizure of personal property. When, however, the seizure of receivables or real property is involved, the enforcement proceeding must be handled by the court.

Usually, the enforcement procedure can be initiated immediately after the rendering of a judgement, and this is true even if the opposing party has the possibility to appeal the judgement. Often, however, before or immediately following the enforcement, the creditor must deposit a security to cover the time period in which avenues of appeal remain available to the debtor. Usually, the security is in the form of a bank guarantee.

A creditor who is enforcing a claim for money most often attempt to have the debtor's bank accounts or regular income seized. Another possibility is the attachment of the debtor's personal or real property. One disadvantage of the enforcement procedure is that the creditor must decide which of these types of assets he wishes to first pursue; pursuing several enforcement measures at the same time is not possible for practical reasons (the original judgement must be presented each time).

If the enforcement procedure is unsuccessful, the creditor can make a motion that the debtor provide a so-called "Eidesstattliche Versicherung" (Par. 807, 899 et. seq. ZPO). In such a document, the debtor must verify under oath whether and if so what property he or she possesses. The fact that the debtor has provided an "Eidesstattliche Versicherung" is noted in a register maintained by the Local Court which has jurisdiction in the geographical area containing the debtor's residence or domicile (Par. 915 ZPO).

This register is open to the public; therefore, its entries typically find their way into the information pages of for example, credit reporting businesses or the Chamber of Industry and Commerce. The entry thus results in the debtor having difficulty in continuing his self-employment or employment activity. In this way, the "Eidesstattliche Versicherung" places a pressure on those debtors, for whom the possibility of raising the funds exists, to satisfy their debts.

On the other hand, it can also occur that the debtor uses his "Eidesstattliche Versicherung" to fend off his creditors; then, he obtains employment, for example, in his wife's business and receives an income which is not subject to attachment. This is possible because whereas all monthly income of a single person over € 930,00 is subject to attachment (assuming he has no support obligations), the amount of income which is not subject to seizure increases depending on the number of persons which the debtor must support. In this way, therefore, sometimes a person, despite his large amount of debt, can enjoy a relatively comfortable standard of living.

Due to multilateral and bilateral international agreements, judgements of foreign courts and arbitration tribunals are, in theory, just as enforceable in Germany as are the judgements of German courts and arbitration tribunals. Nevertheless, holders of foreign judgements are first required to obtain an order from a German court confirming the enforceability of the particular foreign judgement (Par. 722 et. seq. ZPO).

Although the judge does not review the underlying factual or legal correctness of the foreign judgement during this German enforcement proceeding, such proceeding usually lasts quite a long time and results in additional costs. Moreover, there is always the risk that the foreign judgement will fail to meet German legal requirements and therefore be declared "unenforceable". For these reasons, in ,many cases it is advisable (assuming such court is, according to German law, competent to hear the matter) to file the original complaint in the German court.

E. Court costs and attorney fees

In principle, for lawsuits in which the monetary value of the matters in dispute is the same and which are pursued to the same stage of judicial proceeding, the costs are the same throughout Germany. This is due to the existence of statutes which regulate both attorney fees ["Bundesrechtsanwaltsgebührenordnung", "Attorneys Fees Ordinance" (BRAGO)] and court costs ["Gerichtskostengesetz" (GKG)], These laws provide, in part, that regardless of the <u>actual</u> court and attorney time or difficulty of a case, attorney fees and court costs increase depending on

- the monetary value of the matter in dispute
- and –
- the stage of the judicial process the lawsuit reaches (for example: filing of complaint, filing of motion(s), hearing of evidence, settlement, judgement, appeal).

Below are three examples in which these primary cost determining factors are illustrated. The cost figures include court costs, the costs of the client's own attorney(s), the costs of the opponent's attorney(s) and value-added tax. Although an expert witness ("Sachverständiger") is often deemed necessary and, therefore, appointed by the court, this cost is not included in the figures below; it should be kept in mind however, that such additional cost may also arise. Finally, it should be noted that the inclusion of value-added tax can result in a slight overstatement of the costs for many clients because it is not always necessary to include it in an invoice; moreover, even when it is included, it does not represent a real cost for those business clients who are entitled to deduct the VAT they have paid to their customers and would otherwise be required to transmit to the tax department.

Amount in Dispute: € 10.000,00	Amount in Dispute € 100.000,00
1. one court involved no hearing if evidence (i.e. no examination of witness; no expert witness) no settlement	
€ 2.600,00	€ 8.100,00
2. one court involved hearing of evidence settlement	
€ 4.600,00	€ 13.500,00
3. two courts involved (appeal) no hearing of evidence no settlement	
€ 6.500,00	€ 19.000,00

These examples indicate that, in relation to the amount in dispute, the costs increase digressively rather than progressively. In other words, smaller amounts in dispute lead to proportionately higher costs whereas higher amounts in dispute carry with them proportionately lower costs. If, for example, the amount in dispute in example number three above was raised to € 1.000.000,00, then the costs would "only" be € 73.000,00.

The reason that the costs include the fee for the client's own attorney as well as the attorney of the opponent is because, as a rule, such costs are divided between the plaintiff and the defendant depending on the extant one or the other has prevailed in the lawsuit. For example, if a party loses on all issues, then that party must pay all costs burden. [Note: In Labour Court proceedings in the first instance (not on appeal), each party bears their own costs regardless of the outcome].

This rule that the prevailing party is fully reimbursed for costs is only applicable when the party's attorneys have calculated their fees in accordance with the BRAGO, which, with respect to business clients, tends often not to be the case. Since many commercial legal matters involve international facts and issues or an unusually long judicial process. It is not unusual for the attorneys and clients involved in such matters to enter into fee agreements which deviate from the fees fixed by law. Often an hourly fee arrangement is agreed to. The amount of this hourly fee varies depending on the region, the law firm, the importance of the case, etc. Roughly speaking, however, fees agreed to by special contract usually currently range from between € 200,00 and € 350,00 per hour. If the attorney costs of prevailing parties have been agreed to by private contract and exceed the fees fixed by the law, then such parties are only entitled to be reimbursed for the costs in the amount allowed by statue. They must pay anything in excess of that amount themselves.

Of course, it can also occur that the attorneys' costs calculated on an hourly basis are actually less than the statutory fee. This could be the case, for instance, if the lawsuit is resolved very early on in the process. If this happens, however, the attorney must bill the client at the higher statutory rate because he is ethically and legally obliged not to undercut the attorney's fees set by statute. Any type of contingent fee arrangement is strictly prohibited in Germany.

It is important to note that the plaintiff must pay court costs in advance and that this advance payment must include payment for all stages of the judicial proceeding which the lawsuit could theoretically reach. If the lawsuit is resolved at an earlier stage, a refund is provided. In the above three examples, court costs for the lawsuits with a monetary value of € 10.000,00 would be € 600,00 and for the lawsuits worth € 100.000,00 the court costs would be € 2.700,00.

In addition, it is customary for the attorney to require a reasonable retainer ("Vorschuß"). This is an advance payment of fees and is allowed under the Par. 17 BRAGO. Plaintiffs from foreign countries can also be required to provide a security deposit to cover the possibility of losing the law suit, in which case they would be obliged to pay the defendant's costs (Par. 110 ZPO).

Many persons, and as a matter of fact, particularly private persons, are not affected by court costs and attorney fees. Such persons are insured against the costs of legal disputes. This legal costs insurance covers the costs of the insured party's own attorney, court costs as well as the costs of the opposing party.

II. Use of Arbitration Tribunals or Mediation Proceedings to Resolve Disputes

It is becoming more and more common in commercial disputes to turn to arbitration tribunals rather than to the courts. Parties sometimes use the arbitration services of the Arbitration Tribunal of the International Chamber of Commerce in Paris. Usually, however, they submit their disputes to arbitrators who have been appointed by one of the following:

- the Chamber of Industry and Commerce
- appellate judges (for example, the Chief of the Regional Court of Appeals for a particular city) or
- organizations such as the "German Arbitration Institute" in Cologne or the "German Arbitration Committee" in Bonn.

The reasons that parties often agree to arbitration of potential future disputes include cost and time savings as well as the greater confidentiality which an arbitration process affords (unlike a court hearing, an arbitration hearing can be closed). The fact of the matter is, however, that the first objective is often not realized. Once an actual dispute arises, parties frequently spend much time debating whether the dispute is of the type they initially agreed to submit to arbitration and/or arguing over the choice of an arbitrator.

The parties can also find themselves disappointed by the costs of the arbitration process. Because many arbitration agreements specify the appointment of a decision-making panel comprised of three arbitrators, the costs of the arbitration process (particularly in the case of disputes involving relatively low monetary values) can be higher than court costs.

The point here, however, is not to dissuade parties from entering into arbitration agreements but rather to emphasize the importance of exercising great care in the drafting of such agreements. If this is done, arbitration often remains a more efficient and satisfactory dispute resolution method than the courts.

Last but not least, it should be mentioned that mediation procedures, also in Germany, are increasingly becoming the basis of settlement of disputes between parties in events of commercial disagreements arising. In the interim, a considerable number of organisations offer courses to lawyers and other future mediators, in the event of need they also appoint mediators when called upon and have published codes of procedure in this regard.

Institutions of the European Community

Bernd Tremml

I. Overview

The tasks entrusted to the European Community are carried out by five institutions: the Council, the Commission, the European Parliament, the Court of Justice and the Court of Auditors. The most important of these is the Council, in which the most significant governmental functions have been combined. The Council is primarily responsible for passing legislation and making the decisions necessary to realize the goals of the Treaty Establishing the European Community as amended (EC Treaty) as well as the Treaty establishing the European Coal and Steel Community and the Treaty establishing the European Atomic Energy Community. The Council consists of representatives of the governments from each member state (currently 15). It is designed as a body whose function is to represent the national interests. Because all of the Council Ministers have a duty to follow the instructions of their governments, the Council's measurements have the effect of reconciling the differing interests of the member states.

The Commission consists of twenty citizens of the member states who are first nominated by the states and then, following a vote of approval by the European Parliament as a whole, appointed by common accord of the member states. The Commission must include at least one citizen from each member state but may not include more than two members from the same State.

In contrast to the Council, the functions of the Commission are primarily executive rather than legislative, although it does play an authoritative role in shaping Community policy and the legislative process in general. For example, only the Commission is empowered to submit proposed legislation to the Council or the Parliament. The Commission is also in charge of the Community's extensive administrative apparatus and represents the European Community on an international level. If a member state fails to comply with Community law, the Commission can file a complaint with the European Court of Justice and institute enforcement proceedings, thus acting as the "guardian of the Treaties".

Another important institution of the European Community is the European Parliament. The Parliament consists currently of 626 representatives of the member states who are elected by direct universal suffrage. Depending on the type of legislative proposal being considered by the Council, the Parliament is empowered to participate in the legislative process in basically one of two ways either by giving its assent (without which such assent a proposal cannot become law) or by giving an advisory opinion, which is not binding on the Council, but might force the Council to adopt the proposal by unanimous vote if it does not follow the opinion of the Parliament. However, the Parliament cannot enact any law by its sole power against the will of the Council. In this regard it differs greatly from the encompassing legislative powers of any national parliament. But the functions and powers of the European Parliament have been steadily enlarged over the last years and this tendency is supposed to continue the future, thus lessening what is called the "democratic deficit" of the European Community.

The European Court of Justice, which is discussed in greater detail in section III below, consists of fifteen judges who possess the qualifications required for appointment to the highest judicial office in their respective countries. The Court ensures that that European Community law is uniformly interpreted and effectively applied. It safeguards and maintains the rights and duties of the member states, institutions, businesses and individual citizens and rules on questions involving the legality of Community law. A Court of First Instance has been attached to it since 1989.

The Court of Auditors consists of fifteen members with proven auditing experience who are chosen from the population of the member states. This institution is charged, among others, with the duty of examining the accounts of all revenues and expenditures of the Community.

The European Central Bank (ECB), located in Frankfurt (Germany), is not an institution of the European Community according to the EC Treaty. It is an independent body with its own legal personality, which may not be influenced by the institutions of the European Community or the governments of the member states. This corresponds with the European Central Bank's task to define and implement European monetary policy and its primary objective to maintain price stability within the Euro zone.

II. The Sources and the Legislation of the European Community

A. Sources of Community Law

The sources of the European Community Law are:

- The treaties entered into by the member states; they constitute the "primary law" of the Community. Their provisions have "direct applicability" in all member States, which means that they are binding without any further act of transformation by any member state into their national laws. These treaties often empower the Community institutions to enact laws in order to further the treaties' goals.
- The law enacted by the Community institutions themselves is known as "secondary Community law", and usually takes the form of either a regulation or directive. But it also includes the treaties of international public law, which the Community concludes, such as GATT or the WTO agreement.

A typical regulation or directive will be enacted by the Council upon the suggestion of the Commission and after either

- the Council has obtained the opinion of the Parliament, which it is not bound to follow, but might in certain cases only be overruled by a unanimous vote of the Council; or
- the Council has obtained the approval of the Parliament, without which approval enactment is impossible (real veto-right of the Parliament).

It is important to notice that basically the law of the European Community prevails over national law ("priority of the European Community law"). However, this does not mean, that a national law which is incompatible with European Community law automatically becomes void (within the legal order of the member state concerned), but that it is rendered inapplicable in case of a legal conflict with the pertinent European Community law.

Even though in Germany this prevailing character of the European Community law is disputed as far as Fundamental Rights of the Constitution ("Grundrechte des Grundgesetzes") are concerned, the highest Court of the Federal Republic of Germany (the Federal Constitutional Court ["Bundesverfassungsgericht"]) has over the years basically come to accept it under certain preconditions (judgements of Oct. 22, 1986 ["Solange II"] and Oct. 12, 1993 ["Maastricht"]).

B. Some Types of Laws within the European Community

1. European Community Regulations

A regulation is of abstract and general character and, therefore, comparable to the function and objectives of national laws. According to Article 249, paragraph 2 of the EC Treaty, the regulations of the Community are binding in their entirety and directly applicable in all member states. Direct applicability means, that the regulation takes effect automatically upon being published in the Official Journal of the European Community, as mentioned above in the context of the primary law of the Community. No further legislative action on the part of member states is required.

Community regulations have the effect of granting rights as well as imposing responsibilities on the governmental agencies, courts and natural or legal persons of the member states. Any national law, which conflicts with a regulation is rendered inapplicable, due to the priority of European Community law.

2. European Community directives

As a general rule, directives are not directly applicable (compare Article 249 paragraphs 2 and 3 of the EC Treaty). Unlike regulations, they must be incorporated into the law of the member states before they take effect. A Community directive gives the member states the legislative goal to be achieved; the States then have the duty under Article 249, paragraph 3 of the EC Treaty, to incorporate the directive's provisions into their national law. In so doing, the member states cannot change the content of the directive. However, they are given the discretion to determine the form and method of incorporation. Directives serve to harmonize the effect of the laws of the member states. Regulations on the other hand, lead to uniformity and standardization of the laws throughout the Community.

The general principle that a directive cannot be directly applied until acted on by the member state has been considerably modified by the European Court of Justice. In line with its decisions regarding the direct applicability of primary law, the Court has held that under certain specific circumstances, a directive is applicable without member state action. According to the Court of Justice, the individual can seek direct application of a directive by the national courts, even if it is not yet a part of national law, if the requirements set forth in the Court's "Becker" decision are met (Court of Justice, Case 8/81, 1982 E.C.R. 53). The Court of Justice held in "Becker" that the provisions of a directive can be directly applied

- if the member state has not in a timely or sufficient manner incorporated the directive into its national law, and
- if the particular provision in the directive in question is itself sufficiently exact and its content is unconditional.

Whether or not a directive has been incorporated into the member state's national law in a timely fashion is usually easy to determine, because most directives contain a provision stating when this must be accomplished. It is more difficult to prove that this same incorporation has not been performed sufficiently. This requires detailed arguments, which show exactly how the national government fails to comply with the standards set by the directive.

A provision in a directive is considered sufficiently clear or certain if it contains a precise legal proposition. In other words, the content of the provision and the category of persons or entities addressed by it must be determinable, at least through interpretation.

Finally, the content of a directive is unconditional if the obligations imposed by it can be applied and made effective without the necessity of the member states or the institutions passing additional rules or taking any additional action.

A determination of whether or not a directive is directly applicable must be made on a case by case basis. The rationale given by the Court of Justice for allowing the direct application of directives under the above outlined circumstances is that a member state should not be allowed to circumvent its duties with regard to directives by an untimely and/or improper incorporation of the directive into its national law. If the citizens of a member state could be deprived of their individual rights granted by the Community's directives just because of the member state's dereliction of duty, the practical effectiveness of directives would be limited or even completely frustrated. Moreover, direct applicability of directives helps to safeguard the effectiveness of the Community.

From this rational follow two other important aspects of the direct applicability of directives: they may only be invoked by a private individual against the State (and not vice versa or against another private person) and the determination concerned may only be applied in favor of the individual, not to its detriment.

The effect of the Court of Justice's decision has been to carve out another way to sanction member states who fail to timely and sufficiently incorporate directives into their own law, in addition to the Treaty Violation Proceeding of Article 226 of the EC Treaty (discussed below under III.C.).

The German Federal Constitutional Court has upheld the Court of Justice's decision allowing for the direct applicability of directives. The Federal Constitutional Court has found the Court of Justice's decision to be a legitimate, constitutionally acceptable development of the law of the European Community.

In case of a directive which has not been properly implemented by the member state, but which is not directly applicable due to the lack of its provisions being sufficiently exact and unconditional, the Court of Justice has recognized in the "Francovich" decision, that the individual may claim damages from the State concerned under certain preconditions (Court of Justice, Joined Cases C-6 and 9/90, 1991 E.C.R. I-5357).

III. The European Court of Justice

A. The Court of Justice and the Court of First Instance

The European Court of Justice is located in Luxembourg. As mentioned above, the Court of Justice is charged with ensuring that the law is observed in the interpretation and application of the EC Treaty as well as other primary and secondary law. The decision-making tribunal consisting of fifteen judges is served and supported by eight Advocates General. These individuals neither represent a party to the proceeding nor are they members of the bench rather, they serve as legal consultants to the Court. Their position is similar in certain respects to that of a judge insofar as the Advocates General are independent and impartial and responsible solely for the upholding of Community law. They present an advisory opinion to the judges on the relevant facts and the applicable law in each case pending before the Court. As a result, each case is examined by two independent bodies within the Court, thus contributing to an extensive and thorough analysis of all issues raised.

In 1988, in order to ease the burdened Court of Justice, a Court of First Instance was created whose judgments are subject to a right of appeal to the Court of Justice on points of law only. The Court of First Instance is not a new European Community institution; rather, it is a part of the Court of Justice. Both its administrative and budgetary structure is attached to that of the Court of Justice. It is also located in Luxembourg. One important difference between the courts, however, is that the Court of First Instance is not served by the Advocates General.

B. Jurisdiction

The Court of Justice and the Court of First Instance have exclusive jurisdiction in various types of proceedings, which are explicitly enumerated. Two of them will be discussed in greater detail below. There is no general clause defining the jurisdiction of the Court in an abstract way.

Currently, the jurisdiction between the Court of Justice and the Court of First Instance is generally divided as follows:

The Court of First Instance has jurisdiction over all actions brought by natural or legal persons against the European Community institutions. The Court of Justice has original jurisdiction over all actions filed by a member state or an European Community institution. Consequently, the latter do not benefit from a possible appeal on the European level. As a result of this division of jurisdiction between the two tribunals, the Court of Justice decides more on "constitutional" issues, such as the division of power between the Community Institutions themselves or the European Community and the member states, whereas the Court of First Instance is more likely to get involved in "administrative" matters. Both bodies may also take over the role of a "civil" court and render judgements on claims for damages or act as arbitrators.

However, the EC Treaty provides in Article 225, that the Council, upon request of the Court of Justice and following consultation with the European Parliament and the Commission, may transfer further classes of actions and proceedings to the Court of First instance. This sole type of proceeding, which with certainty will not be assigned in the future to the Court of First Instance, is the Preliminary Ruling Proceeding under Article 234 of the EC Treaty, since this proceeding is explicitly excluded from a possible reference.

As long as there is no enumerative, explicit or exclusive jurisdiction of the Court of Justice set forth in the EC Treaty, the national courts remain competent. It is important to emphasize that the Court of Justice has not been placed over the national courts and, therefore, is not empowered to reverse the judicial decisions of the national courts. This is particularly obvious in the Preliminary Ruling Proceeding under Article 234 of the EC Treaty (see D. below).

C. The Treaty Violation Proceeding

The Treaty Violation Proceeding has as its purpose to cause a member state, which is violating Community law, to end the violation by properly fulfilling its obligations under European Community law. Either the Commission (Article 226 of the EC Treaty) or another member state (Article 227 of the EC Treaty) may initiate a Treaty Violation Proceeding, even when the member state is not directly affected by the violation. However, the latter cases are rather rare compared to the very important, frequently initiated proceeding from the Commission.

Individual citizens or legal persons are not entitled to file a Treaty Violation Proceeding with the Court of Justice.

1. Procedural steps of the Treaty Violation Proceeding

If the Commission is convinced that a member state has failed to fulfill any obligation under European Community law, it shall so inform the member state concerned. The state then has the opportunity to respond to the alleged breach and to end the violation at this early stage.

If the state concerned cannot sufficiently convince the Commission that it is has not violated European Community law or that it has come to compliance, the Commission will issue an opinion regarding the violation and lay down a period of time for the state to comply with this opinion. If the state does not follow the opinion in time, the Commission may bring the matter before the Court of Justice.

2. Prerequisites of a Treaty Violation

In order to prevail in a Treaty Violation Proceeding, it must be proven that the underlying act, which constitutes a violation of Community law can be ascribed or imputed to the member state (the Court looks at the legal situation when the specified time period given the member state to respond to the reasoned opinion expires).

a. Treaty Violation

In a Treaty Violation Proceeding, it must be proven that the member state has "failed to fulfill an obligation under this Treaty". Despite the seemingly unequivocal wording of this EC Treaty provision, "an obligation under this Treaty" has been interpreted to refer not only to primary law such as the treaties, but also to secondary law such as regulations and directives, to agreements of the Community with third party States, as well as to the general legal principles of the Community as interpreted by the Court of Justice.

A Member State has "failed to fulfill" its Treaty obligations when it has either not applied Community law at all, incorrectly applied it, or has committed an act which constitutes an affirmative violation of a specific provision of Community law. For example, a frequently occurring Treaty violation consists of the Member States not implementing European Community directives in time.

The party who lodged the complaint (normally the Commission) has the burden of proof.

b. Violation attributable to a member state

From the perspective of Community law, a member state is perceived as one uniform actor, which means that it is held responsible for all violations of Community law which are committed by subordinate institutions, agencies or bodies of the State, which includes the national Parliament, members of the executive branch or its administrative offices and even courts. In countries with a federal system such as Germany, the member state can also be held responsible when one of the legislative bodies of the states violates European Community law, for example, is it refuses to incorporate in a timely manner a Community directive into its own state-wide law. Actions (or failure to act) of private persons, which constitute a violation of Community law, however, cannot be ascribed to the member states unless they exercise an essential influence on the behavior of the private person concerned.

The particular problem of the responsibility of a member state for any failure from the part of public authorities in the widest sense within its territory is obvious. How should the member state end a violation due of an independent body, such as a Parliament or a court? Even if the Court of Justice declares that a treaty violation has occurred, neither the highest national court nor any other branch of the member state's government has the authority to simply set aside the independent body's decision. In such a case, there exist only informal methods of bringing influence by consultations and advice. Surprisingly this method has been successful to date.

Moreover, with regard violations of the national courts, whose decisions neither respect the priority of the Community law nor apply it, it is important to notice that Treaty Violation Proceedings are rarely initiated. This is because more efficient options exist that can bring the national courts into compliance with Community law. One of them is the procedure under Article 234 of the EC Treaty, which empowers national courts to seek a preliminary ruling by the Court of Justice (see D. below). In this way, the court can ensure that a correct interpretation of Community law is applied to its case, and avoid any possible violation of European Community law.

In addition, a party adversely affected by a national court's failure to uphold Community law can make use of methods under German law to challenge the decision. According to German Federal Constitutional Court decisions a court, which violates its duty under Article 234 of the EC Treaty, to request a preliminary ruling, has simultaneously violated Art. 101 paragraph 1, sentence 2 of the German Constitution (which guarantees that no one may be removed from the jurisdiction of his lawful judge ["Recht auf den gesetzlichen Richter"]). On the basis of this violation of German Constitutional law, an aggrieved party is entitled to file a constitutional appeal of the national court's decision.

This check within German law for ensuring that Community law is followed has its limits. First, it requires that the party is harmed rather than advantaged by the national court's decision, which violates Community law. Second, the violation must be due to an arbitrary behavior of the national court. Finally, it is not an available option when the national court has no duty to request a preliminary ruling (see D.2. below).

3. The Decision of the Court of Justice and its enforcement

If a treaty violation is proven, the Court of Justice merely declares that a violation has occurred (declaratory judgment). Acts which violate the Treaty will neither be set aside nor held to be illegal, nor will the Court specify what actions must be taken in order for the member state in violation to come into compliance. Rather, the member state itself is required to determine the necessary compliance measures and to implement those measures. If the Commission subsequently determines that the member state has not done this, it may, after giving the state an opportunity to respond, issue an opinion, which specifies how the member state has failed to comply with the judgment of the Court of Justice. If the member state still fails to come into compliance within the time specified in the Commission's opinion, the Commission may once again bring the matter before the Court of Justice and seek an order imposing a lump-sum penalty on the member state.

D. The Preliminary Ruling Proceeding

The Preliminary Ruling Proceeding under Article 234 of the EC Treaty also plays an important role in Community affairs. To date, approximately one-half of all Court of Justice proceedings have been of this type.

The Preliminary Ruling Proceeding is not a proceeding by way of action, but a proceeding "from court to court". Despite its name, this judicial proceeding does not involve an initial decision by the Court of Justice, followed by a decision of the national court. Rather, it is an interlocutory proceeding in the sense that the underlying case begins in the national court, and after an interlocutory hearing before the Court of Justice in which the national judge seeks an interpretation of Community law relevant to his or her decision, it ends in the national court as well. Applying the Court of Justice's ruling and the rendering of a final judgment in the case remain the province of the national court. This shows that the Preliminary Ruling Procedure does not set up any hierarchical relationship between the Court of Justice and the national courts, but rather institutionalizes a form of co-operation where the Court of Justice provides the national courts with helpful support.

One important purpose of this proceeding can be seen from the goals and mission of the Community as well as from the proceeding's effect, namely, the consistent development of Community law. To the extent that Community law is directly applicable in the member states and, therefore, subject to the interpretation of their national courts, a danger of inconsistent application and interpretation exists. Such a danger runs afoul of the Community goal of integration. If the development of Community law were left solely to the national courts, they would tend to interpret the treaties, regulations, directives, etc. of the Community in light of their own nation's legal tradition and methods.

The Preliminary Ruling Proceeding, therefore, provides a way of preventing the threatened inconsistent interpretations of Community law from nation to nation and instead fosters its standardization and even application throughout the Community. It provides a mechanism whereby the Court of Justice can "flesh out" the meaning of the often generally stated principles of the treaties. At the same time, the proceeding helps the judges of the various nations of the Community with the difficult tasks, which may arise out of the co-existence of national and Community law.

1. The prerequisites of the Preliminary Ruling Procedure

Only a "court or tribunal of a member state" can initiate a Preliminary Ruling Proceeding. The parties of the underlying case (for example, citizens and/or legal persons who have a dispute with a government agency), the institutions of the Community, administrative agencies of the member states as well as courts from countries who do not belong to the Community are not entitled to seek a Preliminary Ruling from the Court of Justice.

The term "court or tribunal of a member state" means an independent tribunal, which derives its judicial power to resolve disputes from the public. Such a tribunal is required to be of permanent character, founded on a legal basis, having obligatory jurisdiction and exercising its judicial powers in a contradictory procedure. For example, administrative agencies and officials which provide citizens an opportunity to be heard or to protest but whose decision-makers lack the requisite independence are not considered to be a "court or tribunal of the member state" in this sense. Also, courts of arbitration are not entitled to present a Preliminary Ruling question since they are not part of the public authority.

As subject matter of a Preliminary Ruling, the most important are:

- the interpretation of the Treaties, which means the whole primary European Community law; and
- the interpretation and validity of acts of the institutions of the Community and the European Central Bank, which means the whole secondary European Community law.

It is important to note, that the Court of Justice is not empowered to rule on the validity of primary European Community law. Also the Court does not decide on the applicability of European Community law in the national case underlying the Preliminary Ruling request or the interpretation of the national law. The Preliminary Ruling Proceeding is concerned solely with the interpretation and in certain cases validity of Community law.

Consequently, in order for a national court to make a request for such a ruling, it must find that a provision of Community law applicable to its case is in need of interpretation, or that there is a justifiable doubt about the legality of the Community law provision under application. The national court must also determine that a decision on its legal question is necessary to its judgment in the pending case.

2. Right and Duty of a National Court to Request a Preliminary Ruling

According to Article 234 paragraph 2 of the EC Treaty, each court of a member state is entitled to request a preliminary ruling. This right, which generally may be exercised on a voluntary basis from the part of the court, turns into a duty in one exceptional case when the national court wants to set aside secondary European Community law and not apply it to the pending case, since the court regards the pertinent European Community law to be invalid. In this regard, the Court of Justice claims to be the sole body who may dismiss secondary European Community law for reasons of invalidity ("Verwerfungsmonopol"). Even though this is not explicitly laid down in Article 234 of the EC Treaty, it follows clearly from the purpose of the Preliminary Ruling Procedure, to assure the uniform application of European Community law throughout the Community.

Under Article 234 paragraph 3 of the EC Treaty, a court or tribunal of a member state against whose decisions there is no judicial remedy under national law shall bring the matter before the Court of Justice. Mostly, this provision is understood to refer not only to the highest courts in the judicial hierarchy of each member state, but to all courts whose decisions may, in a concrete case no longer be appealable. There are exceptions, where national courts of "last instance" have no duty to request a Preliminary Ruling:

- In case the question raised is not necessary for the final decision of the court; or
- in case the question raised has already been decided by the Court of Justice in an earlier request for a Preliminary Ruling, and the national court does intend to follow the earlier decision; or
- in case there is no real doubt possible of how a particular provision of European Community law is to be interpreted ("acte clair"), and there is a common sense of this among the national courts of other member states as well.

The libel of the Article 234 paragraph 2 of the EC Treaty also includes the German Federal Constitutional Court. However, there is a strong and lasting controversy, of whether or not rulings from this highest court should be "submitted" to the Preliminary Ruling Proceeding before the Court of Justice. It is also doubt that the Federal Constitutional Court would request a Preliminary Ruling if it came to question the interpretation of a provision of European Community law. So far, Germany's highest court has carefully managed to avoid an open confrontation with the Court of Justice on this matter by successfully cooperating with the latter.

3. The Decision of the Court of Justice

As mentioned above, the Court of Justice rules only on the question of Community law posed to it, that is it declares what the Community law relevant to the case is. The Court reaches its decision without regard to the final decision in the underlying national case. However, it does take into consideration the concrete facts of the underlying case which the national court initiating the request shall report to the Court of Justice. For example, the concrete structure and tasks of a legal person under the national laws of a member state, can be relevant factual background necessary for the Court of Justice do decide whether the national legal person falls within the scope of a directive or regulation and therefore, has to fulfill the obligations imposed by it.

The Judgement by the Court of Justice is binding of the national court. It must apply the law, as interpreted by the Court of Justice, without modification or distortion to the dispute before it.

4. Effect of the Preliminary Ruling Proceeding for European citizens

Despite the fact that only a court can initiate a Preliminary Ruling Proceeding, this proceeding still serves the important function of protecting the individual's rights under Community law . As a result of the legal decisions of the Court of Justice providing for direct applicability and priority of Community law, citizens are often directly effected by European Community law. They can assert these rights in national court proceedings. The national courts in turn have the right, or sometimes the duty (see above 2.) - to initiate a Preliminary Ruling Proceeding in order to clarify if and to what extent a citizen may claim any rights under European Community law. In this way, citizens' rights under the Community are indirectly protected. For example, parties to a proceeding before a national court can defend themselves against actions of a member state which violate Community law by requesting that the court submit the question of the compatibility of the member state's action (or lack of action) with provisions of Community law to the Court of Justice. Also, the parties involved in the national case underlying the Preliminary Ruling Proceeding may take part in the proceedings before the Court of Justice.

As previously stated, citizens protections are indirect only because citizens cannot compel the national court to submit questions of Community law to the Court of Justice. The citizen can only attempt to persuade the national court of the necessity of initiating a Preliminary Ruling Proceeding. If the national court believes that its case is not significantly impacted by Community law, it is not required to seek a preliminary ruling from the Court of Justice. However, if this constitutes a violation of the duty of a court to request at times a preliminary ruling, the citizen still has the possibility to seek the constitutional relief described in C.2.b. above.

The two proceedings before the Court of Justice examined above, the Preliminary Ruling Proceeding of Article 234 as well as the Treaty Violation Proceeding of Article 226, all involve the submission to the Court of Justice, cases whose resolution has significance and meaning for the entire Community. Both proceedings give the Court the opportunity to interpret Community law in the concrete situations. The development of Community law into a self-contained and unified system is fostered by the Court's gradual development of the law on a case by case basis.

Antitrust Law in the European Community

Bernd Tremml and Andreas Meisterernst

I. Introduction to the Antitrust Law of the European Community

As in the United States, the freedom to do business is subject to many restrictions in the European Community (EC). The EC as well as the Member States of the EC may impose restrictions on trade on the basis of economic, environmental, safety and other grounds. From the perspective of a person engaged in business in the Common Market, the antitrust provisions of the Treaty Establishing the European Economic Community as amended (EC Treaty), which generally encompass Articles 81 to 86, and the regulations adopted pursuant to the treaty, comprise some of the most significant restrictions on the freedom to do business, but foster fair competition and the integration of markets as well. The Commission of the European Community enforces these laws and is empowered to impose fines on businesses in the event of a violation.

In addition to European antitrust law, national antitrust laws exist in most Member States. The purpose of such laws is to control unfair competitive practices within the Member State's internal market. According to the decisions of the European Court of Justice, the European antitrust law takes precedence over national antitrust law. To the extent an antitrust law case has cross-border effects, practices which are allowed under Articles 81 to 86 of the EC Treaty may not be forbidden by a national legislature. Due to the fact that most contemporary business activities have an impact on more than one Member State, the national antitrust laws currently play a limited role and will not be further discussed in this context. However, due to the direct effect of Articles 81 and 82 of the EC Treaty, national authorities can also take action under these provisions until the European Commission itself initiates procedures.

II. Prohibitions Contained in Articles 81-86 of the EC Treaty

A. Article 81

Article 81 of the EC Treaty states:

1. The following shall be prohibited as incompatible with the common market: all agreements between undertakings, decisions by associations of undertakings and concerted practices which may affect trade between Member States and which have as their object or effect the prevention, re-

striction or distortion of competition within the Common Market, and in particular those which:

(a) directly or indirectly fix purchase or selling prices or any other trading conditions;
(b) limit or control production, markets, technical development or investment;
(c) share markets or sources of supply;
(d) apply dissimilar conditions to equivalent transactions with other trading parties, thereby placing them at a competitive disadvantage;
(e) make the conclusion of contracts subject to acceptance by the other parties of supplementary obligations which, by their nature or according to commercial usage, have no connection with the subject of such contracts.

2. Any agreements or decisions prohibited pursuant to this article shall be automatically void.

3. The provisions of paragraph 1 may be declared inapplicable in the case of

- any agreement or category of agreements between undertakings;
- any decision or category of decision by associations of undertakings;
- any concerted practice or category of concerted practices,

which contribute to improving the production or distribution of goods or to promoting technical or economic progress while allowing consumers a fair share of the resulting benefit and which does not

(a) impose on the undertakings concerned restrictions which are not indispensable to the attainment of these objectives;
(b) afford such undertakings the possibility of eliminating competition in respect of a substantial part of the products in question.

The purpose of Article 81 is to establish a common market within the European Community by promoting free competition between enterprises of the private and public sector. Its provisions apply to "horizontal agreements" (agreements between competitors operating at the same level in the economic process) and to "vertical agreements" (agreements between non-competing enterprises operating at different levels). This means that the primary concern of the EC antitrust law is not, in contrast to US antitrust law, to assure inter-brand competition.

The term "agreement" in the sense of Article 81 of the EC Treaty is not limited to formal contracts, but has to be interpreted in a broader sense. The provisions of Article 81 are always applicable when modes of behavior exist which have economic relevance such as informal agreements, imposed agreements and agreements declared to be non-binding. The provisions of Article 81 (1) enumerate several examples of forbidden cartels, such as discount cartels, price cartels, condition-fixing cartels, market-information agencies, tied distribution systems, prohibition of cross deliveries and agreements which discriminate against third persons.

Decisions by associations of undertakings can be made by members of the association as well as by their representatives. According to the decisions of the European Court of Justice, associations of undertakings in the sense of Article 81 do not require a certain legal or organizational structure. By interpreting this term in a very broad sense, the Court aims at enhancing the effect of the antitrust provisions.

A concerted practice as that term is used in Article 81, is even less formal than an agreement and difficult to differentiate from so-called "parallel behavior". The European Court of Justice declared in "ICI vs. Commission" (Case 48/69):

> Although parallel behavior may not by itself be identified with a concerted practice, it may however amount to strong evidence of such a practice if it leads to conditions of competition which do not correspond to the normal condition of the market, having regard to the nature of the products, the size and number of the enterprises and the volume of the said market.

The relevant market is not necessarily the entire market, but only that portion of the Common Market which can be viewed as an independent business area in which competitive relationships can be affected or destroyed. Although Article 81 is primarily intended to apply to deals which affect trade between Member States, it can also apply to internal deals made in one Member State and to deals made between parties located outside of the EC. In "Ahlström Osakyhtio vs. Commission" (1988) ECR 5193, the Court of Justice of the European Community declared:

> It should be noted that the main sources of supply of wood pulp are outside the Community in Canada, the United States, Sweden and Finland and that the market, therefore, has global dimensions. Where wood pulp producers established in those countries sell directly to purchasers established in the Community and engage in price competition in order to win orders from those customers, that constitutes competition within the Common Market.
>
> It follows that where those producers concert on the prices to be charged to their customers in the Community and put that concertation into effect by selling at prices which are actually coordinated, they are taking part in concertation, which has the object and effect of restricting competition within the Common Market within the meaning of Article 81 of the Treaty.

"Restraint of competition" has not been defined abstractly or generally by the Court of Justice of the European Community. Every case must be analyzed individually under the criterion of what possibilities enterprises would have on the open market if the suspect agreement did not exist. The restrictive impact of the agreement or concerted practice on competition must be significant. The European Commission has issued administrative regulations which exclude agreements from the restrictions of Articles 81 to 86 of the EC Treaty, if they affect trade between Member States only insignificantly (Commission Notice on Agreements of Minor Importance [(1986) OJ C231/2, as amended (1997) OJ C372/13]). These provisions will be addressed in III. F. below.

B. Article 82

Article 82 of the EC Treaty states:

> Any abuse by one or more undertakings of a dominant position within the common market or in a substantial part of it shall be prohibited as incompatible with the common market insofar as it may affect trade between Member States.
>
> Such abuse may, in particular, consist in:
> (a) directly or indirectly imposing unfair purchase or selling prices or other unfair trading conditions;
> (b) limiting production, markets or technical development to the prejudice of the consumers;
> (c) applying dissimilar conditions to equivalent transactions with other trading parties, thereby placing them at a competitive disadvantage;
> (d) making the conclusion of contracts subject to acceptance by the other parties of supplementary obligations which, by their nature or according to commercial usage, have no connection with the subject of such contracts.

This provision restricts an enterprise from using its market-controlling position to inflate prices or to drive out competitive enterprises. An enterprise has a controlling market position if it is in a position to avoid participation in competition or to exclude competition on certain cross-border markets for comparable products. For example, a controlling market position is present if a business is able to control the market for raw materials or business channels.

In any case, the most important indicator that an enterprise has a controlling market position is that the market share of the enterprise significantly exceeds the market share of its competitors. A controlling market position is presumed if the market share of an enterprise exceeds 50%.

However, in order to establish a violation of Article 82 it is not enough to show that an enterprise has a controlling market position. Rather, it must also be shown that the enterprise has misused its market controlling position e.g., that it has forced an inappropriate price or unfair business conditions on a competitor.

C. The Control of Mergers

Articles 81 to 86 of the EC Treaty do not directly address the question under which circumstances mergers are consistent with Community Law. But, since Article 3 (1) (g) requires the establishment of "a system ensuring that competition in the internal market is not distorted", the European Court of Justice refers to these provisions (especially to Article 82) in order to prevent mergers that affect trade between Member States. Actions under these provisions are limited to the control of mergers which have already been enacted.

In order to be able to put a preventive control over mergers into effect, the Council of the European Union enacted regulation 4064/89. The main target of this regulation is to maintain effective competition in the free market. Its scope is limited to "megamergers" that have relevance to the functioning of the community wide trade. Mergers of a smaller extent are still subject to the Member States' national antitrust laws.

III. Exemptions to European Antitrust laws

A. Introduction

The practices prohibited by European antitrust law are broadly enough defined to encompass many forms of business relationships which are often desirable from an economic point of view. Such business relationships include patent agreements, licensing agreements, know-how agreements and exclusive distribution or purchase agreements. In order to deal with these types of special cases, the Commission is empowered under Article 81 (3) of the EC Treaty to exclude certain agreements from the restrictions of European antitrust law. The Commission exercises this power through the granting of exemptions on a case-by-case basis, as well as through the adoption of regulations granting categorical exemptions known as "block exemptions."

Besides, the application of the European antitrust law is limited resp. modified in certain community sectors, such as transport and agriculture. Since the provisions governing these issues are very specific, they will not be further discussed in this context.

B. Block Exemptions

The Commission has already issued several regulations under Article 81 (3) which define the criteria for determining certain categories of agreements which are exempt from the European antitrust law. The most important regulations and the corresponding agreements addressed in these regulations are:

- Commission Regulation 1983/83 (exclusive distribution agreements)
- Commission Regulation 1984/83 (exclusive purchasing agreements)
- Commission Regulation 417/85 as amended by Commission Regulation 151/93 (specialization agreements)
- Commission Regulation 418/85 (research and development agreements)
- Commission Regulation 4087/88 (franchise agreements)
- Commission Regulation 240/96 (certain categories of technology transfer agreements)

The structure of the various block exemption regulations is very similar. Typically, Article 1 of such a regulation declares that the agreements defined in it are exempt from the provisions of Article 81 (1) of the EC Treaty. Article 2 typically sets forth additional permissible contract clauses (the so-called "white list"). Article 3 usually contains a list of terms which, when contained in the agreements defined in Article 1, result in the agreement losing its exemption (these terms have come to be known as the "black list"). The remaining articles contain administrative provisions, extend or restrict the scope of Articles 2 and 3 and provide additional definitions.

As a rule, the block exemption regulations are so detailed that it is possible to determine exactly what type of contracts are exempted from Article 81 (1) of the EC Treaty. According to some critics, the extensive detail in the regulations has led to the use of standard types of agreements and a lack of innovation on the part of enterprises in the development of new contracts.

Qualifying for a block exemption requires no application to or formal authorization from the EC Commission. If an agreement meets the requirements of a particular block exemption, it is automatically exempt from the EC antitrust laws.

C. Example of a Block Exemption Regulation: Commission Regulation 240/96 Pertaining to Certain Categories of Technology Transfer Agreements

Because technology transfer agreements are of special economic interest, this section contains a short overview of the most important provisions of the block exemption regulation pertaining to them (Commission Regulation 240/96 of 31 January 1996). This regulation combines the earlier regulations on patent-licensing and know-how licensing into a single regulation.

According to Article 1 (1) of the regulation, Article 81(1) of the EC Treaty shall not apply to pure patent licensing or know-how licensing agreements and mixed patent and know-how licensing agreements, including those agreements containing ancillary provisions relating to intellectual property rights other than patents, to which only two undertakings are party and which include one or more of the following obligations:

- an obligation on the licensor not to grant other undertakings the right to exploit the licensed technology in the licensed territory;
- an obligation on the licensor not to exploit the licensed technology in the licensed territory himself;
- an obligation on the licensee not to exploit the licensed technology in the territory of the licensor within the common market;
- an obligation on the licensee not to manufacture or use the licensed product, or use the licensed process, in territories within the common market which are licensed to other licensees;
- an obligation on the licensee not to pursue an active policy of putting the licensed product on the market in the territories within the common market

which are licensed to other licensees, and in particular not to engage in advertising specifically aimed at those territories or to establish any branch or maintain an distribution depot there;
- an obligation on the licensee not to put the licensed product on the market in the territories licensed to other licensees within the common market in response to unsolicited orders;
- an obligation on the licensee to use only the licensor's trademark or get up to distinguish the licensed product during the term of the agreement, provided that the licensee is not prevented from identifying himself as the manufacturer of the licensed products;
- an obligation on the licensee to limit his production of the licensed product to the quantities he requires in manufacturing his own products and to sell the licensed product only as an integral part of or a replacement part for his own products or otherwise in connection with the sale of his own products, provided that such quantities are freely determined by the licensee.

Article 2 (1) addresses certain agreements that may appear restrictive but are classified as generally not restrictive of competition by the European Commission. According to this provision, Article 1 of the regulation shall apply to the following obligations imposed on the licensee and reservations addressed to the licensee, known as the "white list,":

- an obligation on the licensee not to divulge the know-how communicated by the licensor; the licensee may be held to this obligation after the agreement has expired;
- an obligation on the licensee not to grant sublicences or assign the licence;
- an obligation on the licensee not to exploit the licensed know-how or patents after termination of the agreement in so far and as long as the know-how is still secret or the patents are still in force;
- an obligation on the licensee to grant to the licensor a licence in respect of his own improvements to or his new applications of the licensed technology, provided:
  - that, in the case of severable improvements, such a licence is not exclusive, so that the licensee is free to use his own improvements or to license them to third parties, in so far as that does not involve disclosure of the know-how communicated by the licensor that is still secret, and
  - that the licensor undertakes to grant an exclusive or non-exclusive license of his own improvements to the licensee;
- an obligation on the licensee to observe minimum quality specifications, including technical specifications, for the licensed product or to procure goods or services from the licensor or from an undertaking designated by the licensor, in so far as these quality specifications, products or services are necessary for a technically proper exploitation of the licensed technology or for ensuring that the product of the licensee conforms to the minimum quality specifications that are applicable to the licensor and other licensees, and to allow the licensor to carry out related checks;
- obligations to inform the licensor of misappropriation of the know-how or of infringements of the licensed patents, or to take or to assist the licensor in taking legal action against such misappropriation or infringements;
- an obligation on the licensee to continue paying the royalties:

(a) until the end of the agreement in the amounts, for the periods and according to the methods freely determined by the parties, in the event of the know-how becoming publicly known other than by action of the licensor, without prejudice to the payment of any additional damages in the event of the know-how becoming publicly known by the action of the licensee in breach of the agreement;
(b) over a period going beyond the duration of the licensed patents, in order to facilitate payment;

- an obligation on the licensee to restrict his exploitation of the licensed technology to one or more technical fields of application covered by the licensed technology or to one or more product markets,
- an obligation on the licensee to pay a minimum royalty or to produce a minimum quantity of the licensed product or to carry out a minimum number of operations exploiting the licensed technology;
- an obligation on the licensor to grant the licensee any more favourable terms that the licensor may grant to another undertaking after the agreement is entered into;
- an obligation on the licensee to mark the licensed product with an indication of the licensor's name or of the licensed patent;
- an obligation on the licensee not to use the licensor's technology to construct facilities for third parties; this is without prejudice to the right of the licensee to increase the capacity of his facilities or to set up additional facilities for his own use on normal commercial terms, including the payment of additional royalties;
- an obligation on the licensee to supply only a limited quantity of the licensed product to a particular customer, where the licence was granted so that the customer might have a second source of supply inside the licensed territory; this provision shall also apply where the customer is the licensee, and the licence which was granted in order to provide a second source of supply provides that the customer is himself to manufacture the licensed products or to have them manufactured by a subcontractor;
- a reservation by the licensor of the right to exercise the rights conferred by a patent to oppose the exploitation of the technology by the licensee outside the licensed territory;
- a reservation by the licensor of the right to terminate the agreement if the licensee contests the secret or substantial nature of the licensed know-how or challenges the validity of licensed patents within the common market belonging to the licensor or undertakings connected with him;
- a reservation by the licensor of the right to terminate the licence agreement of a patent if the licensee raises the claim that such a patent is not necessary;
- an obligation on the licensee to use his best endeavours to manufacture and market the licensed product;
- a a reservation by the licensor of the right to terminate the exclusivity granted to the licensee and to stop licensing improvements to him when the licensee enters into competition within the common market with the licensor, with undertakings connected with the licensor or with other undertakings in respect of research and development, production, use or distribution of competing products, and to require the licensee to prove that the licensed know-how is not being used for the production of products and the provision of services other than those licensed.

According to Article 3, Article 81 (1) of the EC Treaty shall nevertheless apply to the agreements defined in Article 1, if such agreements contain one of the following terms (the so-called "black list"):

- one party is restricted in the determination of prices, components of prices, or discounts for the licensed products;
- one party is restricted from competing within the common market with the other party, with undertakings connected with the other party or with other undertakings in respect of research and development, production, use, or distribution of competing products;
- one or both of the parties are required, without any objectively justified reason, to: (a) refuse to meet orders from users or resellers in their respective territories who would market products in other territories within the common market, or (b) make it difficult for users or resellers to obtain the products from other resellers within the common market, and in particular to exercise intellectual property rights or take measures so as to prevent users or resellers from obtaining outside products, or from putting on the market in the licensed territory products which have been lawfully put on the market, within the common market, by the licensor or with the licensor's consent, or (c) do so as a result of a concerted practice between them;
- the parties were already competing manufacturers before the grant of the license and one of them is restricted, within the same technical field of use or within the same product market, as to the customers it may serve, in particular by being prohibited from supplying certain classes of users, employing certain forms of distribution, or with the aim of sharing customers, using certain types of packaging for the products;
- the quantity of the licensed products one party may manufacture or sell, or the number of operations exploiting a licensed technology the party may carry out, are subject to limitations;
- the licensee is obliged to assign, in whole or in part, to the licensor, rights to improvements to or new applications of a licensed technology; or
- the licensor is prohibited (whether in separate agreements or through automatic extension of an agreement's initial duration for a period exceeding the length in Article 1(2) and (3)) from licensing other undertakings to exploit a licensed technology in the licensed territory, or from exploiting a licensed technology in the other party's territory, or other licensees' territories.

Notwithstanding the detailed stipulations of Articles 1 to 3 of Regulation 240/96, those provisions do not cover those agreements which just fall outside their scope, because they contain obligations restrictive of competition that are not listed in Articles 1 and 2, and not expressly ruled out in Article 3. Under Article 4 of Regulation 240/96, these agreements are subject to an opposition procedure, which requires that the agreement in question is notified to the Commission. Unless the Commission formally opposes exemption within a period of four months after notification, the agreement is automatically exempted from Article 81 (1) of the EC Treaty. If the Commission opposes exemption, the parties must either show that the conditions of Article 86 (3) of the EC Treaty are satisfied or amend the agreement.

Article 5 excludes certain kinds of agreements from the scope of the regulation. Article 6 enables the Commission to withdraw the benefit of the Commission Regulation 240/96 in cases where exempted agreements have effects incompatible with Article 81 (3) of the EC Treaty. Articles 7 to 13 contain definitions and additional administrative provisions.

D. Negative Clearances

In the event that an enterprise is uncertain whether a project or transaction contains a competitive practice prohibited by the European antitrust law, it may apply for a negative clearance or certification by the Commission that a specific project or transaction contains no practice which violates European antitrust law. The Commission will not provide a negative clearance, however, if a block exemption is clearly applicable to the intended contract. If the conditions for a negative clearance are not present, the Commission will treat the application as an application for an individual exemption.

E. Individual exemptions

The EC Commission may exempt certain contracts or transactions from the application of Article 81 (1) of the EC Treaty upon application by the enterprise. An enterprise is entitled to apply for an individual exemption if the agreement, transaction or practice in question falls within article 81 (1) and is not allowed by a block exemption.

Often an individual exemption is applied for when the contract is clearly prohibited by a block exemption regulation. In such cases, the application will be granted by the Commission only if the parties are able to submit valid arguments that, in light of the individual circumstances of the agreement, a deviation from the generalized provisions of the regulation is justified.

Article 81 (3) contains four conditions which must be met in order to receive an individual exemption. The applicant must show that the agreement, transaction or practice will:

(1) improve the production of goods or promote technical or economic progress;
(2) will result in the customers obtaining a fair share of the resulting benefit;
(3) is free of unnecessary restraints and
(4) does not eliminate competition.

In practice, an individual exemption will seldom be denied when only one condition has not been met.

Commission Decision 376/17 (Carbon Gas) provides an example of the application of these conditions in an individual exemption proceeding. In that case, the German branch of BP in conjunction with a couple of other enterprises founded a company for the development and commercial exploitation of a new coal gasification procedure. The Commission granted an individual exemption under Article

81(3) of the EC Treaty on the grounds that the agreement would (1) lead to a significant reduction of costs, (2) lead to a stable supply to the consumers, (3) consist of contractual terms which were all necessary in light of the aim of the agreement and (4) not eliminate competition because various other competitive enterprises were involved in developing and testing similar procedures.

The exemption will not be granted if the Commission concludes that it will lead to a monopoly position of the concerned enterprises. For this reason, the Commission often grants an exemption only under the condition that the applicant fulfills enumerated steps designed to protect competition.

An exemption is always granted for a definite time period. Important administrative provisions relating to the exemption proceeding are contained in Council Regulation 17, as amended by the Accession Treaties and Regulations 59/63, 118/63 and 2822/71.

F. Minor Cases

Agreements, decisions by associations or enterprises, and concerted practices which fall within the provisions of the Commission Notice on Agreements of Minor Importance [(1986) OJ C231/2, as amended (1997) OJ C372/13] do not fall under Article 81 (1) of the EC Treaty and, therefore, do not require an exemption.

The Commission will not provide a negative clearance in these cases. If, due to exceptional circumstances, an agreement covered by this notice nevertheless constitutes an antitrust violation under Article 81 (1) of the EC Treaty, the Commission will not impose fines.

Checklist for minor cases

a) Is there an agreement between enterprises?
Participating enterprises are defined as:
- the parties to the agreement
- or -
- enterprises in which a party
  1. owns directly or indirectly more than half the capital or business assets
  - or -
  2. has the power to exercise more than half the voting rights
  - or -
  3. has the power to appoint more than 50% of the members of bodies which legally represent the company
  - or -
  4. has the right to manage the company's affairs
  - and -
enterprises which directly or indirectly exercise the power(s) set forth in 1-4 above over a party to the agreement.

b) Are the enterprises engaged in the production or distribution of goods?

c) Are goods or services the subject of the agreement?
d) Do the participating enterprises offer other goods or services which are viewed by the customers to be equivalent in view of their characteristics, price and intended use?
e) Do the goods and services set forth in (c) together with the goods and services set forth in (d) represent 5 % or less of the total market?
In order to calculate the market share, it is necessary to determine the relevant product market and the relevant geographical market. The relevant product market includes, in addition to the contract goods and services, any other products which are identical or equivalent to them. The products must be interchangeable from the vantage point of the customer. If the contract products comprise a significant component of another product of the participating enterprises, then reference must be made to the latter product. The relevant geographical market is the area within the Community which is affected by the agreement. That market will often be narrower than the whole Common Market, where products are only bought and sold in limited quantities in certain areas or where the nature or characteristics of the products restrict their mobility, for instance, high transport costs.
f) Is the aggregate annual turnover of the participating enterprises equal to or less than 200 million Euro?

Aggregate turnover includes the turnover in all goods and services achieved during the last financial year by the participating enterprises, excluding taxes, and turnover generated between participating enterprises.

Where each of the questions above may be answered in the affirmative, the case in point will be deemed to be a "minor case." Moreover, even if the answer to (e) and/or (f) is *no*, a "minor case" is still shown if the aforementioned market share and/or turnover was, during the last two successive financial years, not exceeded by more than ten percent.

IV. Sanctions and Judicial Review

According to Article 81 (2) of the EC Treaty, agreements which do not comply with the EC antitrust law are void, and the EC Commission as well as national antitrust authorities may impose severe penalties of up to forty million U.S. dollars for such violations.

Decisions of the Commission e.g., the refusal to grant an individual exemption or a negative-clearance certification, as well as decisions of the national authorities can be challenged by the affected enterprises or persons. Suits may be filed by affected parties against individual decisions made by EC institutions as well as against EC regulations. Such suits must be filed in the EC Court of First Instance and instituted within two months of the notification of a decision to a party (in the case of an individual decision) or within two months of the publication of a new regulation.

All appeals based on errors of law alleged to have been made by the European Court of First Instance must be filed with the European Court of Justice. The European Court of Justice does not review factual matters.

Actions of the national authorities may be appealed only in the national courts in accordance with the Member State's law. This applies even if the challenged action exclusively concerns EC law.

If bodies of the EC cause damage to an enterprise or person by illegal acts, compensation from the European Community is also possible. Such claims must be filed in the European Court of First Instance, and in the event the claim is denied, appeal to the European Court of Justice is possible.

Unfair Terms in Consumer Contracts in the European Community

Bernd Tremml and Andreas Meisterernst

I. Introduction

In the light of a European market which is based on ever increasing numbers and types of products and services as well as standardization in the methods used in the marketing and sales of such products and services, consumer protection is more important than ever. Today's consumer is often neither able to understand the terms and conditions used in consumer contracts nor to evaluate the impact of these terms. Until recently, this problem was aggravated by the fact that the laws applicable to the sale of goods and the provision of services to consumers varied significantly throughout Europe - a situation which often left European consumers completely in the dark when they purchased a product or received a service in a foreign country.

For these reasons, among others, the European Community enacted Council Directive 93/13/EEC of 5 April 1993 on Unfair Terms in Consumer Contracts. This directive lays down, for the first time, standardized consumer protection rules to be followed throughout the European Community.

European law makes a distinction between directives and regulations. According to Art. 249 (2) of the of the Treaty Establishing the European Economic Community as amended (EC Treaty), regulations have general applicability. They are binding in their entirety and directly applicable in all Member States of the European Community. This means that regulations, depending on their content, can have a direct impact on the rights and duties of citizens and businesses. Directives, on the other hand, are only directly binding on the Member States to which they are addressed. According to Art. 249 (3) of the EC Treaty, directives are binding on the Member States as to the result to be achieved but leave to the national authorities the choice of how to achieve this result. Therefore, directives often leave a significant amount of discretion to the Member States. In other words, the Member State must observe the aim of the directive when it incorporates the community provisions into national law, but is free to use the form and methods it deems fit to implement the directive (within the scope of discretion provided for in the directive). Usually, directives contain a certain date by which each Member State must have accomplished this incorporation.

Directives, in contrast to regulations, have no direct impact on businesses and citizens. They are neither designed to grant rights nor impose duties on private natural or legal persons but, instead, set common standards which the Member States must incorporate in their laws. However, directives can have direct effect if a Member State has not transformed the directive into its national law in time. But even then, according to the jurisdiction of the European Court of Justice, directives usually evolve merely a vertical as opposed to a horizontal effect. This means that citizens or businesses involved in a Private Law dispute regarding rights which are the subject matter of a directive cannot rely on the provisions of a directive but must observe their national law. This becomes clear in the European Court of Justice decision "Faccini Dori" (Case C-91/92). In its ruling, the Court explicitly stated that Council Directive 85/577/EEC of 20 December 1985 to Protect the Consumer in Respect of Contracts Negotiated Away from Business Premises cannot be directly applied to private citizens and businesses of the European Community, even where a Member State has not transformed the directive into national law in time.

II. Directive 93/13/EEC Pertaining to Unfair Terms in Consumer Contracts

A. Overview

The goal of Directive 93/13/EEC is to ensure a minimum level of consumer protection in the Member States of the European Community. This directive has the dual aim of encouraging the Member States to protect their consumers while at the same time making it easier, through the standardization of consumer protection laws, for businesses to sell their goods and provide services throughout the Community. Competition is thus encouraged and at least some of the distortions which result when products and services are marketed in countries under widely divergent conditions and laws are eliminated.

Accordingly, Article 1 of Directive 93/13/EEC states that the purpose of the directive is to encourage harmonization of the laws, regulations and administrative provisions of the Member States relating to unfair terms in contracts between a seller or supplier and a consumer. Whereas the adoption or retention by Member States of more stringent consumer-protection laws is specifically allowed by Art. 8, the directive sets a minimum level of consumer protection which is obligatory for all Member States.

The Member States had to bring into force the laws, regulations and administrative provisions necessary to comply with Directive 93/13/EEC until December 31, 1994.

B. The Scope of Directive 93/13/EEC

The provisions of Directive 93/13/EEC apply to standard form contracts between consumers and sellers or suppliers of goods and services. A consumer is defined in Article 2 (b) as any natural person who enters into the type of contract covered by the directive for purposes which are not related to his trade, business or profession. Under this definition, it is not the subjective intention of the buyer of goods and services but rather objective circumstances which are capable of being perceived by the seller or supplier that determine his status as a consumer. If the buyer of goods or services is also in business, then all sales contracts which have an objective relationship with the buyer's business are not consumer transactions. If the goods or services sold are used both in the buyer's private as well as business dealings, then the buyer's customer status depends on which use predominates.

Article 2 (c) defines a seller or supplier as a natural or legal person who enters into the types of contracts covered by the directive for the purposes relating to his or her trade, business or profession, which is privately or publicly owned. German law would add that a seller or supplier is one who engages in sales or services for the purposes of making a profit.

The term supplier has to be understood in a broad sense and, therefore, encompasses also rental contracts.

Service contracts are defined in the directive as the provision of services through any form; for example, through work contracts, travel or vacation contracts, and financial services contracts, including loan and insurance contracts.

As it was mentioned before, each Member State transforms the provisions of a directive through national legislation so that the laws which the States accordingly enact are of national, not of international impact. In order to nevertheless ensure effective consumer protection, Art. 6 (2) requires Member States to take all necessary measures to ensure that the consumers do not lose their rights through choice-of-law agreements that render the law of a non-Member country applicable. This provision is necessary, since otherwise the law of a non-Member country (that possibly provides a lower standard of consumer rights than exists in the European Community) could be applied to contracts concerning consumers of Member States, which would essentially vitiate the effect of the directive. Art. 6 (2), though, is restricted to cases in which the consumer contract has a close connection with the territory of a Member State.

C. General definition of an unfair term

Article 3 (1) defines a term as unfair if, contrary to the requirements of good faith, it causes a significant imbalance in the parties' rights and obligations arising under the contract to the detriment of the consumer. The phrase "a significant imbalance" is indefinite and, therefore, open for further interpretation. Important interpretive sources are the laws passed by the Member States transforming Directive 93/13/EEC and the subsequent interpretation of these laws by the national courts.

Here it should be pointed out that the Member States' interpretations of Directive 93/13/EEC are useful only to the extent that such interpretations aim to enhance the purpose and intent of Directive 93/13/EEC, since Member States have a duty to interpret EC-based law independently of their own national law. Meeting this duty (which, in the legal language of European law, is known as the duty to "autonomously interpret directives") is one of the fundamental keys to the ultimate success of the goal of Directive 93/13/EEC to unify consumer protection laws throughout the Community.

A German law entitled "Law for the Regulation of Standard Business Terms" ["Gesetz zur Regelung der Allgemeinen Geschäftsbedingungen" (AGBG)], was the law chosen by Germany as the vehicle for incorporating Directive 93/13/EEC into its national law. The rules of the former AGBG are part of the German Civil Code (BGB) since January 1st 2002 as its Par. 305 to 310 BGB. According to Par. 310 sec. 3 BGB these rules are applicable to consumer contracts. Par. 307 sec. 2 BGB interprets a significant imbalance as one which is present when a particular term is at odds with the essential principles of the consumer protection laws or when the result of a particular term is to restrict the essential rights or contractual obligations to such an extent that the purpose or intention of the contract is in danger of not being met. Whether a term is unfair under German law must be determined by considering the individual interest of both parties and the standard practices in the particular trade or industry. The term has to be assessed in the light of the subject matter, purpose and particular features of the contract involved. Its fairness must be judged in the light of the contract as a whole. A significant imbalance is indicated namely if the consumer, as a result of the term(s) in question, is unreasonably disadvantaged.

According to Article 4 (1) of the directive, an assessment of the unfairness of a contractual term must take into account the nature of the goods or services for which the contract was concluded, other terms in the contract at issue or in any other contract upon which the contract is dependent as well as all given circumstances at the time the parties entered into the contract. Two of these circumstances, which Par. 16 of the preamble particularly stresses, are the respective bargaining positions of the parties and whether or not the consumer has been induced to agree to the challenged term or terms.

Thus, Directive 93/13/EEC contemplates an examination of a challenged term at two levels. First, one must look at the term without considering the situation of the parties in order to determine if, from a generalized, objective perspective, the term itself is unfair. Second, the fairness of the term must be assessed in the light of the individual circumstances of the case. In this second step, it is important to determine whether the circumstances surrounding the conclusion of the contract provide any reason to suspect that the term is unfair. In particular, one should consider whether a consumer has been exploited due to the seller's or supplier's intellectual superiority in business matters or his greater business experience as well as whether there is any evidence of unscrupulous behavior on the part of the seller or supplier.

Article 5 of the directive requires the terms contained in written contracts to be drafted in plain and intelligible language. Where there is doubt about the meaning of a term, the interpretation which is most favorable to the consumer will prevail.

D. Representative list of unfair terms

What exactly constitutes an unfair term under Article 3 (1) of Directive 93/13/EEC is further illuminated by the annex to the directive, which contains an indicative and non-exhaustive list of terms which may be regarded as unfair. Although these terms are merely intended to provide non-binding guidelines, they are an important point of orientation for the Member States in the task of correctly interpreting Article 3 (1). Therefore, each of the terms contained in the Annex to Directive 93/13/EEC will be discussed below. Following an examination of the single terms, a short explanation of the corresponding German law is given. The explanation is provided to illustrate how a Member State typically incorporates the non-mandatory provisions of the Annex to Directive 93/13/EEC into its own national law. It should not be ignored, however, that because the annex is not binding for the Member States, there may be variations between the terms deemed unfair in the annex and terms deemed unfair under national law. This variation in the content of the directive and the national law is not possible in the case of the mandatory articles of Directive 93/13/EEC.

Number 1 (a) of the appendix designates such terms as unfair that have the object or effect of excluding or limiting the legal liability of a seller or supplier in the event of the consumer's personal injury or death resulting from an act or omission of the seller or supplier. This is now adoptped in Par. 309 Number 7 BGB.

Number 1 (b) designates terms which have the object or effect of inappropriately excluding or limiting the legal rights of consumers in their relationships with the seller or supplier or another party in the event of the seller's or supplier's total or partial non-performance or inadequate performance of any of the contractual obligations as unfair. German law provides in Par. 309 Numbers 2,3, and 8 BGB that consumer rights provided by German law may not be inappropriately excluded or limited in the consumer contract. In particular, contractual terms which limit the consumer's ability to terminate the contract or seek damages in the event of partial or total breach by the seller are unenforceable. Moreover, German law designates contractual terms unfair that prohibit the consumer from withholding performance until the seller has performed.

Number 1 (c) designates terms as unfair that have the object or effect of making an agreement binding on the consumer while the seller's or supplier's own performance is subject to a condition whose realization depends on his discretion. Such a provision, while not specifically prohibited in German law, would most likely be deemed unenforceable under the general provisions of Par. 307 BGB. That paragraph is similar to Article 3 of the directive and designates terms which unreasonably disadvantage the consumer as unfair.

Under Number 1 (d), terms are unfair which have the object or effect of permitting the seller or supplier to retain sums paid by the consumer where the latter decides not to conclude or perform the contract, without providing a reciprocal right for the consumer in the event the seller or supplier is the party that cancels the contract. The corresponding German provision renders contractual terms void which allow the seller or supplier, in the event the customer exercises a legal option not to fulfill the contract or otherwise terminates the contract, to withhold an unreasonable sum for the consumer's use of any property or goods, services or rights rendered to the consumer or as remuneration for expenses incurred by the seller or supplier (Par. 308 Number 7 BGB).

Any term which has the object or effect of requiring consumers who fail to fulfill their obligations to pay a disproportionately high sum in compensation is unfair according to Number 1 (e) of the annex. The even more extensive provision of Par. 309 Number 6 BGB prohibits all contract penalties, regardless of their amount, which the seller or supplier seeks to impose in the event that the consumer fails or delays in accepting performance, delays or fails to pay the stipulated sum or backs out of a contract altogether.

Number 1 (f) and (g) deem terms unfair that give the seller or supplier discretion to terminate the contract without providing the consumer the same privilege. Unfair as well are terms which allow a seller or supplier who terminates a contract to retain sums paid by the consumer for a performance which has yet to be delivered. Finally, it is regarded as unfair for the seller or supplier to terminate a contract of indeterminate duration without reasonable notice, unless there are serious grounds for doing so. Par. 308 Number 3 BGB has incorporated this latter provision into German law. This law states that any contractual provision in a standard form contract which gives the seller or supplier the right to refuse performance without a factually justifiable reason is unfair.

Under Number 1 (h), a term whose object or effect is to automatically extend a contract of fixed duration in the absence of affirmative objection by the consumer is unfair if the consumer has to state his objection within an unreasonably short time span. The corresponding provision of German law is found in Par. 309 Number 9 BGB, which provides that in contracts providing for the regular delivery of goods or services, any terms which effect a duration of the contract of more than two years are void. Any automatic extension provisions are limited to one year at a time, and the customer cannot be required to express a desire to cancel the contract more than three months before the expiration of the initial contract or its extension.

Number 1 (i) states that terms which have the object or effect of irrevocably binding customers to terms they had no real opportunity of becoming acquainted with before the conclusion of the contract are unfair. For example, such an unfair term could be a provision in the contract which states that the consumer has read and understood all terms of the contract. Under German law, a corresponding contractual provision in a standard form contract would also be unenforceable because it has the effect of shifting the burden of proof to the consumer regarding his comprehension of the contractual terms. Such a provision therefore violates Par. 309 Number 12 AGBG, which deems as void any terms whose effects are to alter the burden of proof to the disadvantage of a party through the use of a pre-formulated contractual confirmation.

Number 1 (j), (k), (l), and (m) render unfair all terms granting the seller or supplier the right to unilaterally alter the terms in a contract without having a valid reason which is specified in the contract. Such unfair unilateral changes include, in particular, changes to the characteristics of the product or service to be provided, unless there exists a valid reason. Moreover, contractual terms which provide that the seller or supplier at the time of delivery may first determine the price or increase the price are unfair, unless the consumer is given the right to cancel the contract if the final price is too high in relation to the price agreed to at the time the contract was concluded. Finally, giving the seller or supplier the right to determine whether or not the supplied goods or services are in conformity with the contract or the exclusive right to interpret any term in the contract is deemed unfair by the directive. German law has incorporated certain aspects of these proposed prohibitions. Under Par. 309 Number 1 BGB, a term which allows the seller to increase the contract price is unenforceable if the contract has to be executed within four months after its conclusion. According to Par. 308 Number 4 BGB, a term in a standard form contract which allows the seller or supplier to alter his performance is invalid when, in the light of the interests of the seller or supplier, it is unreasonable to expect the consumer to concede to such a unilateral change.

Number 1 (n) designates as unfair any contractual terms that have the objective or effect of limiting the seller's or supplier's obligation to respect the commitments of their agents or which provide that an agent's commitments are not binding on the principal, unless a particular formality is present. This issue is not specifically addressed in the BGB, but principals are generally responsible for their agent's actions under German law.

According to Number 1 (o), terms whose objective or effect is to oblige the consumer to fulfill all of his obligations, even when the seller or supplier does not perform his, are unfair. German law contains a corresponding provision in Par. Number 2 BGB, which provides that contractual terms which prevent or limit the right of the consumer to withhold performance until the seller or supplier has performed are unenforceable.

Number 1 (p) deems a contractual provision to be unfair when it allows the seller or supplier to transfer his rights and obligations under the contract without first obtaining the consumer's consent and when the transfer could reduce the guarantees for the consumer. Similarly, Par. 309 Number 10 BGB provides that a clause in a standard form contract (concerning a sale, service or work and labor) which allows the seller or supplier to unilaterally transfer his rights or responsibilities to a third party is unfair unless this third party is specifically named in the contract or the consumer is given the option of terminating the contract in this case.

Terms whose objective or effect is to exclude or affect a consumer's right to take legal action or exercise any other legal remedy are unfair according to Number 1 (q). This category namely includes terms which require the consumer to take disputes exclusively to an arbitration panel, unduly restrict the evidence available to a consumer or impose on a consumer a burden of proof which, according to the applicable law, should lie with the other party to the contract. According to Par. 309 Number 12 BGB, a contractual term in a standard form contract which shifts the burden of proof to the disadvantage of the consumer, is unfair. Moreover, the directive's suggested intention to render terms inapplicable that restrict the consumer's right to take legal action in a proper and effective way would be deemed adverse to the general provision of Par. 307 BGB.

Number 2 of the annex to Directive 93/13/EEC carves out certain exceptions and modifications of number 1 for particular types of contracts. For example, number 2 (a) modifies number 1 (g) for providers of financial services. As a result, a contractual term reserving to the suppliers of financial services the right to unilaterally terminate a contract of indeterminate duration, without notice, is not unfair where there is a valid reason, provided that the supplier is required to inform the consumer immediately. Number 2 also permits contractual terms which permit the supplier of financial services to alter the rate of interest payable by the consumer or to increase the amount of other financial service charges without notice, as long as there is a valid reason, the consumer is notified of the change at the earliest possible opportunity, and the consumer has the right to terminate the contract due to such change.

According to Number 2 (c) of the annex, number 1 (g), (j), and (l) do not apply to the transactions in transferable securities, financial instruments and other products or services whose price is linked to fluctuations in a stock-exchange quotation or index, or a financial market rate that the seller or supplier does not control. The same exemptions apply for contracts concerning the purchase or sale of foreign currency, traveller's checks or international money orders denominated in foreign currency.

E. General Exclusions from Directive 93/13/EEC

According to Article 1 (2), contractual terms which either reflect mandatory statutory or regulatory provisions and the provisions or principles of international conventions to which the Member States or the Community are party are excluded from Directive 93/13/EEC. This exclusion ensures that terms which the law of a Member State requires to be included in a consumer contract or terms which have been otherwise included as a result of that law are not subject to scrutiny under the directive.

In addition, according to paragraph 10 of the preamble of directive 93/13/EEC, contracts relating to employment, succession rights, rights under family law and to the incorporation and organization of companies as well as partnership agreements are excluded from the coverage of the directive. Further, terms in a consumer contract which describe the main subject matter of the contract or the quality/price ratio of the goods or services supplied are also excluded from coverage. This latter exclusion is necessary to ensure that the directive is not seen or used as a price-control law.

F. Exclusions based on individually negotiated terms

Perhaps the most significant exclusion from Directive 93/13/EEC concerns contractual terms which have been individually negotiated between the consumer and seller or supplier. The directive designates such terms as "individual terms". Directive 93/13/EEC merely defines individual terms negatively: According to Article 3 (2), Sentence 1, a contractual term which has been previously drafted by the seller or supplier, thus providing no real opportunity for a consumer to influence its content, is not an individual term. In particular, terms contained in pre-formulated standard-form contracts are not individual terms.

German case law holds that, even if a consumer has been thoroughly informed about the meaning and impact of a term, this fact does not transform a pre-formulated term into an individual term. Irrelevant as well under German law is a signed declaration by the customer to the effect that the terms of the contract have been individually negotiated. By the same token, the fact that a standard form contract specifically solicits changes or deletions by the consumer or contains blanks for the customer to fill in, does not transform terms of a contract into individual ones.

Much more relevant in determining whether a term in an otherwise standard form contract is an individual term is the examination of whether or not the seller or supplier was, as a matter of fact, ready and prepared to negotiate over the term. The seller's amenability to negotiate must clearly and sincerely be expressed to the consumer. The consumer, in short, must possess the real possibility to influence the contractual term. It is irrelevant that the business person's notary, attorney or other representative drafted the term. Clearly, such a third party has an interest in strengthening or establishing a business relationship with the business person.

According to Article 3 (2), Sentence 2, the fact that one specific term or certain aspects of a term have been individually negotiated does not mean that the directive is inapplicable to the remaining terms, if an overall assessment of the contract indicates that it is nevertheless a pre-formulated standard form contract. Thus, a situation can arise in which certain terms in a contract are subject to the directive's scrutiny, whereas other individual terms are not.

In a pre-formulated standard form contract, the seller or supplier has the burden of proving that one or more of its terms are individual terms. In non-standard form contracts, the burden of proof lies with the consumer to show that a term was not individually negotiated.

G. Impact of unfair terms on the enforcement of the contract

Article 6 (1) of Directive 93/13/EEC requires the Member States to include a provision in their national laws according to which unfair terms used in a contract between a consumer and a seller or supplier shall not be binding, and that the contract shall continue to bind the parties if it is capable of continuing in existence without the unfair terms. This provision corresponds to Par. 306 BGB, which states that, if a contractual term is void, the rest of the contract will remain in function. Furthermore, Par. 306 BGB states that, instead of the unfair clause, the corresponding provisions of German law shall apply to the contract. It is important to keep in mind, though, that the unfair clause itself will not remain into effect. The Bundesgerichtshof, the German appeal court for civil and criminal law cases, has expressly ruled that the practise of so-called "salvatorische Klauseln" (clauses which contain the additional expression "as far as it is permitted by law") is not consistent with Par. 306 BGB. This means that a seller or supplier is not able to place such a clause in a contract and, in case the clause is deemed unfair, to rely on the closest legal approximation to this clause. Such clauses are no longer valid in standard form contracts, because German law mandates that the corresponding provision of German law and not a virtual term which most closely approximates the unfair term applies to the contract.

In addition, German law also clarifies the circumstances under which the contract as a whole will continue to be enforceable despite the unfair term(s). Par. 306 sec. 3 BGB provides that the entire contract is void if its execution would result in an undue hardship to one of the parties under the modified circumstances.

H. Methods of enforcing consumer rights

Member States are required by Article 7 (1) to ensure that adequate and effective means exist to prevent the continued use of unfair terms in contracts between consumers and sellers or suppliers. Article 7 (2) states that those means shall include provisions whereby persons or organizations, having a legitimate interest under national law in protecting consumers, may take action before national courts or before competent administrative bodies for a decision as to the fairness of certain contractual terms which are drawn up for general use. Such a legal action may be directed at a single seller or supplier, at a group of sellers or suppliers from the same economic sector or at seller or supplier associations which use or recommend the use of the challenged term [Article 7 (3)]. In Germany the methods of enforcing consumer rights are now ruled in the "Law for actions for injunction" ["Unterlassungsklagengesetz" (UKlaG)]. A corresponding rule is found in Par. 1 UKlaG.

III. Conclusion

This chapter has provided an overview of the consumer-protection law in the European Community pertaining to unfair terms in standard form contracts. With the enactment of Council Directive 93/13/EEC of 5 April 1993 on Unfair Terms in Consumer Contracts, a significant step has been made in the process of standardizing consumer protection law throughout the European Community. The directive has considerably eased the task of businesses that must remain abreast of the consumer protection laws in effect in the European countries where they transact business. For the European consumer, the directive provides a reasonable amount of assurance that a minimum standard of consumer protection is guaranteed throughout the Community.

The PCT and the Enforcement of Patents in Europe

Kay Rupprecht

I. General Introduction

A. Update of countries

Year by year, the PCT Community of member states is getting larger, since more and more countries recognize the usefulness and the advantages of the PCT for applicants. Use of the PCT saves time, work and money and eases the prosecution of a global patent strategy in a number of countries which has presently increased to 115 (Status on December 31, 2001) contracting states in total.

Albania	Democratic People's	Liberia	South Africa
Algeria	Republic of Korea	Liechtenstein	Spain
Antigua and Barbuda	Denmark	Lithuania	Sri Lanka
Armenia	Domenica	Luxembourg	Sudan
Australia	Ecuador	Madagascar	Swaziland
Austria	Equatorial Guinea	Malati	Sweden
Azerbaijan	Estonia	Mali	Switzerland
Barbados	Finland	Mauritania	Tajikistan
Belarus	France	Mexico	The former Yugoslav
Belgium	Gabon	Monaco	Republic of
Belize	Gambia	Mongolia	Macedonia
Benin	Georgia	Morocco	Togo
Bosnia and Herzegovina	Germany	Mozambique	Trinidad and Tobago
	Ghana	Netherlands	Tunisia
Brazil	Greece	New Zealand	Turkey
Bulgaria	Grenada	Niger	Uganda
Burkina Faso	Guinea	Norway	Ucraine
Cameroon	Guinea-Bissau	Oman	Turkmenistan
Canada	Hungary	Philippines	United Arab Emirates
Central African Republic	Iceland	Poland	United Kingdom
	India	Portugal	United Republic of Tanzania
Chad	Indonesia	Republic of Korea	United States of America
China	Ireland	Republic of Moldova	Uzbekistan

Colombia	Israel	Romania	Viet Nam
Congo	Italy	Russian Federation	Yugoslavia
Costa Rica	Japan	Saint Lucia	Zimbabwe
Côte d'Ivoire	Kazakhstan	Senegal	Zambia
Croatia	Kenya	Sierra Leone	
Cuba	Kyrgyzstan	Singapore	
Cyprus	Latvia	Slovakia	
Czech Republic	Lesotho	Slovenia	

Table 1- Member States

B. Some statistics

The problem with protecting innovations is well-known to all of us:
It has occurred many times that after filing a patent application, the invention is improved by new technical methods. Or in theory, the invention appears promising but the practical function is neither reliable nor good in maintenance or economical. Or it comes to notice at the end of the priority year that the sales or marketing department can not yet make the final selection of countries as the product has not yet been introduced on the market. Thus, more time is appreciated to make a final decision on the selection of countries for patent protection. Important other advantages resulting from using of the PCT route are referred to in the following and interesting aspects will be discussed hereinafter.

The number of International Patent Applications filed since 1985 increased almost like an e-function reaching in the year 2001 a total of applications of 103,947.

Number of international applications received since 1985

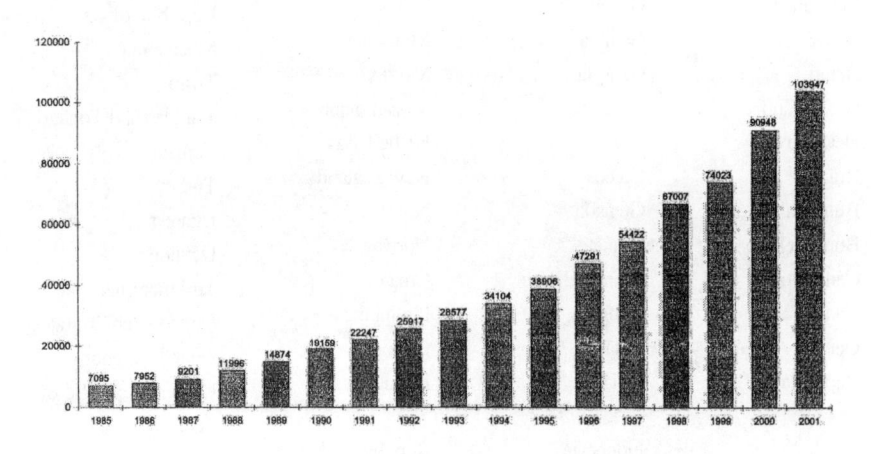

Year	Applications
1985	7095
1986	7952
1987	9201
1988	11996
1989	14874
1990	19169
1991	22247
1992	25917
1993	28577
1994	34104
1995	38906
1996	47291
1997	54422
1998	67007
1999	74023
2000	90948
2001	103947

Diagram 1- Number of International Patent Applications

It will be generally known that the US holds rank No. 1 ahead of Germany and Japan in terms of the filing numbers per country since years. Out of 11,846 applications from Japanese applicants in 2001, approximately 717 or 6 % were filed in English using the European Patent Office as International Search Authority (ISA). As far as the 40,003 PCT applications with US origin are concerned, approximately 19,5 % or 7,783 used the EPO as ISA and another 30 % or 2,334 of these used the EPO also as International Preliminary Examination Authority (IPEA).

Country of origin		Number of applications 2001	(2000)	Percentage 2001	(2000)
US	United States of America	40,003	(38,171)	38.5	(42.0)
DE	Germany	13,616	(12,039)	13.1	(13.2)
JP	Japan	11,846	(9,402)	11.4	(10.3)
GB	United Kingdom	6,233	(5,538)	6.0	(6.1)
FR	France	4,619	(3,601)	4.4	(4.0)
SE	Sweden	3,502	(3,071)	3.4	(3.4)
NL	Netherlands	3,187	(2,587)	3.1	(2.8)
KR	Republic of Korea	2,318	(1,514)	2.2	(1.7)
CA	Canada	2,030	(1,600)	1.9	(1.8)
CH&LI	Switzerland and Liechtenstein	2,011	(1,701)	1.9	(1.9)
AU	Australia	1,754	(1,627)	1.7	(1.8)
CN	China	1,670	(579)	1.6	(0.6)
FI	Finland	1,623	(1,437)	1.6	(1.6)
IT	Italy	1,574	(1,354)	1.5	(1.5)
IL	Israel	1,248	(924)	1.2	(1.0)
DK	Denmark	929	(789)	0.9	(0.9)
BE	Belgium	681	(574)	0.7	(0.6)
AT	Austria	630	(476)	0.6	(0.5)
ES	Spain	575	(519)	0.6	(0.6)
RU	Russian Federation	551	(590)	0.5	(0.7)
NO	Norway	525	(470)	0.5	(0.5)
ZA	South Africa	418	(386)	0.4	(0.4)
IN	India	316	(156)	0.3	(0.2)
NZ	New Zealand	279	(264)	0.3	(0.3)
SG	Singapore	271	(225)	0.3	(0.3)
IE	Ireland	212	(184)	0.2	(0.2)
BR	Brazil	193	(161)	0.2	(0.2)
HU	Hungary	130	(140)	0.1	(0.2)
MX	Mexico	107	(71)	0.1	(0.1)
PL	Poland	105	(104)	0.1	(0.1)
LU	Luxembourg	95	(93)	0.1	(0.1)

CZ	Czech Republic	79	(91)	0.1	(0.1)
TR	Turkey	72	(70)	0.1	(0.1)
HR	Croatia	55	(49)	0.1	(0.1)
GR	Greece	54	(50)	0.1	(0.1)
UA	Ukraine	48	(44)	0.1	(0.1)
SI	Slovenia	41	(38)	< 0.1	(< 0.1)
PT	Portugal	36	(19)	< 0.1	(< 0.1)
YU	Yugoslavia	31	(22)	< 0.1	(< 0.1)
RO	Romania	30	(27)	< 0.1	(< 0.1)
SK	Slovakia	29	(31)	< 0.1	(< 0.1)
IS	Iceland	28	(18)	< 0.1	(< 0.1)
BG	Bulgaria	22	(29)	< 0.1	(< 0.1)
BY	Belarus	18	(10)	< 0.1	(< 0.1)
CY	Cyprus	18	(12)	< 0.1	(< 0.1)
AM	Armenia	15	(5)	< 0.1	(< 0.1)
CO	Colombia	14	n.a.	< 0.1	n.a.
CU	Cuba	10	(5)	< 0.1	(< 0.1)
LV	Latvia	9	(4)	< 0.1	(< 0.1)
AL	Albania	8	(0)	< 0.1	(0)
EE	Estonia	8	(5)	< 0.1	(< 0.1)
KZ	Kazakhstan	6	(5)	< 0.1	(< 0.1)
BB	Barbados	5	(7)	< 0.1	(< 0.1)
CR	Costa Rica	5	(8)	< 0.1	(< 0.1)
GE	Georgia	5	(4)	< 0.1	(< 0.1)
ID	Indonesia	5	(10)	< 0.1	(< 0.1)
MC	Monaco	5	(6)	< 0.1	(< 0.1)
PH	Philippines	5	n.a.	< 0.1	n.a.
AE	United Arab Emirates	4	(1)	< 0.1	(< 0.1)
BA	Bosnia and Herzegovina	4	(4)	< 0.1	(< 0.1)
DZ	Algeria	4	(3)	< 0.1	(< 0.1)
SD	Sudan	4	(5)	< 0.1	(< 0.1)
MK	The former Yugoslav Republic of Macedonia	3	(3)	< 0.1	(< 0.1)
AZ	Azerbaijan	2	(2)	< 0.1	(< 0.1)
CI	Cöte d'Ivoire	2	(1)	< 0.1	(< 0.1)
LK	Sri Lanka	2	(4)	< 0.1	(< 0.1)
LT	Lithuania	2	(1)	< 0.1	(< 0.1)
MA	Morocco	2	(0)	< 0.1	(0)
SN	Senegal	2	(0)	< 0.1	(0)
ZW	Zimbabwe	2	(0)	< 0.1	(0)
AG	Antigua and Barbuda	1	(0)	< 0.1	(0)

TT	Trinidad and Tobago	1	(0)	< 0.1	(0)
CM	Cameroon	0	(2)	0	(< 0.1)
LS	Lesotho	0	(1)	0	(< 0.1)
MD	Republic of Moldova	0	(2)	0	(< 0.1)
UZ	Uzbekistan	0	(2)	0	(< 0.1)
VN	Viet Nam	0	(1)	0	(< 0.1)
	TOTAL	103,947	(90,948)	100.0	(100.0)

Table 2 – Number of Applications per Country

International Searching Authority	Number of applications 2001	(2000)	Percentage 2001	(2000)
European Patent Office	63,128	(55,414)	60.7	(60.9)
United States of America	17,793	(17,386)	17.1	(19.1)
Japan	11,182	(8,850)	10.8	(9.7)
Sweden	4,481	(4,040)	4.3	(4.5)
Australia	2,086	(1,886)	2.0	(2.1)
Republic of Korea	2,033	(1,217)	2.0	(1.3)
China	1,661	(573)	1.6	(0.6)
Russian Federation	556	(595)	0.5	(0.7)
Spain	514	(440)	0.5	(0.5)
Austria	493	(545)	0.5	(0.6)
TOTAL	103,927	(90,946)	100.0	(100.0)

Table 3 – Number of Applications per ISA

Language of filing	Number of applications 2001	(2000)	Percentage 2001	(2000)
English	66,993	(60,571)	64.5	(66.6)
German	14,198	(12,869)	13.7	(14.1)
Japanese	11,129	(8,854)	10.7	(9.7)
French	4,488	(3,588)	4.3	(3.9)
Chinese	1,576	(501)	1.5	(0.6)
Korean	1,445	(786)	1.4	(0.9)
Swedish	1,077	(985)	1.0	(1.1)
Spanish	624	(548)	0.6	(0.6)
Finnish	541	(508)	0.5	(0.6)
Russian	525	(575)	0.5	(0.6)
Dutch	493	(479)	0.5	(0.5)
Italian	372	(240)	0.4	(0.3)
Norwegian	258	(250)	0.2	(0.3)
Danish	153	(147)	0.1	(0.2)
Hungarian	22	(13)	< 0.1	(< 0.1)
Croatian	21	(10)	< 0.1	(< 0.1)
Czech	12	(11)	< 0.1	(< 0.1)

Slovenian	9	(9)	< 0.1	(< 0.1)
Slovakian	7	(2)	< 0.1	(< 0.1)
Turkish	4	(2)	< 0.1	(< 0.1)
TOTAL	**103,947**	**(90,948)**	**100.0**	**(100.0)**

Table 4 – Number of Applications per Language

International Preliminary Examining Authority	Number of demands		Percentage	
	2001	**(2000)**	**2001**	**(2000)**
European Patent Office	44,399	(37,427)	57.3	(58.3)
United States of America	20,203	(16,389)	26.0	(25.5)
Japan	5,383	(4,401)	6.9	(6.9)
Sweden	3,709	(3,420)	4.8	(5.3)
Australia	1,836	(1,372)	2.4	(2.1)
Republic of Korea	829	(346)	1.1	(0.5)
China	625	(244)	0.8	(0.4)
Russian Federation	337	(342)	0.4	(0.5)
Austria	229	(302)	0.3	(0.5)
TOTAL	**77,550**	**(64,243)**	**100.0**	**(100.0)**

Table 5 – Number of Demands per IPEA

Language of publication	Number of applications		Percentage	
	2001	**(2000)**	**2001**	**(2000)**
English	69,287	(56,084)	69.6	(70.2)
German	14,004	(12,010)	14.1	(15.0)
Japanese	9,817	(7,057)	9.9	(8.8)
French	4,138	(3,654)	4.1	(4.6)
Chinese	1,308	(224)	1.3	(0.3)
Spanish	542	(422)	0.5	(0.5)
Russian	510	(496)	0.5	(0.6)
TOTAL	**99,606**	**(79,947)**	**100.0**	**(100.0)**

Table 6 – Number of Applications per Language of Publication

The following should encourage US or Japanese applicants to file their PCT application in English (this recommendation applies of course to Japanese applicants only) and to subsequently use the European Patent Office as ISA and - even more advantageously - as International Preliminary Examining Authority (IPEA). This is possible by inserting "EP" in box number VII of the PCT application form. US-Companies may choose USPTO or WIPO as Receiving Office, in any case the EPO as ISA and IPEA.

Sheet No. ...5...

Box No. VI PRIORITY CLAIM
☐ Further priority claims are indicated in the Supplemental Box.

Filing date of earlier application (day/month/year)	Number of earlier application	Where earlier application is:		
		national application: country	regional application:* regional Office	international application: receiving Office
item (1) 15 July 1999 (15.07.99)	09/997,654	US		
item (2) 14 September 1999 (14.09.99)	99999888.9		EP	
item (3) 17 May 2000 (17.05.00)	PCT/AU00/07777			AU

☒ The receiving Office is requested to prepare and transmit to the International Bureau a certified copy of the earlier application(s) *(only if the earlier application was filed with the Office which for the purposes of the present international application is the receiving Office)* identified above as item(s):   (1)

* Where the earlier application is an ARIPO application, it is mandatory to indicate in the Supplemental Box at least one country party to the Paris Convention for the Protection of Industrial Property for which that earlier application was filed (Rule 4.10(b)(ii)). See Supplemental Box.

Box No. VII INTERNATIONAL SEARCHING AUTHORITY

Choice of International Searching Authority (ISA) *(if two or more International Searching Authorities are competent to carry out the international search, indicate the Authority chosen; the two-letter code may be used)*:	Request to use results of earlier search; reference to that search *(if an earlier search has been carried out by or requested from the International Searching Authority)*.		
	Date (day/month/year)	Number	Country (or regional Office)
ISA /US	15 July 1999 (15.07.99)	09/997,654	US

Box No. VIII CHECK LIST; LANGUAGE OF FILING

This international application contains the following **number of sheets**:

request	:	5
description (excluding sequence listing part)	:	25
claims	:	3
abstract	:	1
drawings	:	3
sequence listing part of description	:	
Total number of sheets :		37

This international application is accompanied by the item(s) marked below:

1. ☒ fee calculation sheet
2. ☒ separate signed power of attorney
3. ☐ copy of general power of attorney; reference number, if any:
4. ☐ statement explaining lack of signature
5. ☒ priority document(s) identified in Box No. VI as item(s): (2) and (3)
6. ☐ translation of international application into (language):
7. ☐ separate indications concerning deposited microorganism or other biological material
8. ☐ nucleotide and/or amino acid sequence listing in computer readable form
9. ☐ other *(specify)*:

Figure of the drawings which should accompany the abstract: 2	Language of filing of the international application: English

Box No. IX SIGNATURE OF APPLICANT OR AGENT

Next to each signature, indicate the name of the person signing and the capacity in which the person signs (if such capacity is not obvious from reading the request).

John Smith
John J. Smith

For receiving Office use only

1. Date of actual receipt of the purported international application:
2. Drawings:
3. Corrected date of actual receipt due to later but timely received papers or drawings completing the purported international application:
   ☐ received:
4. Date of timely receipt of the required corrections under PCT Article 11(2):
   ☐ not received:
5. International Searching Authority (if two or more are competent): ISA /
6. ☐ Transmittal of search copy delayed until search fee is paid.

For International Bureau use only

Date of receipt of the record copy by the International Bureau:

Form PCT/RO/101 (last sheet) (July 1998; reprint July 2000)   *See Notes to the request form*

(July 2000)
Form 1 – Priority Claim

PCT Applicant's Guide – Volume I – Annex C

C	Receiving Offices	C
JP	**JAPAN PATENT OFFICE**	**JP**

Competent receiving Office for nationals and residents of:	Japan
Language in which international applications may be filed:	English or Japanese[1]
Number of copies required by the receiving Office:	1
Does the receiving Office accept the filing of international applications with requests in PCT-EASY format?[2]	Yes
Competent International Searching Authority:	Japan Patent Office or European Patent Office[3]
Competent International Preliminary Examining Authority:	Japan Patent Office or European Patent Office[4]
Fees payable to the receiving Office:	Currency: Japanese yen (JPY)
Transmittal fee:	JPY 18,000
International fee:	
Basic fee:	JPY 47,800
Fee per sheet in excess of 30:	JPY 1,100
Designation fee:	JPY 10,300
PCT-EASY fee reduction:[2]	JPY 14,700
Search fee:	See Annex D (Japan Patent Office or European Patent Office)
Fee for priority document (PCT Rule 17.1(b)):	JPY 1,400
Is an agent required by the receiving Office?	No, if the applicant resides in Japan Yes, if he is a non-resident
Who can act as agent?	Any patent attorney or attorney-at-law resident in Japan

---

[1] If the language in which the international application is filed is not accepted by the International Searching Authority (see Annex D), the applicant will have to furnish a translation (PCT Rule 12.3).

[2] Where the request is filed in PCT-EASY format together with a PCT-EASY diskette and the receiving Office accepts such filings (see *PCT Gazette* No. 51/1998, pages 17330 and 17332), the total amount of the international fee is reduced.

[3] The European Patent Office is competent only if the international application is filed in English.

[4] The European Patent Office is competent only if the international search is or has been performed by that Office.

(1 January 2002)

Form 2 – Japanese Patent Office

PCT Applicant's Guide – Volume I – Annex C

C   Receiving Offices   C

US   UNITED STATES PATENT AND TRADEMARK OFFICE (USPTO)   US

Competent receiving Office for nationals and residents of:	United States of America
Language in which international applications may be filed:	English
Number of copies required by the receiving Office:	1
Does the receiving Office accept the filing of international applications with requests in PCT-EASY format?[1]	Yes
Competent International Searching Authority:	United States Patent and Trademark Office or European Patent Office[2]
Competent International Preliminary Examining Authority:	United States Patent and Trademark Office or European Patent Office[2,3]
Fees payable to the receiving Office:[4]	Currency: US dollar (USD)
Transmittal fee:	USD 240
International fee:	
Basic fee:	USD 407
Fee per sheet in excess of 30:	USD 9
Designation fee:	USD 88
PCT-EASY fee reduction:[1]	USD 125
Search fee:	See Annex D (United States Patent and Trademark Office or European Patent Office)
Fee for priority document (PCT Rule 17.1(b)):	USD 15
Is an agent required by the receiving Office?	No
Who can act as agent?	Patent attorneys and patent agents registered to practice before the Office. A list of registered patent attorneys and agents may be obtained from: Superintendent of Documents, U.S. Government Printing Office, Washington, D.C. 20402, and on the Internet at http://www.uspto.gov/web/offices/dcom/olia/oed/roster/index.html.

---

[1] Where the request is filed in PCT-EASY format together with a PCT-EASY diskette and the receiving Office accepts such filings (see *PCT Gazette* No. 51/1998, pages 17330 and 17332), the total amount of the international fee is reduced.

[2] The availability of the European Patent Office as an International Searching Authority and/or International Preliminary Examining Authority is restricted. For details, see Annexes D(EP), E(EP) and *PCT Gazette* No. 52/2001, page 24248.

[3] The European Patent Office is competent only if the international search is or has been performed by that Office.

[4] The amounts of these fees change periodically. The receiving Office or the *Official Gazette* of the United States Patent and Trademark Office should be consulted for the applicable amounts.

(1 March 2002)

Form 3 – US Patent and Trademark Office

C. Time frame of a PCT application

Let us now have a brief look at the PCT time frame, i.e. at the periods, dates and terms in the course of a PCT application. Once the PCT application has been filed, there are three crucial terms which have to be carefully surveyed: The first term is the term for filing a request for International Preliminary Examination ("Demand") and will expire 19 months from the priority date (i.e. in practice about 7 months after the PCT filing date). If a request for International Preliminary Examination is not filed in time, the next crucial date is the entry of the National/Regional phases either 20/21 months after the priority date (i.e. in practice 8/9 months after the PCT filing date) or – since April 1, 2002 and if applicable to the particular designated state – 30/31 months after the priority date (i.e. in practice 18/19 months after the PCT filing date) In some states this entry of the National/Regional phases is only extended to 30 or 31 months if a request for International Preliminary Examination has been filed in time, namely when "*Chapter II*" has been entered before expiry of the 19 months term. Those Regional and National offices having the extended term of 21 and 31 months, respectively, after the priority date or which automatically have the 30/31 months period from the priority date for entering the Regional/National Phase without the necessity of filing a Demand within the 19 months term may be taken from Table 7.

PCT-TERMS

PCT-Application at the End of the Priority Year

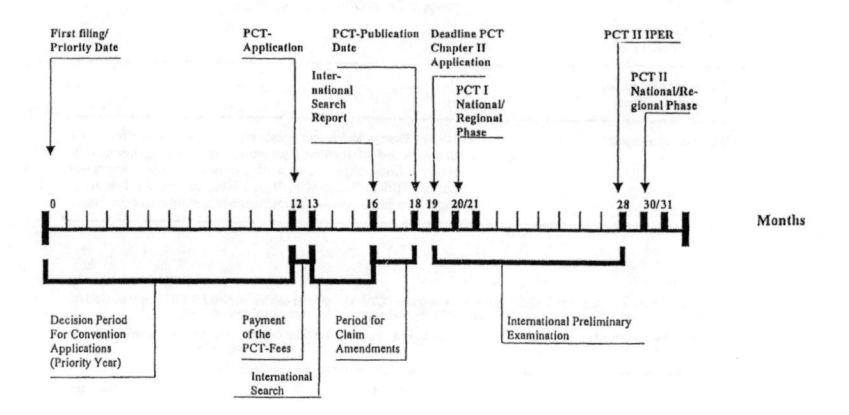

Diagram 2 – PCT-Terms

The PCT and the Enforcement of Patents in Europe 213

DO/EO	Chapter I	Chapter II	DO/EO	Chapter I	Chapter II	DO/EO	Chapter I	Chapter II
Regional Offices			National Offices [continued]			National Offices [continued]		
AP	21	31	ES	20	30	MW	20	30
EA	21	31	FI	20	30	MX	20	30
AP	21	31	GB	21	31	MZ	21	31
OA	20	30	GD	20	30	NO	20	30
National Offices			GE	21	31	NZ	21	31
AE	20	30	GH	20	30	PL	20	30
AG	20	30	GM	21	31	PT	20	30
AL	21	31	HR	21	31	RO	20	30
AM	21	31	HU	21	31	RU	21	31
AT	20	30	ID	21	31	SD	20	30
AU	21	31	IL	20	30	SE	20	30
AZ	21	31	IN	21	31	SG	20	30
BA	21	31	IS	20	30	SI	21	31
BB	20	30	JP	20	30	SK	21	30
BG	21	31	KE	20	30	SL	21	31
BR	20	30	KG	21	31	TJ	21	31
BY	21	31	KP	20	30	TM	21	31
BZ	21	31	KR	20	30	TR	20 (23)	30 (33)
CA	20 (32)	30 (42)	KZ	21 (23)	31 (33)	TT	21	31
CH+LI	20	30	LC	20	30	TZ	21	31
CN	20	30	LK	20	30	UA	21	31
CO	20	30	LR	21	31	UG	21	31
CR	21	31	LS	21	31	US	20	30
CU	20	30	LT	21	31	UZ	21	31
CZ	21	30	LU	20	30	VN	21	31
DE	20	30	LV	21	31	YU	20 (21)	30 (31)
DK	20	30	MA	21	31	ZA	21	31
DM	20	30	MD	21	31	ZW	21	31
DZ	21	31	MG	20	30			
EC	20	30	MK	21	31			
EE	20	30	MN	21	31			

Table 7 – PCT-Time Limits

Time Limits for entering National/Regional Phase under PCT Chapters I and II (in months from priority date, or from international filing date if there is no Priority claim) - situation as of March 2002.

You may retrieve a lot of useful information from the WIPO's Internet site **www.wipo.int**, the entry page of which is shown in the following.

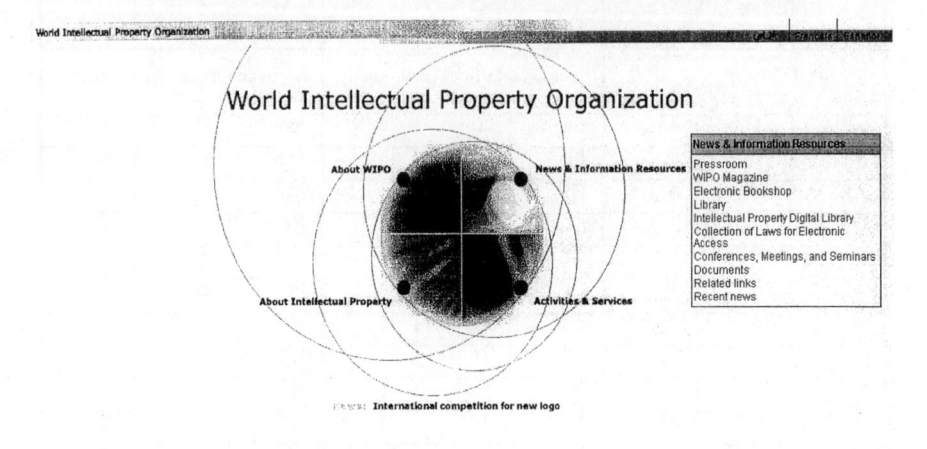

Picture 1 – WIPO-Site

II. Filing of PCT Patent Applications

A. Claim Drafting under the PCT and the EPC

A granted patent confers an exclusive right upon the patentee and reserves various commercial advantages. Hence, particular attention should be paid when drafting patent claims since they define the scope of protection granted by the exclusive right. Also, care should be taken to obtain smoothly a complete search report and to avoid unnecessary formal problems due to an inexpedient approach of the wording.

In order to obtain a more detailed insight into and an improved understanding of patent claims in their structure under the PCT and the European patent system, we would like to summarize at first some legal provisions relating to patent claims and comment on the situation thereafter.

As is well known, the PCT and the EPC are very much interrelated with each other, and a great deal of practical PCT work, in particular searches and preliminary examination, is carried out by the European Patent Office. Moreover, many PCT applications are later prosecuted as EPC applications. Therefore, in the following, particular attention is paid to the EPC provisions which are also applied by the EPO in the PCT procedure.

B. Case Papers

According to PCT and EPC law, a patent application must contain the following components:

- Request for grant
- Description
- One or more patent claims
- Drawings, if any.

In the following, we shall focus on the claims as the "heart" of every patent application, in particular under the aspect of unity.

C. Unity of Invention

The term "unity of invention" is an essential administrative regulation in the PCT and European patent system which must be taken into account when drafting patent claims. The aim is always the same, namely to avoid separate inventions being covered by one and the same patent.

Under European law, the legal provisions are very detailed. The principle is defined in Article 82 EPC:

> "The European patent application shall relate to one invention only or to a group of inventions so linked as to form a single general inventive concept."

Further details are set forth in Rule 30 EPC as follows:

> (1) Where a group of inventions is claimed in one and the same European patent application, the requirement of unity of invention referred to in Article 82 EPC shall be fulfilled only when there is a technical relationship among those inventions involving one or more of the same or corresponding special technical features. The expression "special technical features" shall mean those features which define a contribution which each of the claimed inventions considered as a whole makes over the prior art.

> (2) The determination whether a group of inventions is so linked as to form a single general inventive concept shall be made without regard to whether the inventions are claimed in separate claims or as alternatives within a single claim.

With respect to the PCT search, in particular when carried out by the European Patent Office, it is not appropriate to use claims in the U.S. format with several independent claims approaching the invention from various sides with partly over-

- Incomplete search report
- Invitation to pay further search fee(s)
- Delay in prosecution and time pressure
- with respect to the 20 month period.

Rather, the following is highly recommended to avoid unity objections:

- Only <u>one</u> independent claim per category (product, method and apparatus, where appropriate)
- Reasonable number of <u>sub-claims</u> for each independent claim using <u>multiple dependencies</u>. (Reference signs in all the claims support the understanding and are highly recommended).

Such claims will result in one complete search report relating to all claims without additional search fees. The applicant has still all options to modify the claims during prosecution.

III. The International Search Report

A. Amendments to the Application

As the questions of amendments to the International Application are always a big issue, the following table shows various possibilities and some restrictions.

	AMENDMENTS TO THE INTERNATIONAL APPLICATION		
	INTERNATIONAL PHASE		NATIONAL PHASE
Abbreviations: IPEA=International Preliminary Examination Authority IPER=International Preliminary Examination Report	Amendments under PCT Chapter I (only if an international search report has been established) PCT Article 19 and Rule 46	Amendments under PCT Chapter II (only if an applicant files a demand for international preliminary examination) PCT Article 34 and Rules 53.9 and 66	Amendments upon entering the National Phase PCT Articles 28 and 41 and Rules 52 and 78
Which part(s) of the international application may be amended ?	Claims only	Claims, descriptions and drawings	Claims, description and drawings. Different amendments are possible for different designated/elected Offices
Where must the amendments be filed ?	With the international Bureau.	With the IPEA	With the designated/elected Offices

When must the amendments be filed?	Within two months from the date of transmittal of the international search report, or 16 months from the priority date, or before the technical preparations for the international publication have been completed, whichever time limit expires/event occurs later.	May be filed with the demand or during international preliminary examination. They should, however, be filed before the IPEA begins to draw up the IPER.	May be filed within one month from the date of fulfillment of the requirements for entry into the national phase. Later time limits may apply – see relevant National Chapter in the *PCT Applicant's Guide*, Vol. II.
In what language must the amendments be filed?	In the language of the international application, if that language is Chinese, English, French, German, Japanese, Russian or Spanish, or in English where the international applications was filed in another language.		Where the designated/elected Office requires a translation of the international application, the amendments must be in the language of the translation.
What is the allowable scope of the amendments?	Amendments must not go beyond the disclosure in the international application as filed. Although this requirement is not directly enforceable during the international phase, failure to comply may have adverse consequences during international preliminary examination and in the national phase.	Amendments must not go beyond the disclosure in the international application as filed. Although this requirement is not directly enforceable during the international phase, if any amendment does not comply, the IPEA will make comments in the written opinion and the IPER, and the IPER will be established as if the amendment had not been made.	Amendments must stay behind the disclosure in the international application as filed unless the national law of the designated/elected State permits them to go beyond that disclosure – see National Chapters in the PCT *Applicant's Guide*, Vol. II.
Where do the amendments have effect?	In all designated/elected Offices.	In all elected Offices.	In those designated/elected Offices with which they are filed.
For what procedures do the amendments serve as a basis?	For examination by the IPEA (unless reversed or superseded) and for examination by the designated/elected Offices in the national phase (unless superseded by later amendments).	For examination by the IPEA, and, in the national phase, by elected Offices (unless superseded by later amendments).	For examination by the designated/elected Offices in the national phase.

May amendments be made more than once ?	No.	Yes, depending on when the IPER is established. But note that amendments need not be taken into account by the IPEA if they are received after it has begun to draw up a written opinion or the IPER.	Depends on the national law.
Are the amendments confidential ?	They are confidential before international publication. After publication of the international application, amendments published by the International Bureau as part of the Pamphlet are no longer confidential.	They are confidential until transmittal of the IPER to the elected Offices. Once the IPER has been transmitted to the elected Offices, any amendments which form part of the annexes to the IPER may be made available by any elected Office whose national law so permits.	Depends on national law.

Table 8 Amendments to the International Application

According to Article 19 PCT, the applicant has - upon receipt of the International Search Report - once the opportunity to amend the claims of the International Application (there will be another opportunity for amendments to the claims, description and drawings during the International Preliminary Examination Procedure according to Article 34 PCT). Amendments to the claims could be advisable if the prior art cited in the International Search Report is so close to the application as claimed that it is desirable to enter either the International Preliminary Examination Procedure or the national/regional examination procedure with fresh claims in order to cut down the time needed for substantive examination.

1. What parts of the International Application may be amended?

As a reaction to the International Search Report, only the claims may be amended once (Article 19 PCT).

Remark: During the International Preliminary Examination and upon entry into the national or regional phase, all parts of the International Application may be amended.

2. Until when may the International Application be amended?

Within 2 months from the date of transmittal of the International Search Report or within 16 months from the priority date, whichever time limit expires later. It should be noted, however, that the amendments will also be considered as having been received in time if they are received by the International Bureau even after the expiration of the applicable time limit, but before the completion of the technical preparations for the International Publication (15 days).

3. Where to file the amendments?

The amendments may only be filed directly with the

> International Bureau of WIPO
> 34, Chemin des Colombettes,
> CH-1211 Geneva 20,
> Switzerland

and not with the Receiving Office or the International Searching Authority (Rule 46.2 PCT).

Remark: Where a demand for International Preliminary Examination has been filed or is filed, the applicant must preferably, at the same time of filing the amendments with the International Bureau, also file a copy of such amendments with the International Preliminary Examining Authority (Rule 62.2(a), first sentence PCT).

4. How to file the amendments?

Either by cancelling one or more claims entirely, by adding one or more new claims or by amending the text of one or more of the claims as filed. A replacement sheet must be submitted for each sheet of the claims which, on account of an amendment or amendments, differs from the sheet as originally filed. All the claims appearing on a replacement sheet must be numbered in Arabic numerals. Where a claim is cancelled, no renumbering of the other claims is required. In all cases where claims are renumbered, they must be renumbered consecutively. The US system of cancelling e.g. claims 1 to 12 and filing new claims 13 to 24 it not applicable.

The amendments must be made in the language in which the International Application is to be published.

5. What documents must or may accompany the amendments?

The amendments must be submitted with an accompanying letter which will not be published with the International Application. This accompanying letter should not be confused with the "Statement under Article 19(1)" which will be explained hereinafter. The accompanying letter just serves to clarify in a more formal way which claims remain unchanged, which claims are being cancelled, which claims are new, and which claim shall replace which claim.

The Statement under Article 19(1) PCT and according to Rule 46.4 PCT may be added and should explain the amendments and indicate any impacts that such amendments might have on the description and the drawings. This Statement will be published with the International Application and the amended claims. It must be in the language in which the International Application is to be published and must not exceed 500 words.

6. **Consequence with regard to the translation of the International Application upon entry into the national/regional phase.**

Article 19 PCT

Amendment of the Claims before the International Bureau

(1) The applicant shall, after having received the international search report, be entitled to one opportunity to amned the claims of the international application by filing amendments with the International Bureau within the prescribed time limit. He may, at the same time, file a brief statement, as provided in the Regulations, explaining the amendments and indication any impact that such amendments might have on the desciption and the drawings.

(2) The amendments shall not go beyond the disclosure in the international application as filed.

(3) If the national law of any designated State permits amendments to go beyond the said disclosure, failure to comply with paragraph (2) shall have no consequence in that State.

Statute 1 – Article 19 PCT

B. Fee Reductions

The following table shows a breakdown of the official fees for an International Application including the International Search, the International Preliminary Examination, the subsequent Examination and the supplementary search at the European Patent Office.

Case	(a)	(b)	(c)	(d)	(e)
Fee in USD (US-Dollars)	EPO=ISA EPO=IPEA	EPO=ISA JPO=IPEA	EPO=ISA USPTO=IPEA	JPO=ISA JPO=IPEA	USPTO=ISA USPTO=IPEA
Intern. Search fee	866.00	866.00	866.00	610.00	450.00[1] (700.00)[2]
Prelim. Exam. fee	1,402.00	240.00	750.00	240.00	490.00
Exam. fee	715.00	1,430.00	1,430.00	1,430.00	1,430.00
Suppl. Search fee	-	-	-	552.00[3]	552.00[3]
TOTAL	2,983.00	2,536.00	3,046.00	2,832.00	2,922.00 (3,172.00)

1   Payable when a corresponding prior US national application has been filed and the basic filing fee for that application has been paid.
2   Regular fee
3   This fee is already reduced by 20 %; the regular fee would have been 690.00

Table 9 – Fee Reductions

Case a) denotes entering the Regional Phase at the EPO under the condition that the International Search and the International Preliminary Examination were carried out by the EPO; case b) denotes entering the Regional Phase at the EPO under the condition that the International Search was carried out by the EPO, but the International Preliminary Examination by the JPO; case c) denotes entering the Regional Phase at the EPO under the condition that the International Search was carried out by the EPO, but the International Preliminary Examination by the USPTO; case d) denotes entering the Regional Phase at the EPO under the condition that the International Search and the International Preliminary Examination were carried out by the JPO; case e) denotes entering the Regional Phase at the EPO under the condition that the International Search and the International Preliminary Examination were carried out by the USPTO.

Remark: International Preliminary Examination at the EPO presupposes that the EPO also performed the International Search.

Fee reductions are applicable in all five cases, but in a different way: Article 157(2)(a) provides that a Supplementary European Search Report shall be drawn up in respect of all International Applications. However, Article 157(3) says that the Administrative Council of the EPO may decide under what conditions and to what extent the EPO can waive the necessity of a Supplementary European Search Report or the Supplementary Search fee is to be reduced. This has been done in terms of the Japanese Patent Office and the US Patent and Trademark Office in case (d) and (e), where the Supplementary Search fee is reduced by 20%. In cases (a), (b) and (c) however, where the EPO has drawn up the International Search Report, no Supplementary Search fee is due. In case (a), where the EPO has conducted the International Preliminary Examination and has drawn up an International Search Report, the examination fee upon entering the Regional Phase is being reduced by 50 %. This cost advantage and others will be addressed again in chapter IV dealing with the International Preliminary Examination Procedure.

Remark: Since March 1, 2002, the EPO does, however, not act as ISA in respect of any PCT application filed on or after March 1, 2002 by a national or resident of the USA where such application contains one or more claims relating to certain fields of biotechnology or business methods. The EPO does also not act as IPEA in respect of the afore-mentioned applications and further not in respect of those applications relating to certain fields of telecommunication. The initial duration of these limitations shall be tree years. More limitations cannot be excluded to happen.

C. Scope of Prior Art considered in the International Search Report

The International Searching Authority shall endeavor to discover as much of the relevant prior art as its facilities permit, and shall, in any case, consider the documentation specified in the PCT Regulations (Article 15(4) PCT). This is the official definition of a so-called "minimum documentation", which shall consist of the prior art documents as shown in the following.

The minimum documentation forming the basis of an International Search shall consist of:

- the patents issued in and after the year 1920 by France, the former *Reichspatentamt* of Germany, Japan, the former Soviet Union, Switzerland (in French and German languages only), the United Kingdom and the United States of America;
- the patents issued by the Federal Republic of Germany;
- the patent applications published in and after the year 1920 in the aforementioned countries;
- the inventors certificates issued by the former Soviet Union;
- the utility certificates issued by, and the published applications for utility certificates of France;
- such patents issued by, and such patent applications published in any other country after the year 1920 as are in the English, French or Spanish language and in which no priority is claimed, provided that the national office of the interested country does sort out these documents and place them at the disposal of the International Searching Authorities;
- the published International (PCT) applications, the published regional applications for patents and inventors certificates, and the published regional patents and inventors certificates;
- selected items of non-patent literature.

Article 157 EPC
International Search Report

(1) Without prejudice to the provisions of paragraphs 2 to 4, the international search report under Article 18 of the Cooperation Treaty or any declaration under Article 17, paragraph 2(a), of that Treaty and their publication under Article 21 of that Treaty shall take place of the European search report and the mention of its publication in the European Patent Bulletin.

(2) Subject to the decisions of the Administrative Council referred to in paragraph 3:

    (a) a supplementary European search report shall be drawn up in respect of all international applications;

(b) the applicant shall pay the search fee, which shall be paid at the same time as the national fee provided for in Article 22, paragraph 1, or Article 39, paragraph 1, of the Cooperation Treaty. If the search fee is not paid in due time the application shall be deemed to be withdrawn.

(3) The Administrative Council may decide under what conditions and to what extent:

(a) *the supplementary European search report is to be dispensed with;

(b) **the search fee is to be reduced.

(4) The Administrative Council may at any time rescind the decisions taken pursuant to paragraph 3.

* See the decisions of the Administrative Council of 21.12.1978, 17.05.1979 and 09.06.1995 on cases where the Supplementary European Search Report is to be dispensed with (OJ EPO 1979, 4, 50 and 248; 1995, 511)
** See the decisions of the Administrative Council of 14.09.1979, 11.12.1980 and 09.12.1993 on the reduction of the Search fee for the Supplementary European Search Report (OJ EPO 1979, 368; 1981, 5; 1994, 6)

Statute 2 – Article 157 EPC

IV. The International Preliminary Examination Procedure

A. Advantages of International Preliminary Examination

When the end of the priority year approaches, the question is: In which countries shall foreign applications be filed? In many cases, however, a final selection is not possible at this early stage. A PCT application already grants a minimum postponement of the entry of the National Phases for 8 or 9 months, at the majority of national offices and at all regional offices even for 18 or 19 months. But going "Chapter II", i.e. applying for International Preliminary Examination, may even have more advantages.

There are basically three major arguments in favor of International Preliminary Examination:

(a) Getting more time for the decision as to where national or regional phases should be entered;

(b) Getting a preliminary and non-binding opinion on the questions whether the claimed invention appears to be novel, to involve an inventive step (i.e. to be non-obvious), and to be industrially applicable; and

(c) Further amendments of the application are possible.

Advantage (a) is as of April 1, 2002 only effective for a minority of countries since the majority and all regional offices already grant a postponement of the due date for the National/Regional Phase until 30/31 months from the priority date, irrespective of the condition that International Preliminary Examination ("Chapter II") has been entered by filing a Demand before the expiry of 19 months from the priority date. However, in said minority of countries (those in Table 7 which have 20 or 21 months in the Chapter I column), only filing said Demand and electing at least one of the designated states will extend the term for entry of the National Phase - and this is what usually incurs a lot of costs - by further 10 months.

Advantage (b), i.e. the preliminary and non-binding opinion by the International Preliminary Examining Authority (IPEA), has two impacts: first of all, it can serve as a basis for the decision, where the national or regional phases should be entered because it enables the applicant to make an assessment of the chances to get a patent granted. Secondly, since the criteria on which the International Preliminary Examination is based correspond to internationally accepted criteria for patentability, the International Preliminary Examination Report (IPER) will of course influence the national/regional examiners who will be provided with the IPER by the International Bureau.

Advantage (c) is apparent from Table 8 - Amendments to the International Application mentioned above. Article 34 PCT governs the International Preliminary Examination Procedure wherein the applicant may amend the claims, the description and the drawings as often as deemed necessary in communication with the examiner at the International Preliminary Examining Authority. The time provided for this interaction between the applicant and the examiner is, as a rule, not less than 6 months and the final date by which the International Preliminary Examination Report must be established, is always given on the first page of any office action in the course of these proceedings.

H Demand *filled-in sample* H

The demand must be filed directly with the competent International Preliminary Examining Authority or, if two or more Authorities are competent, with the one chosen by the applicant. The full name or two-letter code of that Authority may be indicated by the applicant on the line below:

IPEA/ US

PCT

DEMAND

under Article 31 of the Patent Cooperation Treaty:
The undersigned requests that the international application specified below be the subject of international preliminary examination according to the Patent Cooperation Treaty and hereby elects all eligible States (except where otherwise indicated).

CHAPTER II

For International Preliminary Examining Authority use only

Identification of IPEA	Date of receipt of DEMAND

Box No. I IDENTIFICATION OF THE INTERNATIONAL APPLICATION		Applicant's or agent's file reference 480-PCT-1
International application No. PCT/US00/65432	International filing date *(day/month/year)* 7 July 2000 (07.07.00)	(Earliest) Priority date *(day/month/year)* 15 July 1999 (15.07.99)

Title of invention
WEAVING MACHINE

Box No. II APPLICANT(S)

Name and address: *(Family name followed by given name; for a legal entity, full official designation. The address must include postal code and name of country.)*	
WALSH AND COMPANY 2500 Virginia Avenue, N.W. Washington, D.C. 20037-0456 United States of America	Telephone No.: (202) 557-3054 Facsimile No.: (202) 557-3100 Teleprinter No.:

State *(that is, country)* of nationality: US	State *(that is, country)* of residence: US

Name and address: *(Family name followed by given name; for a legal entity, full official designation. The address must include postal code and name of country.)*

JONES, Mary
1600 South Eads Street
Arlington, Virginia 22202
United States of America

State *(that is, country)* of nationality: US	State *(that is, country)* of residence: US

Name and address: *(Family name followed by given name; for a legal entity, full official designation. The address must include postal code and name of country.)*

RUDD, David
54 Harfield Street
Wollongong, NSW 2500
Australia

State *(that is, country)* of nationality: AU	State *(that is, country)* of residence: AU

[X] Further applicants are indicated on a continuation sheet.

Form PCT/IPEA/401 (first sheet) (July 1998; reprint July 2000)   *See Notes to the demand form*

(July 2000)

Form 4 – PCT-Demand, Page 1

Sheet No. 2	International application No. PCT/US00/65432

Continuation of Box No. II   APPLICANT(S)

If none of the following sub-boxes is used, this sheet should not be included in the demand.

Name and address: *(Family name followed by given name; for a legal entity, full official designation. The address must include postal code and name of country.)*

SILVER, James
12 Oxford Street
Richmond, Ontario K0A 2Z0
Canada

State *(that is, country)* of nationality: CA	State *(that is, country)* of residence: CA

Name and address: *(Family name followed by given name; for a legal entity, full official designation. The address must include postal code and name of country.)*

CRUZ, Jose
7B J.P. Rizal Street
Project 4, Quezon City 1109
Philippines

State *(that is, country)* of nationality: PH	State *(that is, country)* of residence: PH

Name and address: *(Family name followed by given name; for a legal entity, full official designation. The address must include postal code and name of country.)*

State *(that is, country)* of nationality:	State *(that is, country)* of residence:

Name and address: *(Family name followed by given name; for a legal entity, full official designation. The address must include postal code and name of country.)*

State *(that is, country)* of nationality:	State *(that is, country)* of residence:

☐ Further applicants are indicated on another continuation sheet.

Form PCT/IPEA/401 (continuation sheet) (July 1998; reprint July 2000)   *See Notes to the demand form*

Form 5 – PCT-Demand, Page 2

	Sheet No. 3.	International application No. PCT/US00/65432

Box No. III AGENT OR COMMON REPRESENTATIVE; OR ADDRESS FOR CORRESPONDENCE

The following person is [X] agent [ ] common representative

and [X] has been appointed earlier and represents the applicant(s) also for international preliminary examination.

[ ] is hereby appointed and any earlier appointment of (an) agent(s)/common representative is hereby revoked.

[ ] is hereby appointed, specifically for the procedure before the International Preliminary Examining Authority, in addition to the agent(s)/common representative appointed earlier.

Name and address: *(Family name followed by given name; for a legal entity, full official designation. The address must include postal code and name of country.)*

SMITH, John J.; HILLARD, Steven; MEYER, David
220 Jefferson Avenue
Arlington, Virginia 22202-0234
United States of America

Telephone No.: (703) 545-2212

Facsimile No.: (703) 545-2200

Teleprinter No.:

[ ] **Address for correspondence:** Mark this check-box where no agent or common representative is/has been appointed and the space above is used instead to indicate a special address to which correspondence should be sent.

Box No. IV BASIS FOR INTERNATIONAL PRELIMINARY EXAMINATION

Statement concerning amendments:*

1. The applicant wishes the international preliminary examination to start on the basis of:

    [ ] the international application as originally filed

    the description [ ] as originally filed
    [X] as amended under Article 34

    the claims [ ] as originally filed
    [ ] as amended under Article 19 (together with any accompanying statement)
    [X] as amended under Article 34

    the drawings [X] as originally filed
    [ ] as amended under Article 34

2. [ ] The applicant wishes any amendment to the claims under Article 19 to be considered as reversed.

3. [ ] The applicant wishes the start of the international preliminary examination **to be postponed** until the expiration of 20 months from the priority date unless the International Preliminary Examining Authority receives a copy of any amendments made under Article 19 or a notice from the applicant that he does not wish to make such amendments (Rule 69.1(d)). *(This check-box may be marked only where the time limit under Article 19 has not yet expired.)*

* Where no check-box is marked, international preliminary examination will start on the basis of the international application as originally filed or, where a copy of amendments to the claims under Article 19 and/or amendments of the international application under Article 34 are received by the International Preliminary Examining Authority before it has begun to draw up a written opinion or the international preliminary examination report, as so amended.

Language for the purposes of international preliminary examination: .... English ....

[X] which is the language in which the international application was filed.

[ ] which is the language of a translation furnished for the purposes of international search.

[ ] which is the language of publication of the international application.

[ ] which is the language of the translation (to be) furnished for the purposes of international preliminary examination.

Box No. V ELECTION OF STATES

The applicant hereby elects **all eligible States** *(that is, all States which have been designated and which are bound by Chapter II of the PCT)*

excluding the following States which the applicant wishes **not to elect**:

Form PCT/IPEA/401 (second sheet) (July 1998; reprint July 2000)   *See Notes to the demand form*

(July 2000)

Form 6 – PCT-Demand, Page 3

Sheet No. 4.

International application No. PCT/US00/65432

Box No. VI CHECK LIST

The demand is accompanied by the following elements, in the language referred to in Box No. IV, for the purposes of international preliminary examination:

For International Preliminary Examining Authority use only

				received	not received
1. translation of international application	:		sheets	☐	☐
2. amendments under Article 34	:	3	sheets	☐	☐
3. copy (or, where required, translation) of amendments under Article 19	:		sheets	☐	☐
4. copy (or, where required, translation) of statement under Article 19	:		sheets	☐	☐
5. letter	:	4	sheets	☐	☐
6. other (specify)	:		sheets	☐	☐

The demand is also accompanied by the item(s) marked below:

1. [X] fee calculation sheet
2. ☐ separate signed power of attorney
3. ☐ copy of general power of attorney; reference number, if any:
4. ☐ statement explaining lack of signature
5. ☐ nucleotide and or amino acid sequence listing in computer readable form
6. ☐ other (specify):

Box No. VII SIGNATURE OF APPLICANT, AGENT OR COMMON REPRESENTATIVE

Next to each signature, indicate the name of the person signing and the capacity in which the person signs (if such capacity is not obvious from reading the demand).

John Smith
John J. Smith

For International Preliminary Examining Authority use only

1. Date of actual receipt of DEMAND:

2. Adjusted date of receipt of demand due to CORRECTIONS under Rule 60.1(b):

3. ☐ The date of receipt of the demand is AFTER the expiration of 19 months from the priority date and item 4 or 5, below, does not apply. ☐ The applicant has been informed accordingly.

4. ☐ The date of receipt of the demand is WITHIN the period of 19 months from the priority date as extended by virtue of Rule 80.5.

5. ☐ Although the date of receipt of the demand is after the expiration of 19 months from the priority date, the delay in arrival is EXCUSED pursuant to Rule 82.

For International Bureau use only

Demand received from IPEA on:

Form PCT/IPEA/401 (last sheet) (July 1998; reprint July 2000)   See Notes to the demand form

PCT

FEE CALCULATION SHEET

Annex to the Demand for international preliminary examination

International application No.	PCT/US00/65432
Applicant's or agent's file reference	480-PCT-1
Applicant	WALSH AND COMPANY, et al.

For International Preliminary Examining Authority use only

Date stamp of the IPEA

CHAPTER II

Calculation of prescribed fees

1. Preliminary examination fee .... **490** P

2. Handling fee *(Applicants from certain States are entitled to a reduction of 75% of the handling fee. Where the applicant is (or all applicants are) so entitled, the amount to be entered at H is 25% of the handling fee.)* .... **153** H

3. Total of prescribed fees
   Add the amounts entered at P and H
   and enter total in the TOTAL box .... **USD 643** TOTAL

Mode of Payment

[X] authorization to charge deposit account with the IPEA (see below)
[ ] cheque
[ ] postal money order
[ ] bank draft
[ ] cash
[ ] revenue stamps
[ ] coupons
[ ] other *(specify)*:

Deposit Account Authorization *(this mode of payment may not be available at all IPEAs)*

The IPEA/ **US** [X] is hereby authorized to charge the total fees indicated above to my deposit account.

[X] *(this check-box may be marked only if the conditions for deposit accounts of the IPEA so permit)* is hereby authorized to charge any deficiency or credit any overpayment in the total fees indicated above to my deposit account.

12-3456	10 January 2001	*John Smith*
Deposit Account Number	Date *(day/month/year)*	Signature John J. Smith

Form PCT/IPEA/401 (Annex) (July 1998; reprint July 2000) *See Notes to the fee calculation sheet*

(July 2000)

Form 8 – PCT-Demand, Page 5

PATENT COOPERATION TREATY

From the
INTERNATIONAL PRELIMINARY EXAMINING AUTHORITY

To:

PCT

WRITTEN OPINION

(PCT Rule 66)

Date of Mailing (day/month/year)	07 FEB 1997

Applicant's or agent's file reference	REPLY DUE	within TWO months from the above date of mailing

International application No.	International filing date (day/month/year) 08 MAY 1996	Priority date (day/month/year) 17 MAY 1995

International Patent Classification (IPC) or both national classification and IPC
IPC(6): G06F 13/00, 13/14 and US Cl.: 395/200.10; 370/67; 340/825.06

Applicant

1. This written opinion is the **first** (first, etc.) drawn by this International Preliminary Examining Authority.

2. This opinion contains indications relating to the following items:

   - I [X] Basis of the opinion
   - II [ ] Priority
   - III [ ] Non-establishment of opinion with regard to novelty, inventive step or industrial applicability
   - IV [ ] Lack of unity of invention
   - V [X] Reasoned statement under Rule 66.2(a)(ii) with regard to novelty, inventive step or industrial applicability; citations and explanations supporting such statement
   - VI [ ] Certain documents cited
   - VII [ ] Certain defects in the international application
   - VIII [ ] Certain observations on the international application

3. The applicant is hereby invited to reply to this opinion.

   When? See the time limit indicated above. ~~The applicant may, before the expiration of that time limit, request this Authority to grant an extension., see Rule 66.2(d).~~

   How? By submitting a written reply, accompanied, where appropriate, by amendments, according to Rule 66.3. For the form and the language of the amendments, see Rules 66.8 and 66.9.

   Also
   ir an additional opportunity to submit amendments, see Rule 66.4.
   ir the examiner's obligation to consider amendments and/or arguments, see Rule 66.4 bis.
   ir an informal communication with the examiner, see Rule 66.6.

   If no reply is filed, the international preliminary examination report will be established on the basis of this opinion.

4. The final date by which the international preliminary examination report must be established according to Rule 69.2 is: **17 SEPTEMBER 1997**

Name and mailing address of the IPEA/US	Authorized officer
Commissioner of Patents and Trademarks Box PCT Washington, D.C. 20231	ALPESH M. SHAH
Facsimile No. (703) 305-3230	Telephone No. (703) 305-9698

Form PCT/IPEA/408 (cover sheet) (January 1994)*

Form 9 – PCT-WrittenOpinion

B. The EURO-PCT-Way: A valuable Choice

Even more advantages can be achieved by filing a request for International Preliminary Examination ("Demand") if the EPO is elected to be the International Preliminary Examination Authority (case (a) of table 9 – "Breakdown of Official Fees"). It is highly recommendable to do so because extraordinarily good results may be achieved going the EURO-PCT-way with International Preliminary Examination at the EPO. Of course, this way is open to Japanese applicants, as is apparent from Form 2, field "Competent International Preliminary Examination Authority" and. With the current exclusion of certain technical fields, also to US applicants, as is apparent from Form 3 (again field " Competent International Preliminary Examination Authority"). The Demand must be filed directly with the competent IPEA or, if two or more authorities are competent, with the one chosen by the applicant. This choice can be made on the first page of the Chapter II demand by inserting "EP" behind "IPEA/" (see Form 4 to Form 8 "PCT-Demand, Page 1 - 5"). Approximately 3 months after filing said Demand, the elected authority will issue a first office action ("Written Opinion") in the International Preliminary Examination Proceedings prepared by the regular examiner who also did the search for the ISR. On the first page of this Written Opinion, the applicant is notified the date by which the IPER will have to be established. Since January 3, 2002, the EPO provides for either a "rationalized" or a "detailed" International Preliminary Examination Procedure as follows:

1. Rationalized Procedure

In the rationalized procedure, the International Search Report ("ISR") will serve as a basis for the International Preliminary Examination, without involving the examiner again unless the applicant filed or files amendments and/or arguments under Article 19 PCT (upon receipt of the ISR) or under Article 34 (2)(b) PCT (during Preliminary Examination) and expressly requests "detailed" procedure, all of said reactions by the applicant leading directly to a detailed Preliminary Examination (see b) hereinafter). Hence, the applicant is in a position to determine whether the ISR directly becomes the basis of the later International Preliminary Examination Report ("IPER") or whether a more detailed substantive examination – still preliminary – is made.

If the ISR contains at least one "X" or "Y" document and, again, since we are still in the rationalized procedure, if the applicant has neither filed amendments nor a request for "detailed" examination, the ISR becomes the basis for a negative Written Opinion without involving the substantive examiner again. If this Rationalized Written Opinion prompts no response by the applicant (Rule 66.3 PCT), the EPO will draw up the IPER with the same content as that Written Opinion and will refund 2/3 of the Preliminary Examination fee at the same time as it transmits the IPER.

If the ISR contains only "A" documents and, again, if the applicant has neither filed amendments nor a request for "detailed" examination, the ISR becomes the basis for a positive IPER without involving the substantive examiner again and the EPO will refund 2/3 of the Preliminary Examination fee at the same time as it transmits the IPER.

As to the fees or refunds incurred with the Rationalized procedure, it should be noted that the advantage of the 50% reduction of the examination fee upon entry of the Regional Phase cannot be achieved since this reduction does not apply in connection with rationalized Preliminary Examination.

It seems to be obvious that "Rationalized" Preliminary Examination is advisable if the ISR is either very positive for the applicant, i.e. contains merely "A" documents, or is very bad, i.e. contains such "X" or "Y" documents which are in fact beating and which cannot be circumvented by amending the claims. However, the latter case is pretty rare and thus, the alternative "detailed" Preliminary Examination is a valuable option for those cases where the "X" or "Y" documents may be countered by amendments or if the applicant is of the opinion that these documents received their classification unjustified. On the other hand, if there are only "A" documents cited in the ISR, it does not make sense any more to enter detailed preliminary examination (by filing an expressed request with the EPO) although the 50% reduction of the examination fee upon entry of the Regional Phase will be lost. Namely, the 2/3 refund of the International Preliminary Examination fee is a better deal than the 50 % reduction.

2. Detailed Procedure

In the detailed procedure, that is if the applicant either filed amendments and/or arguments under Article 19 PCT (upon receipt of the ISR) or under Article 34 (2)(b) PCT (during Preliminary Examination) and expressly requests "detailed" procedure (either when filing the Demand or later), the PCT application will always be dealt with by the examiner again. It should be standing practice to make use of the granted time to the greatest possible extent by exchanging as many arguments as possible with the examiner. Hence, precedence should be given to Written Opinions stemming from International Preliminary Examination, and in the (first) response to said Written Opinion, even a phone interview should be offered to the examiner if this is deemed to be helpful to discuss all relevant aspects and to achieve a positive IPER at the end. This IPER will be distributed to all offices of the elected countries, i.e. to all offices of the designated Chapter II countries.

Moreover, there is a special advantage in using the EPO as International Preliminary Examination Authority: the examiner processing the application during the International Preliminary Examination is the very same who previously did the search for the ISR and, later on, will deal with the examination at the European Patent Office after the regional phase has been entered. This is the result of the introduction of the EPO's **BEST** (**B**ringing **E**xamination and **S**earch **T**ogether) project. Thus, when the examiner opens the file again during the regional phase, he first looks at what he pointed out during the International Preliminary Examination Proceedings and, in most cases, the first office action during the regional phase merely refers to the IPER. If the IPER was positive and the only remaining deficiency is that the description has not yet been brought into conformity with the amended claims, the first Office Action in the Regional Phase could well be as short as

> "The result of the International Preliminary Examination Report (IPER) is made subject of the present Office Action. The applicant is requested to adapt the description to the result of the IPER."

The applicant may even happen to receive an intention to grant (Communication under Rule 51(4) EPC) as first office action from the EPO on the basis of the IPER.

It is apparent that it is highly advantageous to elect the EPO as IPEA because the

- Result of the IPER has a direct impact on the European examination procedure covering up to 20 member states;
- Examiner of the International Preliminary Examination is the same one during the regional phase at the EPO;
- EPO provides for several steps to accelerate the proceedings;
- EPO provides for a choice between "rationalized" and "detailed" Preliminary Examination procedure.

Thus, the overall advantage of choosing the EPO as IPEA is a cooperative, quick and straight forward prosecution of the International Application.

V. Considerations with Respect to Enforcement after Grant

A. How to Prepare Claims which are Advantageous for Search, Prosecution and Infringement Litigation

1. General outline

Under European law, the following aspects of Rule 29 EPC should be observed concerning the form and content of claims. In particular, the claims shall contain:

a) A statement indicating the designation of the subject matter of the invention and those technical features which are necessary for the definition of the claimed subject matter but which, in combination, are part of the prior art.

b) A characterizing portion - preceded by the expression "characterized in that" or "characterized by" - stating the technical features which, in combination with the features stated in sub-paragraph (a), it is desired to protect.

c) Subject to Article 82 EPC, a European patent application may contain two or more independent claims in the same category (product, process, apparatus or use) where it is not appropriate, having regard to the subject matter of the application, to cover this subject matter by a single claim.

d) Any claims stating the essential features of an invention may be followed by one or more claims concerning particular embodiments of that invention.

e) Any claim which includes all the features of any other claim (dependent claim) shall contain, if possible at the beginning, a reference to the other claim and then state the additional features which it is desired to protect. A dependent claim shall also be admissible where the claim, to which it directly refers, is itself a dependent claim. All dependent claims referring back to a single previous claim, and all dependent claims referring back to several previous claims, shall be grouped together to the extent and in the most appropriate way possible.

2. Patent Claims and Possibilities of Amendments

As mentioned above, the extent of protection is defined by the patent claim or claims of a European patent. Since the patent should give an appropriate award to the inventors, it is fully legitimate that the patent claims be worded as broadly as possible. The limits are presented by the prior art on the one hand and the original disclosure on the other hand.

In PCT and European examination procedure, the claims may be modified and amended using the full disclosure of the original case papers, including description, claims and drawings; even such features may be claimed which are only shown in the drawings but not mentioned in the description.

Even though the complete disclosure of the application can be used for amending claims during prosecution, this does not apply to the abstract, even if the abstract is very detailed and clearly comprises further features in addition to the specification. This is ruled by Article 85 EPC.

Moreover, it is established case law that any priority document is not a part of the patent application even if it is filed together with the specification. Therefore, no feature may be claimed after filing which is only disclosed in the priority document. Hence, utmost care is to be taken that the specification comprises full disclosure from the very beginning, in particular when several (Japanese) priority applications are combined with each other for filing one PCT or EPC patent application claiming convention priority.

One problem can arise in practice, when the original patent claims as filed are very narrow due to a plurality of features. Many EPO Examiners are reluctant to agree to cancelling a feature from the original main claim and hold that this is an inadmissible enlargement under Article 123 EPC. However, the essential provision in such cases is Article 84 EPC:

> "The claims shall define the matter for which protection is sought. They shall be clear and concise and be supported by the description."

Nevertheless, the applicant has the difficulty and time consuming task of convincing the Examiner that the new (broader) patent claim is fully supported by the description and represents a complete solution of the problem underlying the invention.

Therefore, it is highly recommended to start with broad original claims comprising a minimum number of features defining the invention. Advantageous features and further developments should be covered by sub-claims using multiple dependencies.

3. Structure of Patent Claims

Patent claims can be drafted in the one-part form or the two-part form. In the two-part form, which is preferred by many Examiners and facilitates arguments in favour of the inventive activity, the preamble should comprise those features which are known from the closest prior art. Reference should be made to one document only, not to a mixture of two or more prior-art documents.

It is sufficient to include those features which are of relevance and are essential to the invention. For example, if the invention relates to a photographic camera, but the inventive step relates entirely to the shutter, then it is fully sufficient for the preamble of the claim to read: "A photographic camera including a focal plane shutter". It is not necessary to include other known features of a photographic camera, such as the lens and the view-finder.

The characterizing portion comprises those features which are not known from the closest prior art and which define the invention concisely and precisely together with the features of the preamble. Of course, only the essential features should be specified in the claims without giving a full list of instructions of how to build the apparatus in question.

Where appropriate, the independent claims can be drafted in the one-part form. This is expedient in some cases. For example, the one-part form is appropriate when the prior-art documents have only some relation to the invention but do not really form the starting point of the invention. When some steps of a method are known from the closest prior art, it is appropriate to draft the main claim in the one-part form giving a clear time sequence of the steps.

Claims in the one-part form are also expedient when the closest prior art is not prepublished but only the content of an older patent application filed prior to the invention in question but not published prior to the filing date of the invention.

Of course, the arrangement and order of features in the preamble or the characterizing portion have no effect on the extent of protection which is only defined by the entirety of the features defining the claim.

4. Clarity of Claims

The claims should define the invention in a clear and concise manner so that it is readily apparent to everybody what is protected as patentable matter. Only the essential technical features have to be specified which give a clear and complete technical teaching.

Concerning non-technical features, which contribute to a better understanding of the technical teaching and statements of effect and advantages obtained thereby, the practice has become more liberal in the past in the practice of the European Patent Office. Therefore, it is always worth trying to include statements of effect or function to obtain a broad scope of protection - instead of including features with restricting effect.

The EPO Examiners are usually rather lenient in this regard and readily allow non-technical statements for reasons of explanation. Also, statements of function and effect are admissible for defining the invention if a person skilled in the art will readily know which means can be used for carrying out the function without needing inventive activities of his own.

However, indefinite statements should be avoided in the claims, in particular statements like "approximately", "as small as possible", "relatively thin, wide or strong". Such general statements are only admissible when they have a well-recognized meaning in the art, for example "high-frequency" or "thin film technology".

Also, optional statements like "in particular" or "preferably" are not allowable in the claims. Rather, these expressions should be used in the description for explanation purposes, whereas the technical features can be the subject matter of respective claims.

5. Main Claim

A main claim is an independent claim comprising all the technical features essential to the invention without making reference to any other claim. A main claim must comprise all the features which are necessary for solving the object underlying the invention.

On filing and during examination, it is always recommendable to use a minimum number of features in the main claim even though the inventive step may be doubtful. Namely, it is easy to later include features from the sub-claims into the main claim, taking account of the relevant prior art. As outlined above, cancelling features in the main claim, however, is very complicated and often considered as "inadmissible enlargement" of the scope under Article 123 EPC.

6. Independent Claims

In a set of claims comprising several independent claims, the main claim is the first independent claim. All the independent claims must comprise their own invention and, like the main claim, all features which are essential for the solution of the object in question. If a main claim is patentable and another independent claim is not allowable, and the applicant insists on such a further independent claim, the patent application is to be rejected in its entirety.

There are cases where it may not be appropriate to cover the subject matter of an invention in one single independent patent claim of the same category. Assume that the invention relates to a socket and a plug which correspond to each other but can be marketed separately. Then, independent claims should be drafted to cover the respective subject matters.

Of course, the principle of unity of invention must be fulfilled when drafting independent claims. This will be explained later.

7. Sub-claims

Sub-claims are dependent claims and comprise all features of another claim, usually in the preamble thereof. Sub-claims may relate to one or several or all of the preceding claims. Also, indirect relations are possible. (For example claim 8 may relate to claim 4 when depending on claim 2.) In such a manner, a tree-like structure of claims can be drafted with multiple dependencies in PCT and European proceedings without any limitation in this regard. This differs completely from practice in the USA.

There is no limitation as to the number of claims in Europe. However, a large number of claims may be expensive under the EPC where each claim beyond claim 10 requires one further claim fee. This may result in considerable expenses. Therefore, the claims should be grouped together to the extent and in the most appropriate way possible.

As mentioned above, multiple dependencies should be used as far as possible because it saves claim fees and provides the broadest scope of protection.

If a device can consist of various materials, it is not necessary to list them in single separate sub-claims. Rather, it is possible to draft a sub-claim of the type "A closing mechanism having a sealing cap consisting of a material selected from the group comprising iron, brass, nickel, aluminum, resin and combinations thereof". Any preferred material could be specified in the description.

Sub-claims may comprise a specific expedient further development of the invention. The features may be known as such but not from the closest prior art defining the preamble of the main claim. Sub-claims may also comprise their own invention, but in such a case it should be carefully checked as to whether the content thereof should be used for drafting an independent claim. Of course, a sub-claim must relate to the same category of claims as the main claim or independent claim to which it relates.

8. Categories of Claims

In principle, there are two categories of claims, namely product and substance claims on the one hand and method, process and use claims on the other hand. The differentiation is essential for the extent of protection conferred by the patent and for determining whether the further claims are sub-claims or independent claims with respect to the main claim.

9. Several Categories of Claims

In principle, the applicant is free to select several categories of claims. The condition is that the principle of unity of invention be complied with and that the applicant have a legitimate interest for all the claimed categories. The following table comprises a summary of admissible claim categories which may be claimed in combination:

- a) Product or substance + plus manufacturing process therefor
- b) Product or substance + manufacturing process therefor + apparatus or means for carrying out the process or method
- c) Product or substance + manufacturing process + use of the new product or substance
- d) Substance plus manufacturing process + new intermediate products
- e) Intermediate product + final product
- f) Intermediate product + manufacturing process + process for further processing of the intermediate product
- g) Substance plus analogous process + (pharmaceutical) agent
- h) Process or method + means for carrying out the process or method
- i) Process or method + apparatus for carrying out the process or method
- j) Manufacturing process + use of the products obtained thereby
- k) Apparatus + product produced by means of the apparatus.

In particular, care should be taken that all the categories of interest are covered by the original patent claims. This is the only way to obtain a complete search from the EPO and avoid problems during prosecution. Please bear in mind that the EPO search is carried out in The Hague (Netherlands) whereas substantive examination is usually carried out later by a totally different person in the main office of the EPO in Munich (Germany).

10. Specific aspects with respect to unity of invention

The guidelines for examination in the EPO are consistent with and based upon an agreement between the EPO, the Japanese Patent Office and the US Patent and Trademark Office, concluded in 1988 with a view to harmonizing unity of invention practices in the three Offices.

According to Article 82 EPC, the European application must "relate to one invention only, or to a group of inventions so linked as to form a single general inventive concept". The second of these alternatives - the single-concept linked group - may give rise to a plurality of independent claims in the same category, but the more usual case is a plurality of independent claims in different categories.

Rule 30 EPC indicates how to determine whether or not the requirement of Article 82 EPC is fulfilled when more than one invention appears to be present. The link between the inventions required by Article 82 EPC must be a technical relationship which finds expression in the claims in terms of the same or corresponding special technical features. The expression "special technical features" means, in any one claim, the particular technical feature or features that define a contribution that the claimed invention considered as a whole makes over the prior art.

Once the special technical features of each invention have been identified, one must determine whether or not there is a technical relationship between the inventions and, furthermore, whether or not this relationship involves these special technical features. Moreover, it is not necessary that the special technical features in each invention be the same. Rule 30 EPC makes clear that the required relationship may be found between corresponding technical features.

An example of this correspondence can be the following: in one claim, the special technical feature which provides resilience or elasticity can be a metal spring, whereas in another claim, the special technical feature which provides the resilience or elasticity can be a block of rubber.

Another example is electrical bridge-rectifier circuits where it may be necessary to include separate independent claims relating to single-phase and polyphase arrangements incorporating such circuits since the number of circuits needed per phase is different in the two arrangements.

A further example is a transmitter and a receiver which are separate items which can be marketed separately. Such a pair of receiver and transmitter can be linked, for example, by the common inventive concept of controlling and maintaining the operation frequency.

In particular, the following combinations or groups of independent claims are acceptable under the EPC as one group of inventions in the same application:

(i) In addition to an independent claim for a given product, an independent claim for a process specially adapted for the manufacture of the product, and an independent claim for a use of the product; or

(ii) in addition to an independent claim for a given process, an independent claim for an apparatus or means specifically designed for carrying out the process; or

(iii) in addition to an independent claim for a given product, an independent claim for a process specially adapted for the manufacture of the product, and an independent claim for an apparatus or means specifically designed for carrying out the process.

While a single set of such independent claims according to any one of the combinations (i), (ii) or (iii) above is always permissible, an Examiner is not obliged to accept a plurality of such sets. Rather, the general provision of Rule 30 EPC applies. In other words, if two independent claims for a process specially adapted for the manufacture of the product are claimed, then they must also be linked by special technical features or a general inventive concept.

The requirement that the process be specially adapted for the manufacture of the product is fulfilled if the claimed process inherently results in the claimed product. On the other hand, it is clearly not sufficient for the wording "specially adapted" to be used in the claim itself because such wording does not necessarily imply that a single general inventive concept is really present.

The requirement that the apparatus or means be specifically designed for carrying out the process is fulfilled if the apparatus or means is suitable for carrying out the process and if there is a technical relationship as defined in Rule 30 EPC between the claimed apparatus or means and the claimed process. It is not sufficient for unity that the apparatus or means is merely capable of being used in carrying out the process. On the other hand, the expression "specifically designed" does not exclude that the apparatus or means could also be used for carrying out another process, or that the process could also be carried out using an alternative apparatus or means.

Unity of invention should be considered to be present in the context of intermediate and final products where:

(i) the intermediate and final products have the same essential structural element, i.e. their basic chemical structures are the same or, their chemical structures are technically closely interrelated, the intermediate incorporating an essential structural element into the final product, and

(ii) the intermediate and final products are technically interrelated, which means that the final product is manufactured directly from the intermediate or is separated from it by a small number of intermediates all containing the same essential structural element.

Unity of invention may also be present between intermediate and final products of which the structures are not known - for example, as between an intermediate having a known structure and a final product with unknown structure, or as between an intermediate of unknown structure and a final product of unknown structure. In such cases, there should be sufficient evidence to lead one to conclude that the intermediate and final products are technically closely interrelated as, for example, when the intermediate contains the same essential element as the final product or incorporates an essential element into the final product.

Different intermediate products used in different processes for the preparation of the final product may be claimed provided that they have the same essential structural element. The intermediate and final products should not be separated, in the process leading from one to the other, by an intermediate which is not new. Where different intermediates for different structural parts of the final product are claimed, unity should not be regarded as being present between the intermediates. If the intermediate and final products are families of compounds, each intermediate compound should correspond to a compound claimed in the family of the final products. However, some of the final products may have no corresponding compound in the family of the intermediate products so that the two families need not be absolutely congruent.

The mere fact that, besides the ability to be used to produce final products, the intermediates also exhibit other possible effects or activities should not prejudice unity of invention.

Alternative forms of an invention may be claimed either in a plurality of independent claims, or in a single claim. In the latter case, the presence of the two alternatives as independent forms may not be immediately apparent. In either case, however, the same criteria should be applied in deciding whether or not there is unity of invention, and lack of unity of invention may then also exist within a single claim.

Where a single claim defines (chemical or non-chemical) alternatives, i.e. a socalled "Markush grouping", unity of invention should be considered to be present when the alternatives are of a similar nature. Namely, it is in line with European law that a claim, whether independent or dependent, can refer to alternatives provided those alternatives are of a similar nature and can fairly be substituted one for another and provided also that the number and presentation of alternatives in a single claim does not make the claim obscure or difficult to construe.

Lack of unity may be directly evident a priori, in other words before considering the claims in relation to the prior art, or may only become apparent a posteriori, namely after taking the prior art into consideration. The former case is present when the independent claims clearly follow different technical directions and principles. The latter case may arise when prior art is revealed during examination which leads to limitation of the independent claims where the common concept is not inventive any more. Then, two or more independent claims may be left, but even if they are patentable, they are not linked any more by "special technical features".

No objection on account of lack of unity is justified in respect of a dependent claim and the claim from which it depends, even when the dependent claim contains an independent invention. For example, suppose claim 1 claims a turbine rotor blade shaped in a specified manner, while claim 2 relates to claim 1 and is characterized in that it is produced from an alloy Z. Then, no objection under Article 82 EPC arises either because alloy Z was new and its composition was not obvious and thus the alloy itself already contains the essential features of an independent patentable invention, or because although alloy Z was not new, but its application in respect of turbine rotor blades was not obvious, and thus represents an independent invention in conjunction with turbine rotor blades.

11. Example

The amendments of claims in connection with the aspect of unity will be explained by means of an example defined by the following claims. Assume that the object underlying the invention is "to provide a cooling chamber for accommodating various goods and which is to be protected against undesirable temperature losses". The claims may read as follows:

(1) A cooling chamber, comprising
   a) storing means for accommodating goods,
   b) cooling means for cooling the interior of the chamber,
   c) control means for controlling the operation of cooling means, and
   d) closing means adapted for closing the chamber which is accessible from outside,
   characterized in that
   e) the closing means comprise a sliding door,
   f) the sliding door is provided with automatically operating return means adapted for returning it into its closing position.

(2) The cooling chamber according to claim 1,
   characterized in that
   g) the return means comprise pusher means operated by spring means prestressing the sliding door towards its closing position.

(3) The cooling chamber according to claim 1,
   characterized in that
   h) the return means comprise a cable operated by a weight adapted to draw the sliding door into its closing position.

(4) The cooling chamber according to claim 1,
   characterized in that
   i) the return means comprise a linear motor adapted to operate on the door by energizing electric coil means thereof moving the sliding door into its closing position.

(5) The cooling chamber according to any of claims 1 to 4,
   characterized in that
   k) the return means include actuation means operated by means of a timer and/or temperature sensing means in order to maintain the temperature under a predetermined maximum room temperature in the cooling chamber.

The main claim is in the two-part form reflecting a prior-art document comprising features a) to d).

Of course, such a set of claims is readily acceptable both under the PCT and European patent law under the aspect of unity. Please note that the aspects of novelty and inventive activity are completely neglected in this context.

Now, assume that further prior art is revealed which anticipates not only features a) to d) in the preamble of claim 1, but also features e) and f) of the characterizing portion in claim 1.

Then, three new independent claims could be drafted comprising

(i)   features a) to f) plus feature g)   (= new claim 1);
(ii) features a) to f) plus feature h)   (= new claim 2); and
(iii) features a) to f) and feature i)   (= new claim 3).

Original claim 5 could follow as new claim 4.

(1) A cooling chamber, comprising
   a) storing means for accommodating goods,
   b) cooling means for cooling the interior of the chamber,
   c) control means for controlling the operation of cooling means, and
   d) closing means adapted for closing the chamber which is accessible from outside,
   wherein
   e) the closing means comprise a sliding door,
   f) the sliding door is provided with automatically operating return means adapted for returning it into its closing position,
   characterized in that
   g) the returning means comprise pusher means operated by spring means prestressing the sliding door towards its closing position.

(2) A cooling chamber, comprising
   a) storing means for accommodating goods,
   b) cooling means for cooling the interior of the chamber,
   c) control means for controlling the operation of cooling means, and
   d) closing means adapted for closing the chamber which is accessible from outside, wherein
   e) the closing means comprise a sliding door,
   f) the sliding door is provided with automatically operating return means adapted for returning it into its closing position,
   characterized in that
   h) the return means comprise a cable operated by a weight adapted to draw the sliding door into its closing position.

(3) A cooling chamber comprising
   a) storing means for accommodating goods,
   b) cooling means for cooling the interior of the chamber,
   c) control means for controlling the operation of cooling means, and

d) closing means adapted for closing the chamber which is accessible from outside, wherein
e) the closing means comprise a sliding door,
f) the sliding door is provided with automatically operating return means adapted for returning it into its closing position,
characterized in that
i) the return means comprise a linear motor adapted to operate on the door by energizing electric coil means thereof moving the sliding door into its closing position.

(4) The cooling chamber according to any of claims 1 to 3,
characterized in that
k) the return means include actuation means operated by means of a timer and/or temperature sensing means in order to maintain the temperature under a predetermined maximum room temperature in the cooling chamber.

Under European law, and also under the PCT, such a set of (new) claims is lacking unity because the three independent claims are not linked by a general inventive concept, in other words special technical features any more. Namely, the original link provided by features e) and f) is already part of the prior art and cannot form the general inventive concept any more.

In such a case, the applicant has to decide which invention (independent claim) is further prosecuted in the application; the other alternatives can be made the subject matter of divisional applications. The other possibility is to find another single general inventive concept in the disclosure of the invention which is capable of uniting them.

Now, with respect to the Example, there is a fall-back position represented by original claim 5 comprising feature k). Namely, when original claim 1 is anticipated by some prior art, features a) to f) would form the preamble of a new main claim while feature k) could form the characterizing portion of the new main claim. Then, original claims 2 to 4 could readily follow as sub-claims defining further developments of the subject matter.

(1) A cooling chamber, comprising
a) storing means for accommodating goods,
b) cooling means for cooling the interior of the chamber,
c) control means for controlling the operation of cooling means, and
d) closing means adapted for closing the chamber which is accessible from outside, wherein
e) the closing means comprise a sliding door,
f) the sliding door is provided with automatically operating return means adapted for returning it into its closing position,
characterized in that
k) the return means include actuation means operated by means of a timer and/or temperature sensing means in order to maintain the temperature

under a predetermined maximum room temperature in the cooling chamber.

(2) The cooling chamber according to claim 1,
characterized in that
g) the return means comprise pusher means operated by spring means prestressing the sliding door towards its closing position.

(3) The cooling chamber according to claim 1,
characterized in that
h) the return means comprise a cable operated by a weight adapted to draw the sliding door into its closing position.

(4) The cooling chamber according to claim1,
characterized in that
i) the return means comprise a linear motor adapted to operate on the door by energizing electric coil means thereof moving the sliding door into its closing position.

On the other hand, it is possible to draft three independent claims, namely

(i) features a) to f), plus features k) and g) (= new claim 1);
(ii) features a) to f), plus features k) and h) (= new claim 2); and
(iii) features a) to f), plus features k) and i) (= new claim 3).

(1) A cooling chamber, comprising
a) storing means for accommodating goods,
b) cooling means for cooling the interior of the chamber,
c) control means for controlling the operation of cooling means, and
d) closing means adapted for closing the chamber which is accessible from outside,
wherein
e) the closing means comprise a sliding door,
f) the sliding door is provided with automatically operating return means adapted for returning it into its closing position,
characterized in that
k) the return means include actuation means operated by means of a timer and/or temperature sensing means in order to maintain the temperature under a predetermined maximum room-temperature in the cooling chamber,
g) the return means comprise pusher means operated by spring means prestressing the sliding door towards its closing position.

(2) A cooling chamber, comprising
a) storing means for accommodating goods,
b) cooling means for cooling the interior of the chamber,
c) control means for controlling the operation of cooling means, and
d) closing means adapted for closing the chamber which is accessible from outside,

wherein
e) the closing means comprise a sliding door,
f) the sliding door is provided with automatically operating return means adapted for returning it into its closing position,
characterized in that
k) the return means include actuation means operated by means of a timer and/or temperature sensing means in order to maintain the temperature under a predetermined maximum room
temperature in the cooling chamber,
h) the return means comprise a cable operated by weight adapted to draw the sliding door into its closing position.

(3) A cooling chamber, comprising
a) storing means for accommodating goods,
b) cooling means for cooling the interior of the chamber,
c) control means for controlling the operation of cooling means, and
d) closing means adapted for closing the chamber which is accessible from outside,
wherein
e) the closing means comprise a sliding door,
f) the sliding door is provided with automatically operating return means adapted for returning it into its closing position,
characterized in that
k) the return means include actuation means operated by means of a timer and/or temperature sensing means in order to maintain the temperature under a predetermined maximum room temperature in the cooling chamber,
i) the return means comprise a linear motor adapted to operate on the door by energizing electric coil means thereof moving the sliding door into its closing position.

Such a set of claims is clearly admissible under the aspect of unity of invention, both under the PCT and European patent law. The reason is that in each case feature k) forms the "special technical feature" required under Rule 30 EPC, and of course these sets of revised claims also solve the specific problem underlying the invention as outlined above.

The alternatives according to the third amended set of claims may appear somewhat limited - but sometimes there is no other choice in view of pertinent prior art.

B. PATENT INFRINGEMENT LITGATION- PROBLEMS AND POINTS TO CONSIDER

1. Extent of protection

When a European patent has been granted, the most important component is the patent claims.

Under the EPC, the protection is defined in Article 69 EPC:

Article 69 EPC

Extent of Protection

(1) The extent of the protection conferred by a patent or a patent application shall be determined by the terms of the claims. Nevertheless, the description and the drawings shall be used to interpret the claims.

Statute 3 – Article 69 EPC

Due to European harmonization, the same or similar wording is used in national patent law of the respective member states.

Since interpretation of claims may be difficult on the one hand and on the other hand should be carried out in a similar manner throughout Europe, the Protocol on the Interpretation of Article 69 EPC was adopted at the Munich Diplomatic Conference for the setting up of a European System for the Grant of Patents on October 5, 1973, as set out below:

"Article 69 EPC should not be interpreted in the sense that the extent of the protection conferred by a European patent is to be understood as that defined by the strict, literal meaning of the wording used in the claims, the description and the drawings being employed only for the purpose of resolving an ambiguity found in the claims. Neither should it be interpreted in the sense that the claims serve only as a guideline and that the actual protection conferred may extend to what, from a consideration of the description and drawings by a person skilled in the art, the patentee has contemplated. On the contrary, it is to be interpreted as defining a position between these extremes which combines a fair protection for the patentee with a reasonable degree of certainty for third parties."

Accordingly, legal and commercial disadvantages for the patentee can only be avoided, if utmost care was taken when drafting claims during prosecution.

Experience has shown that claims with the broadest scope of protection are those which comprise a minimum number of features and/or claims of the so-called "means plus function" type. The reason is that such claims can cover a huge number of embodiments and provide a strong position to the patentee.

2. Excursion: Situation in the U.S.A.

We note that recent case law in the U.S.A., in particular the decision of the Court of Appeals in re. Donaldson has changed the situation in the United States considerably with respect to the scope of protection granted by U.S. patents. Namely, the U.S. Patent Act is very detailed as to the drafting of claims and the scope thereof, see for example 35 U.S.C. § 112 Paragraph 6, quoted in the pertinent case law and reading as follows:

> "An element in a claim for a combination may be expressed as a means or step for performing a specified function without the recital of structure, material or acts in support thereof, and such claim shall be construed to cover the corresponding structures, materials, or acts described in the specification and equivalents thereof."

However, such a restrictive rule does not exist in European patent law, neither in the EPC itself nor in the rules relating thereto.

3. Situation in Europe

The decisive provision is found in Article 84 EPC concerning the claims and giving only a general indication as follows:

> "The claims shall define the matter for which protection is sought. They shall be clear and concise and be supported by the description."

According to the European harmonization among the member states to the EPC, similar provisions can be found in the national Patent Acts.

Further aspects can be found in Rule 29 EPC relating to the form and content of the claims. Of course, the claims must be drafted in terms of the "technical features of the invention", and the claims should not contain any statements relating, for example, to commercial advantages or other non-technical matters. However, statements of purpose or effect or function are allowed if they assist in defining the invention. Also, it is not necessary that every feature be expressed in terms of a structural limitation. Functional features may readily be included provided that a person skilled in the art would have no difficulty in providing some means of performing this function without exercising inventive skill. Hence, claims to the use of the invention in the sense of the technical application thereof are allowable.

From the above explanations, it should be clear that, in principle, patent claims written in the "means plus function format" are well acceptable under the EPC, in particular when their functional statement contributes to the clarity of the feature to be defined thereby. There are no rules in the EPC to readily reject such claims.

Also, they are not limited in scope in the sense as provided in the U.S. patent law. Of course, it is to be decided case by case as to whether the "means plus function format" is really appropriate and acceptable to the respective Examiner in charge.

4. Problems of broad claims

One problem which arises with claims giving only a general outline and/or comprising the "means plus function format" resides in that the scope thereof is very broad. For example, "locking means with safety function" may cover a huge variety of embodiments. Therefore, a broad patent claim comprising a "means plus function format" will attract a huge number of prior-art references because various conventional locking means with safety function may already exist. Even if the specific means according to prior-art documents may differ completely from the specific embodiments described in a new patent specification, they can readily anticipate the broad feature "locking means with safety function". In such a situation, the applicant cannot but restrict the patent claim to the specific embodiments in order to escape from such prior art.

However, once a patent has been granted comprising features in the "means plus function format", they give the full broad protection without being limited down to the specific embodiments as described in the patent specification (unlike the situation in the U.S.A.). When the applicant has made an invention which comprises a generalized teaching going beyond specific embodiments, the full scope of protection is awarded to such an applicant and patentee.

This is due to the fact that interpretation of European claims is ruled by Article 69 EPC and the Protocol of the Interpretation of Article 69 of the European Convention, as quoted above. In particular, emphasis is put on the fact that according to the Protocol the ... "description and drawings being employed only for the purpose of resolving an ambiguity found in the claims".

Please bear in mind that the quoted Protocol is an integral part of the EPC pursuant to Article 164 EPC and is directly applicable law in the contracting states to the EPC.

5. Re-examination of granted European patents

Once a European patent has been granted, the EPO Examiners can only be involved with one aspect of such claims, namely when opposition proceedings and/or opposition appeal proceedings are started. Then, they have to re-examine the granted claims as to patentability when considering additional prior art cited by an opponent. However, the EPO Examiners are never involved in patent litigation matters after grant of a European patent. The reason is that any such patent litigations are handled by the national Civil Courts in the respective contracting states where an infringement may take place.

In other words, during re-examination under opposition or appeal, the EPO Examiners compare a granted claim comprising a "means plus function format" in its broad meaning with every prior-art document cited by an opponent. Then, it may readily happen that such a broad claim must be restricted in opposition or appeal due to prior art which is pertinent to such a broad coverage as defined by the general wording of the claim.

When it comes to patent litigation, however, the national Civil Courts are bound by Article 69 EPC and corresponding provisions in the national patent laws as well as the Protocol quoted above.

6. Scope of protection

By tradition, the scope of protection awarded by German Civil Courts based upon granted patents is rather wide, no matter whether national German patents or German patents based upon granted European patents are concerned.

Before the EPC came into force, we had a so-called trinity of protection awarded by a patent, namely (a) scope of protection awarded by the literal wording of the claims, (b) scope of protection awarded by the claims and the equivalents thereof, and (c) the scope of protection awarded by the so-called general inventive concept which could be derived from the teaching of the patent.

Due to European harmonization, the "general inventive concept" was abandoned in Germany, but the scope of protection is still very broad under the doctrine of equivalence. Hence, it is well established German practice that claims comprising a "means plus function format" are understood as claims giving a broad scope of protection because any such means are covered thereby without being limited by specific details in the description of preferred embodiments.

7. Situation in other European countries

According to information from British colleagues, the situation is quite similar in the United Kingdom. In other words, they also contribute a broad scope of protection to such a claim comprising a "means plus function format" and also apply the doctrine of equivalence. Sometimes, the scope of equivalence in the United Kingdom seems to be somewhat smaller than in Germany, at least according to estimation of our British colleagues. But it is difficult to give evidence in this regard because it is a rare case that you have both identical patents and identical infringements in both countries which are decided in Court so that they would result in directly comparable Court Decisions.

It goes without saying that a similar situation applies to France where they also apply the broad scope of protection awarded by a claim comprising a "means plus function format". This is not surprising in view of the provisions provided by Article 69 EPC and the Protocol relating thereto.

With respect to France, however, one particularity should be considered. According to long-lasting practice in France, patent applications are not examined as to patentability before grant. Even though a search report is established, the applicant is free to modify the claims in the light of prior art cited in the search report, or to obtain registration of the patent on the basis of the original case papers.

Therefore, it is well established practice in France that in litigation matters handled by the Civil Courts, the defendant presents two arguments, namely

(a) he does not infringe the patent in question, and
(b) the patent is not valid in view of the prior art.

Accordingly, it is common practice that in one and the same patent litigation proceedings, the Civil Courts in France decide both on the question of nullity and the question of infringement.

This practice also applies to granted European patents having protection in France where a defendant may readily attack the granted patent because of nullity reasons presenting prior art which may be the same as at the EPO or also some additional prior art. Then, it may turn out in practice in such French patent litigation proceedings that the French Civil Court awards a limited scope of protection in such litigation proceedings. However, the reason is not based upon the "means plus function format" of the claim, rather such narrow protection is due to the fact that in view of the (additional) prior art cited against the patent in question, the judges hold that the scope of protection is to be reduced.

VI. Summary

Patent claims granted under the EPC provide a broad scope of protection, provided that they have carefully been drafted with a strong main claim comprising a minimum number of features, whereas various embodiments are covered by the features in sub-claims connected by the use of multiple dependencies.

In infringement situations, the competitor can be attacked on the basis of the main claim and suitable sub-claims which are combined with each other to cover the infringing subject. In nullity situations, the patentee has various fall-back positions by supplementing an attacked main claim by one or more sub-claims in order to survive.

Since the doctrine of equivalence is applied throughout Europe by the member states to the EPC the patentee has a strong position after grant of a patent.

Trademark Protection in Germany and Europe

Eugen Popp

I. The Profession of Patent Attorneys in Germany

Until the year 1900, professional advice and representation in matters of patents, trade marks and registered designs was not regulated.

This shortcoming was removed by the Patent Attorney Law of 21 May 1900. Patent Attorneys could only now be persons who, after a university technical education, had passed a legal examination. The title "Patent Attorney" was legally protected.

In 1933 the Patent Attorney Law was adapted to the general regulation for Attorneys at Law. A Patent Bar Association was established, which obtained the authority to supervise Patent Attorneys. Also, the Patent Bar Association obtained competence in cases of first instance on discipline matters.

Moreover, Patent Attorneys, along with Attorneys at Law obtained a monopoly of professional representation in intellectual property matters. Patent Attorneys got the right to plead before courts (right of hearing and participation).

On September 7, 1966 the Patent Attorneys Law was replaced by a Patent Attorney Act in which the areas of authority of the Patent Attorney were clearly defined and since when the training of the Patent Attorney has also been regulated. In supplement to this, the Federal Minister for Justice has issued a "Training and Examination Rule".

Par. 1 of the Patent Attorney Act defines the position of the Patent Attorney in the administration of justice and, within the framework of his activities, declares him to be an independent organ of the administration of justice.

The position of the Attorney as an independent organ of justice has its roots in the history of the status of attorney in general. It follows the development from state-dependency to free advocacy in the modern legal systems.

The term "organ" is assigned to persons having functions within the society. The function of the Patent Attorney as "organ" is his legal administrative activity together with State authorities. From this arises his responsibility to properly implement the law.

1. His professional activity must be guided exclusively by the needs for aid and security of the person seeking justice who is overburdened by complex legal systems and not by his financial interests.

2. The Patent Attorney must be fully committed to the purpose of law. This includes for example the duty of the Patent Attorney with his qualifications and objectivity to strive for a fair decision of the Patent Office, the Patent Court or the Civil Courts:

The Patent Attorney should not be an "accomplice of the State". Rather, Par. 1 of the Patent Attorney Act clearly states that the Patent Attorney is an "independent" organ in the administration of justice. The independence requires that he is not partial to the State or his client.

Certainly, the activity of the Patent Attorney, just like the Attorney at Law, is integrated into the judicial system; however, he does not have executive power.

The Patent Attorney however is not independent of his client in the sense that he may act on his own voluntary discretion. He must fulfill his legal administrative duties, independently assess the factual matter and respond, based on his own assessment.

3. The activity of the Patent Attorney is restricted by the scope of activities set down under Par. 1 of the Patent Attorney Act. Those activities are defined in Par. 3 and 4 of the Patent Attorney Act. Accordingly, the Patent Attorney has the professional duty

- to advise and represent parties in matters of attainment, maintenance, defence and enforcement of a patent, of a protective certificate supplementing a Patent (pharmaceuticals and plant protective agents), of a Utility Model, of a protected topography, of a Trademark or of another sign protected by the Trademark Law, e.g., company name, etc., or of a protective right for plant varieties;
- to represent parties before the Patent and Trademark Office and the Patent Court in matters for which these Anthorities are compentent;
- to represent parties before the Federal Supreme Court in proceedings relating to nullity suits or withdrawal of a patent or of a supplementary protective certificate, or pertaining to granting of a compulsory license;
- to represent parties before the Federal Authority for plant varieties in matters relating to plant variety protection;
- to advise and represent parties on questions which relate to an Intellectual Property right, a design patent, a data processing program, an unprotected invention or other technical development, a protective right for plant varieties or an unprotected plant cultivation or to advise on legal questions directly related to such matters; and
- to participate and plead before the competent court in litigation deriving from the activities of the Patent Attorney.

As already mentioned, with the Patent Attorney Law of 1933, the Patent Attorney obtained a monopoly for professional representation in matters of

Intellectual Property protection. This monopoly is guaranteed by the so-called "Legal Consultation Law", which also protects legal advice by

- Attorneys at Law
- Public Notaries
- Certified Accountants
- Tax Advisers

According to Par. 2 of the Patent Attorney Act, the Patent Attorney exercises a so-called "free profession" and not a "trade". The essential features of the free profession are:

- the lack of profit motive, i.e., the maximisation of profit should not dominate, but rather assistance for those seeking justice. Naturally, the Patent Attorney like any other legal adviser must operate his business in a profitable way, in order to maintain independence from the State as well as from clients, i.e., if necessary, also to be able to refuse a client;
- prohibition of offering services for a success-related fee (commission);
- binding of the professional law firm to its proprietors or members;
- the provision of personal services;
- independence of the market.

Despite the independence under Par. 1 of the Patent Attorney Act and the exercise of a free profession according to Par. 2, the Patent Attorney as an "organ of legal administration" is naturally obligated to ensure the function of the legal system. Therefore, the Patent Attorney, like anyother legal adviser is obligated to ensure that his clients behave in accordance with the law. This influence of the attorney on the client is assumed by the state; therefore, the attorney also enjoys a certain amount of "trust" when presenting the factual case.

To this extent the Patent Attorney is obligated to the "truth", but naturally also has a "loyalty" with respect to what his client entrusted to him.

If there is a conflict here, the Patent Attorney must refuse his services. In concrete terms this may be when a client requires the Patent Attorney to present an un-truth, e.g., to make statements known to be incorrect in trade mark matters with respect to use of the Trademark.

Naturally, the Patent Attorney, as an "organ of legal administration" is not under any obligation to betray his client. To this extent the Patent Attorney, like an Attorney at Law or notary, is protected by law. He need not make any statements relating to information entrusted to him by his client, but is subject to a secrecy obligation. He can only be relieved of this obligation by his client. In order that the interaction between the law and best representation of the client (trust) can function, the Patent Attorney is bound by a so-called Professional Act.

- conscientiousness (in exercise of the profession);
- independence (both of State and society, i.e., independence of the client);
- secrecy (betrayal of party is a punishable offence)
- objectivity (in disagreements with Authorities, Courts and Opponents, the personal emotions of the clients must be kept out of the discussion);
- prohibition of opposing interests (e.g., opposition to a trade mark, the registration of which the Patent Attorney has previously persued);
- administering assets (moneys of the client must be held and used for the intended purpose);
- duty of access (office accessible to the public);
- restricted advertising (advertising allowed, if objective; no comparative advertisements, such as "I am better than Attorney X and in addition even cheaper!"
- professional behaviour (only objective disagreement with other colleagues; avoidance of personal insults);
- duty of training.

The supervision of Patent Attorneys is carried out by the Patent Bar already mentioned. It is an institution of public law, with its seat in Munich.

The Patent Bar Association has the duty to protect and further the interests of the profession and to ensure that its members observe their professional responsibilities.

The agents of the Patent Bar Association are :

- the Executive Board;
- the Assembly of the Bar.

The President of the German Patent Office exercises State supervision of the Patent Bar Association. This supervision is restricted to seeing that the law and the constitution regulating the organization and administration of the Patent Bar Association are observed.

The duties of the Executive Board of the Patent Bar Association are :

- to advise and instruct the members, i.e., the individual Patent Attorneys, in questions of professional duties;
- when requested to mediate in disagreements between members of the Bar;
- when requested, to mediate in disagreements between the members of the Bar and their clients;
- to monitor fulfillment of the duties placed on the Patent Attorneys, and to exercise disciplinary action (Council for the first instance disciplinary matters);
- to provide yearly accounts of the assets of the Bar;

- to issue expert opinions, as required by the Federal Ministry of Justice, a Court or an administrative authority, in particular the German Patent Office;
- to participate in the training of candidates to become a Patent Attorney;
- to nominate Patent Attorneys as members of the examining commission.

Before which Authorities and Courts is and may the Patent Attorney be active?

In all application proceedings, Trademark cancellation proceedings (absolute bars) and Utility Model cancellation proceedings before the **German Patent- and Trademark Office**	In Nullity and Compulsory License proceedings before the	In infringement proceedings (participatory) before the
Federal Patent Court (Appeal Level)	**Federal Patent Court**	**District Court**
Federal Supreme Court (legal appeal, participatory)	**Federal Supreme Court** (appeal level)	**District Appeals Court**
		Federal Supreme Court (legal appeal)
In piracy proceedings (confiscation, etc. before the	In EU Trademark matters before the	In European Patent matters before the
Upper Finance Directorate Munich	**OHIM**	**European Patent Office** (1st and 2nd instance)
	Court of First Instance of European Court of Justice (participatory)	

Lastly, it should be pointed out that according to the Patent Attorney Act, Patent Attorneys may undertake the common practice of their profession with:

- Attorneys at Law;

- Tax Advisers;
- Certified Accountants;
- Attorneys at Law who are also Notaries.

Due to his experience and training as well as his daily business, the Patent Attorney is certainly the first person to contact when seeking counsel in the field of Intellectual Property. This applies in particular to persons from abroad, as the Patent Attorney is professionally qualified to handle international matters for example under the Paris Convention, the Strasbourg Patent Convention, the European Patent Convention, the Community Trademark Convention or the Madrid Trademark Agreement. Accordingly, the Patent Attorney as a rule has adequate language skills and a number of contacts at home and abroad. The Patent Attorney can carry out and evaluate searches as a basis for a patent application, TM application, etc.

In an infringement suit, the Patent Attorney can appoint a suitable Attorney at Law in the respective jurisdiction who has the experience in Intellectual Property. In this respect it should also be pointed out that it is a legal requirement that foreigners, e.g., patent or trade mark applicants from abroad, appoint a representative from within Germany. As such either a Patent Attorney or an Attorney at law may be appointed, because only these two professions have the corresponding monopoly under the law.

II. Trademark Protection in Germany

A. A new Product - Five Types of Protection

The illustrated activities of a Patent Attorney show that he is the competent person to consult on the question of which type of protection is available for a new product. This will now be demonstrated with the example of a

new telephone.

1. Patent Protection

A company develops a new telephone able to identify and executing acoustic signals as commands, e.g., dialing certain pre-stored numbers, redialing a number, etc. The hardware elements of the memory and identification module of the acoustic receiver are patentable because they provide a completely new technical solution of high inventive quality.

ACOUSTIC RECEIVER

Patent Application

2. Utility Model

The telephone receiver can be disassembled and transformed into a headphone. This has the advantage that the operator can speak freely and at the same time has his hands are free to take notes. One can sort through papers; notes on the conversation can even be typed into a computer. The inventive step in solving this problem, which is somewhat smaller than for patent protection, would suggest the filing of a Utility Model.

Utility Model Application

3. Design Protection

The external appearance of the telephone is different from other devices. It has a distinctive character and is therefore suited for the filing of a Design Patent at the German Patent and Trademark Office. The design is then protected against imitations. However, novelty and distinctiveness of the design, the basic requirements of this protection right, are only examined during an infringement suit.

Design Application

4. Trademark Protection

The telephone is sold under the product name Pronton®. The product name is legally protected only when it is entered into the Trademark register at the German Patent and Trademark Office, assuming that no older claims on the product name are in force. If not registered, protection can arise if the mark attains "market recognition". This will be addressed further hereinafter. Also, a service mark could be obtained by the company which services such telephone systems.

Trademark Application

5. Copyright Protection

The telephone is accompanied by a user manual containing instructions, graphics and tables. The manual is copyright protected. The right need not be registered in Germany, since it automatically belongs to the creator under the law.

Copyright Application

B. The Trademark Law in Germany

The new Trademark Act, in force since January 1, 1995, was conceived as a uniform regulation for <u>all</u> commercially used signs. Thus it includes not only the product and service marks obtained by registration or by intensive use, but also the trade designations previously protected by unfair competition laws. This includes trade names (companies) and titles such as newspaper titles, titles of theatre productions, TV shows, etc. Also included are appellations of geographic origin.

C. Signs Protectable as Trademarks

According to Par. 3 of the German Trademark Act, all of the following signs can be protected :

- words including personal names
- designs
- letters
- numerals
- acoustic signs
- three-dimensional configurations, including
  - the shape or packaging of a product
- other dressings including
  - colors and color combinations
  - taste
  - smells
  - animated pictures

The above signs are naturally only protectable if they are able to be represented graphically and distinguish the goods or services of one enterprise from those of another. These prerequisites will be discussed in more detail later.

In the following some examples of protectable signs are shown as publication copies :

1. **Words**

a. *A single word mark:*

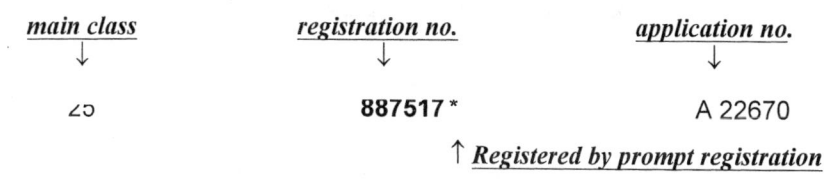

main class ↓	*registration no.* ↓	*application no.* ↓
25	**887517***	A 22670

↑ *Registered by prompt registration*

adidas

filing date ↓		*applicant* ↓

13.8.71. adidas Sports Shoe Factory Adi Dassler KG,
8522 Herzogenaurach Am Bahnhof.

Business Activity: Manufacture and selling of sportswear and sports apparatus, selling of promotional articles.
Goods: Shoes, insoles, spikes and studs for sports shoes, spike key, stud key, shoe laces, shoe care products and equipment, shoe boxes, bags for shoe boxes; clothing (including mechanicall knitted and hand knitted), stockings, gloves, bags and suitcases sports apparatus, balls, miniature shoes, miniature balls; promotional articles, namely card games, electric light bulbs as small key illuminators, ball point pens, pin brooches (not made pfecious metal), shoe cleaning materials, key rings made from plastics and/or non-precious metal). GK. 25, 3, 6, 8, 11, 16, 18, 20, 21, 26, 28.

↑*classes*

71/2684	16.11.71	72/65
↑	↑	↑
publication of application	*registration date*	*publication of registration*

Remark: This is a publication under the former German Tradmark Act („Warenzeichengesetz", in force until Dec. 31, 1994).

b. *A multiple word mark:*

12   **937 689**   R 31398

ROLLS - ROYCE

25.9.74. **Rolls-Royce (1971) Ltd.**, London (United Kingdom).
Representative: Lederer, F., Dr. , Pat-Anw., 8000 Munich.

Business Activity: Manufacture and sales of motor and jet engines.
Goods: Gas turbines – combustion engines for land, sea and air vehicles and for use as stationery motors; jet engines as well as parts of such motors and engines. GK. 12, 7.

75/1199   12.11.75   75/3294

12   **1 082 589**   A39427/12 Wz

ALFA ROMEO

11.1.85. **ALFA ROMEO Marketing company, mbH**, 6230 Frankfurt 80, Lärchenstr. 110.

Business Activity: Manufacture and repairs of motor vehicles.
Goods/services: Motor vehicles of Italian origin; repairs of motor vehicles. GK 12,37.

15.5.85   3.10.85   15.11.85

c. *Personal Names:*

3   **1 060 901***   S 39116/3 Wz

JIL SANDER

16.7.83. Heide-Marie Sander (Pseudonym: Jil Sander),
2000 Hamburg 13, Milchstr. 8-9.

Business Activity: Manufacture and sales of all type of goods, trading concern, manufacture of designs and advertising for third parties.
Goods/Services: Soaps, perfumery, essential oils, cosmetics, hair lotions; dentifrices; deodorants; manicure sets, shaving apparatus; optical instruments, in particular spectacles, sun glasses, correction spectacles, contact lenses, spectacle frames, lens glass; spectacle cases; electrical curling tongs; massage apparatus; hair drying apparatus; jewellery; real and imitation jewellery, also from different materials; precious stones; time pieces; goods made of leather or of leather imitations, namely handbags and other cases not adapted to the product as they are intended to contain as well as small articles of leather, in particular purses, pocket wallets, key cases; hides and animal skins; trunks and travelling bags; travel and handbags; umbrellas, parasols and walking-sticks; appliances and apparatus for the care of the body and beauty care namely combs and sponges, brushes, tooth brushes, mouth rinses; textiles; bed and table covers; household linen, in particular hand towels, face cloths, bath towels, makeup removal tissues, bed linen; clothing, in particular men's and ladies outer garments of textiles, leather, fur and other materials, bath robes, hats, gloves as well as boots, shoes and slippers, belts; laces and embroidery, ribbons and braids; buttons, hooks and eyes, needles; artificial flowers, clothing accessories, in particular brooches (without precious metal and no imitation jewellery), needles (without precious metal), clasps; product design and packaging for third parties. GK. 3, 5, 8, 9, 10, 11, 14, 18, 21, 24, 25, 26, 42.

14.4.84   14.3.84   30.4.84

d. *Advertising Slogans:*

16a 785777 P 11982

good..........

better........

Paulaner

22.12.62. Paulaner-Salvator-Thomasbräu-A.G.,
Munich 9, Regerstr. 28.

Business Activity: Beer brewery.
Goods: Beer. GK. 16a. Int. Cl. 32.

63/1763 18.3.64 64/1110

Signs comprising several words can be put together to form a slogan. Protection is then possible when the slogan includes the actual product mark, here "Paulaner".

2. Letters and numerals

9   **1 090 536**   A 40306/9 Wz

AEG

20.8.85. AEG Corporation, 6000 Frankfurt 70, Theodor-Stern-Kai 1.

Business Activity: Manufacture and sales of all types of goods, in particular of electronic, mechanical engineering and chemical products and equipment, import and export business, building and repair, planning and information/advice, training, renting and leasing.
Goods/services: Combustible elements for nuclear reactors, chemical products for technical purposes, namely fixing agents, synthetic resins, adhesives and hardening substances; tempering, welding and solder preparations; partially processed precious and non-precious metals and their alloys; current collectors – super Structures for electric driven land vehicles; small iron mongery, Locksmith and smithy work. Cabling and finishing; carrying out calculations for third parties; carrying out developments, tests and research assignments; technical advice and expert opinions; leasing of data processing equipment. GK. 9, 1, 6, 7, 8, 10, 11, 12, 14, 16, 17, 19, 20, 21, 35, 37, 41, 42.

31.12.85   21.4.86   31.5.86

[511] 41   [210] 39627364.5   [111] **396 27 364**
      42
[220] **21.06.1996**   [151] 25.10.1996   [450] 30.01.1997

[540] **MTV**

[732] **Kahle, Regina**, Friedrich-List-Str. 2/1,70736, Fellbach, Germany

[750] Patent Attorneys Jackisch-Kohl & Kohl, Stuttgarter Str. 115, 70469 Stuttgart
[740] Jackisch-Kohl and Associates, Stuttgarter Str. 115, 70469 Stuttgart
[510] catering for and entertainment of guests in gastronomic sectors.

34   **206680**   E 11265

4711

1/3 1915. Eau de Cologne and Perfume Factory "Glockengasse No. 4711"
gegenüber der Pferdepost von Ferd. Mühlens, Cologne. 28/10 1915.

Business Activity: Perfume and soap factory.
Goods: Eau de Cologne, hair lotions and toilet water, perfumery, cosmetic products, hair, beard, mouth, dental and skin care products, pomades, powder, sachets, smelling salts, shaving, toilet and glycerine soaps.- Descr. (GK 34, 2)

15/1409   52/234

25   **2 074 951***   L 37963/25 Wz

501

21.12.93. Levi Strauss & Co., a Corporation under the law of the State of Delware, San Francisco, California (USA).
Representative: Droste, attorney, 20354 Hamburg.

Goods/Services: Jeans. GK. 25.

30.7.94   12.8.94   30.9.94

3. Designs, Emblems, e. g.

39   **2 008 220***   M 70792/39 Wz

25.9.91. Mercedes-Benz AG, 7000 Stuttgart 60, Mercedesstr. 136.

Business Activity: Development, manufacture and sales of vehicles, motors and other technical drives, equipment, machines and other technical equipment, other industrial products, technical systems and methods on the aforementioned areas; trade with all raw materials and processing materials, unfinished and finished products and goods, those that have connection with articles commonly used in these business sectors; Providing services in the area of the afore-mentioned activities.
Goods/Services: Repairs or maintenance of motor vehicles, in particular utility vehicles, their tractors, trailers, flat-bed trailers and/or interchangeable open body trailers; mobile services (breakdown services) and towing of motor vehicles.

4. Combined Words and Designs, e. g.

3   **894 504***   W 23569

WELLA

29.10.71. Wella AG, 6100 Darmstadt, Berliner Allee 65.

Business Activity: Manufacture and sales of chemical and electronic products such as the operation of a general trade, import and export business.
Goods: Bleaching preparations and other substances for laundry use; cleaning, polishing, scouring and abrasive preparations; soaps; perfumery, essential oils, cosmetics, hair lotions; dentifrices; substances for cleaning, shoe laces; buttons; press studs, hooks and eyes, pins; artificial flowers. GK. 3, 5, 11, 21, 26.

72/1480   21.6.72   72/1857

5. Melodies and Tunes

> e.g., recognized melody of a TV program (jingle) or
> the sound of a "HARLEY DAVIDSON" or the like

It should be noted that to file such acoustic signs, they must be represented graphically, whether this is in the form of

- written music,

HARIBO

or in the form of

- a sonogram, i.e., graphic representation of acoustic vibrations

The same holds for odour marks, taste marks (chromatographical representations), touch marks (surface representations) or animated picture marks. The principal consideration is that these marks must be graphically represented. This however is not a legal matter but only a technical problem to be solved.

6. Three-Dimensional Marks

This concerns especially the shape of an article, e.g., soap in a specific form, e.g., in the shape of an animal or the fragance of an Eau de Cologne.

[511] 3 [210] 39505775.2 [111] **395 05 775**
[220] **09.02.1995** [151] 22.08.1996 [450] 30.11.1996
[540]

[732] **Calvin Klein Cosmetic Corp. Wilmington**, US
[750] Attorney Association: Boehmert & Boehmert, Hollerallee 32, 28209 Bremen
[740] BOEHMERT & BOEHMERT, Holleralle 32, 28209 Bremen
[510] 03: Eau de Cologne
[544] three dimensional marks

[511] 3 [210] 39409236.8 [111] **394 09 236**
09, 14, 16, 18, 25
[220] **01.01.1995** [151] 20.08.1996 [450] 30.11.1996
[540]

[732] **Hohe-Modelle Maria Hohe GmbH & Co.** Bahnhofsteig 8
Pegnitz, Germany
[750] Patent attorneys Dipl.-Ing. E. Tergau, Dipl.-Ing. D. Tergau,
Mögeldorfer Hauptstr 51, 90482 Nuremburg
[740] E. Tergau and Colleagues, Mögeldorfer Hauptstr 51,
90482 Nuremburg
[510] Soaps, Perfumes, essential oils, cosmetics, hair lotions a
dentifrices; children's outer garments, paper, cardboard and goods
made from these materials (as far as contained in Class 16);
stationery; jeweller products, jewellery; watches and timing
instruments; leather and leather imitations as well as goods
made thereof (as far as contained in Class 18), in particular
rucksack kitbags and bags made from textile materials; cases
made for spectacles.

Remark : This is a publication under the new German Trademark Act as
in force since Jan. 1, 1995.

Codes

[511] classes [210] appl. no. [111] reg. no.
[220] appl. date [151] reg. date [450] publ. date of reg.
[540] representation of the mark
[732] applicant/owner
[750] agents
[740] address of service
[510] specification of goods/services

In such cases, the shape should represent a "distinguishing" <u>addition</u> to the goods. For this reason, a shape determined by the goods itself is excluded from protection, e.g., the illustration of a common book for the protection of books is excluded as a trade mark.

3   **943 653***   L 20926

2.3.76. LINGNER + FISCHER GMBH, 7580 Bühl, Hermann-Str. 7.

Business Activity: Manufacture and sales of chemical/pharmaceutical, cosmetic and chemical/technical products.
Goods: medications, chemical products for healing purposes and health care, pharmaceutical drugs, preparations for body and beauty care, soaps, bleaching preparations and other substances for laundry use; starches and starching products for cosmetic purposes, all mentioned goods in fluid form. GK. 3, 5.

76/1195   22.4.76   76/1436

The above bottle represents a very peculiar packaging for mouth wash.

The following is an International Registration ("IR-Marke") showing the famous "Michelin man" as example for advertising figures or emblems which may be protected as trade mark.

registration date   *period of protection*   *registration no.*
↓   ↓   ↓

1er décembre 1980   20 ans   457 818

MICHELIN & CIE (COMPAGNIE GÉNÉRALE
DES ÉTABLISSEMENTS MICHELIN),
Société en commandite par actions
4, rue du Terrail, F-63 000 CLERMONT-FERRAND
(France)

↑
applicant/owner

specification of goods/services
↓

Cl.9: Appareils et instruments électriques (y compris la T.S.F.), optiques, de mesurage, de signalisation * Cl.11:Appareils et instruments d'éclairage * Cl.14:Produits d'horlogerie et articles de bijouterie, joaillerie, orfèvre-rie en vrai et en faux * Cl.16: Articles en papier, im-primés, matières adhésives, papeterie, cartes à jouer, sty-los, portecrayon * Cl.20: Articles décoratifs en matières plastiques * Cl.21: Articles de verrerie, porcelaine, faïence et récipients portatifs pour le ménage et la cuisine * Cl.24: Articles textiles décoratifs et, particulièrement, fanions, écussons * Cl.25: Blousons, anoraks, maillots à manches courtes, cravates, casquettes * Cl.26: Épingles de cravate, boutons de manchette, fleurs artificielles ; in-signes * Cl.28: Jeux, jouets, articles de sport * Cl.34: Briquets, cendriers, allumettes.

prior home registration

Origine: France,
26 juin 1980, Nos 4492/1 150 623 (premier dépôt au sens de   ←
l'article 4 de la Convention de Paris, selon déclaration du déposant).

designated states

Pays intéressés: Allemagne, République fédérale d'; Autriche;   ←
Benelux; Espagne; Italie; Liechtenstein; Monaco; Portugal; Saint-Marin; Suisse.

7. Colors and Color Combinations

Few would disagree that we are influenced by colors, that we associate colors with specific phenomena and that they arouse our emotions. That is why consistent use of a color or a combination of colors is utilized for profiling and marketing of companies, products and services. But even so, is it possible to claim the sole right to a color? Is it perhaps even possible to register a color as a trade mark?

Yellow, red and orange are warm colors, while blue, green and violet are cold ones. Warm colors are seen as stimulating and cold ones as calming. While evidence for these assertions is often sketch, they are used in such widely differing disciplines as architecture, therapeutic treatments and naturally in marketing. Whether we believe the assertions or not, we can agree that colors affect people differently. In some situations, color identifies function, just as words or pictures do. Still, in comparison with words, color is more flexible since it can be used in different ways, while a word or picture always looks the same. With this in mind, shouldn't it be possible to assert the identification and role of color in support of claiming the sole right to that identification?

For some years now there has existed a theoretical possibility of registering colors, as well as fragrances and sounds as Trademarks in Germany. The trade mark must, as already mentioned, be able to be depicted graphically and the basic requirement of distinctness applies to colors as well. The color should be able to distinguish one company's goods and services from another's.

Seen from the perspective of traditional Trademark law, it is difficult to imagine that a color has distinctness. A color is not normally used to delineate a company's goods and services, and all colors must be available for everyone to use in marketing. Nor is it intended that anyone should be able to monopolize a color for certain goods and services and block all use of that special color in connection with other goods and services. However, there might exist a justifiable interest in being able to reserve the sole right to the use of a special color as an identification for a limited number of goods and services.

The requirement for distinctness must include the restriction that the color to be used for these goods and services is not used publicly, such as yellow and red for traffic signs. Nor may it have a practical or functional meaning, such as the bright yellow used for alpine rescue services. But in situations where the registration of the color would not restrict other uses, and where there does not already exist a justifiable need for others to use that exact color, it should be possible to register the color.

Still, it isn't that easy to register a color. The possibility is still relatively new and lacks precedents in German practice. However, interest for these somewhat unusual trade marks is growing, which should create such precedents in future. The description of the goods and services will probably have to be very specific and descriptions which are too general or comprehensive will hardly be approved. In addition, the color must be carefully indicated, using such systems as the RAL -

German standard - system. Finally, it is probable that at least in the foreseeable future evidence of trade mark establishment must be presented. One of the best ways to prove that a trade mark has distinctness is to demonstrate that it is actually perceived as a trade mark, e.g., the color violet for chocolate (violet wrapping) from Jacobs Suchard.

Even if the sole right to the color cannot be registered as a trade mark, it is important to continue to use the color as a trade mark consistently. If possible, action should be taken against any infringement of the right developed in this way.

There exist a number of cases in other countries where a color has been protected. France has granted trade mark status to a traditional pink color long used for baking powder and a specific shade of green-gold color registered in the U.S. for the clothes press pads used in dry-cleaning.

In conclusion it is worth noting that a combination of colors has a higher degree of distinctness and is probably easier both to get registered and to defend as an established trade mark.

GERMAN TELECOM

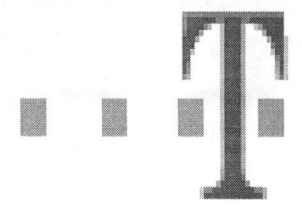

8. Applications of Geographical Origin

Concerning applications of geographical origin which also fall under the new Trademark Act, only the following brief explanation is being given. Under Par. 126, sec 1 Trademark Act, such appellations include the names of :

- places
- regions
- countries

Such signs can include words and/or pictures.
- The "Eifel Tower" indicates for example "Paris".
- The word "Champagne" characterizes a sparkling wine from the region of "Champagne" (France).
- "Made in Thailand" indicates a product manufactured in Thailand.

In contrast to trade marks and other trade names, the appellations of geographical origin do not distinguish goods or services of one enterprise from another. For example, "WALLIS" is not registrablefor cosmetic products because it is a well known Region in Switzerland. There have to be at last negative connotations in the target country kept in mind, which can be seen from for example "IRISH MIST" i.e. "Irish Manure" in German, or "NIX" i.e. "Nothing" in German.

Class 33 : The IRISH MIST Liqueur

Class 3 : The NIX detergent

Basically, they may be used by all enterprises located in the geographic region in question. Thus such appellations incorporate a

collective good will

to which all enterprises concerned are commonly entitled.

On the other hand, so called pseudo-designations of origin suggest a geographic region. In reality however they have no geographic origin or have lost their original geographic meaning through improper use, e.g.,

"Wienerschnitzel"

for a special type of breaded veal, or

"Pilsener" or "Pils"

for a special type of beer (Note : "Pilsener-Urquell" is a protected designation). These pseudo-designations are not protected by the Trademark Act.

D. Acquiring Trademark Protection

According to Par. 4 of the Trademark Act, protection arises through:

- the registration of a sign as a trade mark in the register at the German Patent Office,
- the commercial use of the sign in the market, provided that the sign has acquired prominence as a trade mark within the relevant trade circles, or
- the notoriety of a mark, i.e., it has become well known in the sense of Article 6 of the Paris Convention.

  1. Concerning protection of a trade mark by registration, details will be provided later.

  2. When trade mark protection is asserted based on use and corresponding prominence of a mark in Germany, it is necessary to prove a sufficient

     Degree of Reputation.

     If the mark is distinctive per se, no reputation is required. For less distinctive marks, extensive use is required, whereby the origin should be apparent.

  3. In Germany, the "notoriety" of a mark does not require that the mark also be used in Germany. In practice, this is difficult to imagine, however, use in Germany is not a prerequisite for "attaining notoriety".

     A rather extreme example relates to the former East Germany (DDR). The mark "NIVEA" was a very well known mark for skin creme. In the former East Germany, it doubtless had notoriety, although the product was not available there.

To give you a feeling for the relationship between a mark being well known and acquiring protection, I refer to the following illustration:

4. Relationship between Notoriety and Protection

Type of Mark	Degree of Reputation				
	No Reputation Required	Well Known Mark > 33 %	Established Mark > 50 %	Notorious Mark > 60 %	Famous Mark > 80 %
Registered Mark	Start of Protection by Registration	Protection against Dilution or Exploitation			
Non-Registered Mark			Start of Protection	Protection against Dilution or Exploitation	
Mark not used and not registered in Germany				Start of Protection	Protection against Dilution or Exploitation

The proof of sufficient prominence of a mark can be provided on the basis of a

demographic poll

e.g., for a mark relating to clothing, kitchen appliances or dishes, about 2000 should be questioned who are representative of the entire population according to age, sex, occupation and income. The costs for such a poll range from € 10,000 to € 20,000.

Instead of demographic polls, other types of evidence are recognized, such as

- information from professional organizations
- information from Chambers of Commerce
- proven expenses for advertising
- sales figures compared to the competition.

E. Protection obtained by Registration

The normal and usually simpler method of obtaining trade mark protection is by

<u>application</u>

at the German Patent Office and by

<u>registration</u>

in the Register. The requirements include:

- an official application and
- payment of the prescribed office fees.

A separate application at the German Patent Office is required for each mark to be protected. The minimal requirements for the application according to Par. 32, sec 2 Trademark Act are:

1. the name and address of the applicant
2. a reproduction of the trade mark
3. a list of the goods and/or services.

In addition, the application should state in which <u>form</u> the mark is to be registered, i.e., as a

- word mark
- design mark
- three dimensional mark
- acoustic mark, etc.

For design marks, combined word and design marks as well as three dimensional marks, a two dimensional reproduction should be provided. For the three dimensional marks, views from six different angles are allowed.

A mark can be registered for goods and/or services of several classes according to the Nice Classification Convention of June 15, 1957. It is not necessary as in some other countries to file a separate application for each class of goods or services.

According to Par. 32, sec 4 Trademark Act, a fee of € 300.- is to be paid with the application. The application fee includes up to three classes of goods and/or services. For each additional class, a class fee of € 100.- is due.

If the applicant wishes to claim priority of an earlier foreign application, this can be done within two months after the German filing date (Par. 34 sec. 3 Trademark Act). The priority period is six months according to Article 4 of the Paris Convention. Instead of the Paris Convention, it is also possible that a

reciprocity agreement

exists with the country of the applicant.

Finally, it should be noted that an applicant without residency or a place of business in Germany requires a

local representative

namely, a German Patent Attorney or lawyer. He represents the case before the German Patent Office or the Federal Patent Court (Par. 96 Trademark Act).

According to Par. 35 Trademark Act it is also possible to claim a

trade fair priority.

In such a case, it must be an officially recognized domestic or international exhibition, at which the goods or services are offered under the trade mark in question. This priority by means of a trade fair can be claimed by domestic or foreign applicants. The priority period is six months.

F. Procedures for Registering a Trademark

1. Examination of the Filing Requirements

Upon filing, it is examined whether the above mentioned

Formalities

for application of a mark are fulfilled. If the Patent Office finds deficiencies and if these are not remedied within a term set by the Patent Office, the application is considered not to have been filed. When the deficiencies are subsequently overcome, the application date is shifted to the day the deficiencies have been remedied.

2. Examination by the Patent Office with respect to Absolute Bars to Protection

The substantive law (Par. 8 Trademark Act) provides for examination of the mark with respect to absolute bars to protection. Excluded from protection are:

- signs which cannot be graphically represented (Par. 3 Trademark Act)
- signs which are devoid of any distinctive character, i.e., are not suited to distinguish the goods and/or services of one enterprise from those of another (Par. 3, sec 1 Trademark Act)
- signs that should belong to the public domain, i.e., signs which in the market could denote the kind, composition, quantity, intended purpose, value, geographic origin, date of production of the goods or of providing services or other characteristics of the goods or services
- signs which have become customary everyday language or which have become common usage in established practice in trade for the goods or services (Par. 8, sec 2, nos. 2 and 3 Trademark Act)
- national emblems, national coats of arms, inspection signs or signs of quality
- marks offending against public order or decency and morality
- signs which would obviously confuse the public as to the type, composition or geographical origin of the goods or services
- signs whose use would obviously be prohibited in view of public interest
- signs which would collide with a well known foreign mark.

If the German Patent Office finds such bars to protection with respect to all or part of the goods or services, the application is either partially or completely rejected. The applicant can respond with a first instance appeal

if the decision came from the "First Examiner". In addition, a

second instance appeal

is possible if the decision resulted from a "first instance examiner". The second appeal is handled by the Federal Patent Court. If the Federal Patent Court finds that basic legal issues require clarification, it may allow the

legal appeal (revision)

which goes to the

Federal Supreme Court.

Repetitive: The sequence of instances

Second Instance Appeal
(Federal Supreme Court)

⇧

First Instance Appeal
(Federal Patent and Trademark Court)

⇧

Reconsideration Proceedings
(Senior Examiner, legally educated)

⇧

Examiner

It should be mentioned that the applicant may <u>limit</u> the list of goods and/or services in examination proceedings, however, cannot extend the list. In addition, nothing can be amended with respect to the presentation of the trade mark itself.

Example: The filed trade mark comprises a part which includes the Thai national emblem. The objection to this cannot be remedied in that the applicant requests that this part of the trade mark be removed.

The same holds if a filed trade mark contains a part including a well known sign, e.g., the auto mark FORD. Amending the mark by removing the FORD emblem is also not possible.

When all of the objections of the German Patent Office or of the Federal Patent Court are overcome, possibly by limiting the goods and/or services, the trade mark is registered in the Register with all relevant data. The applicant receives a registration document and a detailed certificate with all essential data of the registration.

An illustration of the trade mark with all of the data (also later amendments such as name changes, assignments, legal actions, etc.) are published in the Trademark Gazette published by the Patent Office.

20.10.1997 B 13783
Heft 29
Seiten 12987–13278
Seiten N 579–N 590
3. Jahrgang
ISSN 0947-787X

MARKENBLATT

Veröffentlichungen auf Grund des Markengesetzes
Herausgegeben vom Deutschen Patentamt

INHALTSVERZEICHNIS

TEIL 1 Eingetragene Marken	12988
a) gegen die Widerspruch erhoben werden kann	12989
b) gegen die kein Widerspruch mehr erhoben werden kann	13198
TEIL 2 Widersprüche	13200
TEIL 3 Teilungen, Rechtsübergänge, Teilweise Rechtsübergänge	13209
TEIL 4 Verlängerungen	13212
TEIL 5 Löschungen, Teillöschungen	13219
TEIL 6 Dingliche Rechte, Zwangsvollstreckung, Konkursverfahren	13227
TEIL 7 Geographische Angaben/Ursprungsbezeichnungen (VO (EWG) Nr. 2081/92)	–
TEIL 8 Änderungen, Berichtigungen	13228
Früher bekanntgemachte Zeichen, die nicht eingetragen wurden	13241
Vergleichshinweise	13242
Nach Registernummern geordnetes Verzeichnis	13248
International registrierte Marken	–

Klasse 32   −1006−   Teil II / Heft 5 vom 15.3.1990

32   1 153 368   P 38153/32 Wz

10.6.89. Privatbrauerei Dortmunder Kronen GmbH & Co., 4600 Dortmund 1, Märkische Str. 85.
Geschäftsbetrieb: Brauerei

Waren/Dienstleistungen: Exportbier. − Farbig. GK. 32.
15.9.89   1.2.90   15.3.90

The publication allows owners of older trade marks to examine whether the newly entered marks collide with existing marks or company names. Such watches are conducted by Patent Attorneys or patent information firms, such as COMPUMARK or the like. The costs for watching a mark in one class are about € 500.- per year.

3. Relative Bars to Protection

Starting from the publication date in the Trademark Gazette a

three month Opposition term

begins. Within this term, the owners of older marks of prior time rank or owners of prior applications may file

Opposition.

The filing of an Opposition requires payment of an Official fee of € 120.-. The owners of <u>other</u> older signs such as

- Companies
- company logos
- work titles, such as book titles, magazine titles, film titles, music titles, theatre titles, etc.
- design rights in respect of graphic signs
- copyrights

are required to file a

cancellation action

before a civil court and/or to prohibit the use of such a mark before a civil court with a request for

injunction.

In all of the above cases it is examined whether

a. a similarity exists between the goods or services of the older sign with those of the opposed trade mark, and

b. a similarity between the compared signs exists with respect to :

- phonetics
- conceptual content, or
- graphic representation including character type for word marks.

Prior copyrights go beyond the similarity of goods or services. Again, in opposition cases the possibility of a

first instance appeal

exists against the decision of a "first examiner". A

<u>second instance appeal</u>

is possible against a decision of the first instance examiner. Further, if basic legal issues are in question a

<u>legal appeal (revision)</u>

is possible.

The course of the legal procedures in Opposition proceedings are the same as those in prosecution proceedings, except that in Opposition, two parties are present.

An extended protection exists for owners of

<u>well known or notorious trade marks.</u>

Such marks can have validity beyond the scope of similar goods and/or services. The protection scope is broader, the more notorious the mark is. The enforcement of such marks is made before a civil court because an Opposition at the German Patent Office, as mentioned above, can only be based on an older trade mark application or trade mark registration.

The owner of a trade mark

<u>well known in Germany</u>

can prohibit the use by third parties of an identical or similar sign even for non-similar goods/services in so far as the use of the sign in the market <u>exploits</u> or <u>diminishes</u> the value of the well known mark.

Example: "Dimple" is a well known mark for Whisky of higher quality. The owner of that mark could prohibit the use of it for "men's cosmetics".

An even further extended protection is enjoyed by "notorious" trade marks. Notorious marks enjoy absolute protection in all branches of the market. Notorious marks in Germany are, e.g.,

CAMEL	(originally only cigarettes)
4711	(cologne for men)
Mercedes	(Mercedes Star)

Repetitive: Well known and notorious Trademark

Well known or notorious Trademarks
validity beyond the scope of similar goods and/or services

Example: CAMEL (originally only cigarettes)
4711   (cologne for men)
Mercedes (Mercedes Star)

Well known in Germany
prohibition of use for identical or similar signs even for non-similar goods/services

Example: „Dimple" prohibited for „men´s cosmetics"

4. Acquisition and Loss of Trade Marks

a. The owner of a trade mark can prolong the protection of a registered mark (for all or part of the registered goods/services) repeatedly in ten year periods by payment of the extension fee. The fee is € 600.- per mark for up to three classes. For each additional class, an additional fee of € 260.- is due. The extension of a mark is published in the Trademark Gazette.

b. According to Par. 49 Trademark Act, the registration of a trade mark can be cancelled upon request by any third party. This is the case if the trade mark is <u>not used</u> in an uninterrupted time period of five years according to Par. 26 Trademark Act from the date of registration or from the conclusion of an Opposition proceeding. The request by the third party can be made at the German Patent Office (Par. 53 Trademark Act). If the owner of the trade mark does not react to the request within two months from the date of service of the cancellation request, the trade mark registration is being cancelled. If the owner opposes the request, the third party is required to take further legal action, i.e., a cancellation action before a civil court.

The objection of lack of use can also be made in an Opposition proceeding before the German Patent Office or before the Federal Patent Court. This also applies to the mark asserted in Opposition in so far as this mark has been registered longer than five years. If the Opponent in such a case cannot substantiate sufficient use, the Opposition is dismissed without any examination of the matter of confusion.

With respect to the requirement of use, Par. 26 Trademark Act was mentioned. This provision specifies the necessary form of the use of a trade mark such that its validity can be maintained. Basically, the <u>registered trade mark</u> must be used in the form in which it is <u>registered</u>, i.e., with all of the word, graphics, form or acoustic elements of which it consists, without leaving out or adding anything.

Repetitive: Renewal and Cancellation of registered Trademarks

Renewal of registered Trademark
for all or part of the registerd goods/services repeatedly in a ten years period by payment of extension fee

Cancellation upon request by a third party
if not used in an uninterrupted period of five years (Grace period : First five years after registration)

but :

No Office Action requesting proof of use

Modifications by the owner can only be allowed if they do not alter the distinctive character of the trade mark. Whether this is true or not depends on the particular market, i.e., on the particular case. In the following two cases, it was found that a valid use of the registered mark had taken place.

1. The Appeals Court in Munich had to make a decision in the following case. The trade mark "ALISEO" was registered for hair dryers as shown below

Registered

aliseo

The trade mark was, however, only used as a word mark according to

Actually Used

ALISEO

The usage of this Trademark is different from the registered form only in details, thus protected. Moreover, the trade mark was only used on business papers and not on hair driers.

The Appeal Court held in its judgment of January 25, 1996 that there was a use preserving rights in spite of the modified form of use. The distinctive character of the trade mark was the word "ALISEO", the picture component was only an addition. The change of the type face from a wavelike form into normal type was an insignificant modification. The fact that the trade mark was only used on business papers also had no negative effects. According to the new trade mark law the described use is sufficient.

2. There is a similar decision of the Federal Patents Court. The trade mark "Manhattan" was registered for cigarettes. The trade mark was, however, only used in the form shown below

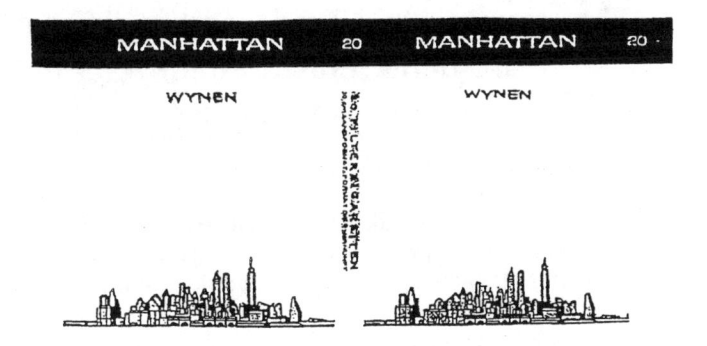

that is to say together with the word "wynen" as well as the skyline of a city with high-rise buildings.

Also, in this case the Federal Patents Court confirmed a use preserving rights in its decision of February 1, 1995. These two examples show that a use preserving rights is taken for granted if the trade mark as such is clearly recognisable.

Repetitive: Registered and actually used Trademarks

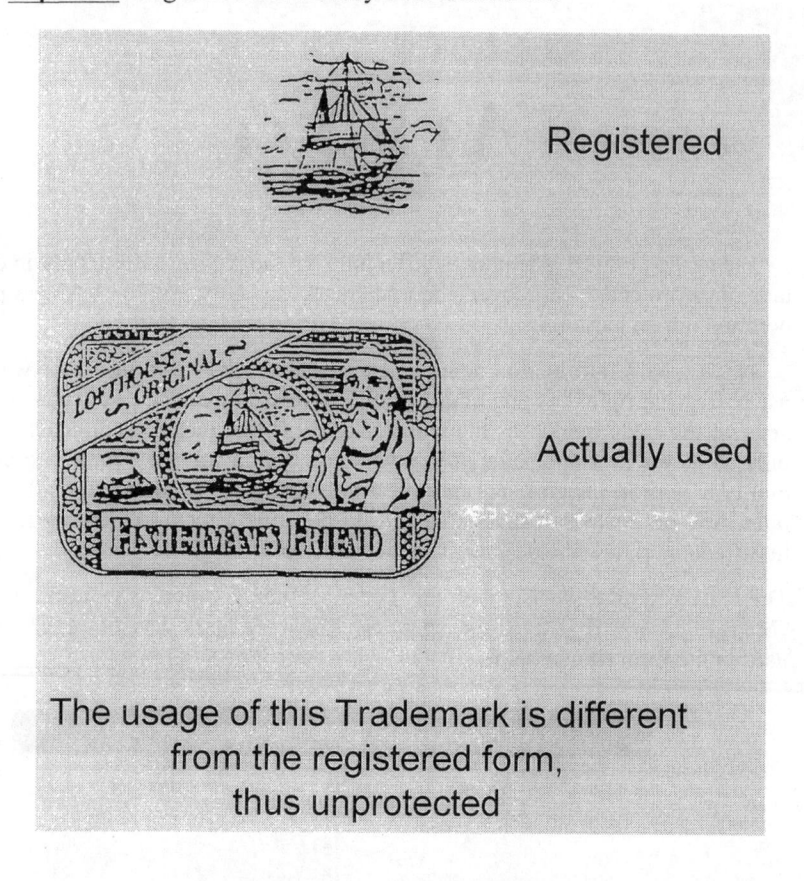

Registered

Actually used

The usage of this Trademark is different from the registered form, thus unprotected

Before the new German Trademark Act entered into force on January 1, 1995, the case law was much more restricted. For example, the use of the registered single word ARTREXFORTE, but in the modified form with a hyphen, i.e., AR-TREX-FORTE was not found to be sufficient to preserve the trade mark right. The above two examples show that the previous restrictive interpretation is no longer applicable. The newer case law accounts for the rapid transition in marketing and the corresponding representations of registered trade marks.

Example: A trade mark registered for "pharmaceutical products" is used for "bandages". Although bandages and pharmaceutical products have similarity, the use does not support the registered goods "pharmaceutical products".

The scope of use must be serious, even a small volume of sales can be sufficient if it is commercially relevant. Unsubstantiated business transactions are not sufficient to preserve the right of a trade mark.

G. Miscellaneous

1. Searches for Older Signs

The extensive effort required in developing a new trade mark can be worthless if a conflict exists with an already existing trade mark. Since the German Patent Office only investigates absolute bars to protection in the registration proceedings, a conflicting older trade mark or an older sign, e.g., an older company name, only becomes apparent in an <u>Opposition</u> before the German Patent Office or the Federal Patents Court or in a <u>cancellation action</u> before a civil court. To avoid this possibility and in particular also to avoid infringing a registered mark, an older title, e.g., a newspaper or film title, or an older company name, it is indispensable and legally advisable (negligence and possibility liability damages by infringement) to investigate whether an identical or similar trade mark, company or title already exists for the same or similar goods and/or services. The corresponding investigation is made by a search in the relevant documents including:

- trade mark register of the German Patent Office
- international trade mark register (W.I.P.O.)
- for design marks, the German and International design registers
- the register of the Community Trademarks
- registered and used titles (books, films, computer software)
- register of companies.

To carry out such searches, a Patent Attorney, specialized lawyer or a specialized firm, e.g., COMPUMARK should be commissioned. The latter, however, is not authorized to provide advice as to the relevance of the signs located. For this a Patent Attorney or attorney at law must be consulted. The costs of such searches are as follows:

Schedule of Charges 2002 Searches for Trademarks valid in Germany (German National Marks, IR-Marks and EU-Marks)	
Type of Search	Attorneys Fee €
Full Availability Search	approx. 400.-
Identity Search	approx. 90.-
Proprietor Search	approx. 460.-
Status Search	approx. 20.-
Costs for an Opinion	approx. 100.- to 225.- per target mark

Note : The searches are for target mark in a maximum of 2 classes and do not include disbursements for copies, etc. For any extra the price is increased by € 150.00 per class. Costs are given for normal turn-around times, that is max. 11 working days.

Type of Search	Germany only €
Searches for the Use of Word and Design Marks (e.g. to check wether a trade mark registered for more than five years has been used or to determine the prominence of a mark)	approx. 700.-
Design Registrations (important for design or graphic trade marks	approx. 700.-

Based on experience, a search of registered marks, company designations, copyrights, etc. is highly recommended before filing a trade mark application in Germany or a Community Trademark application at the OHIM or in particular before using such a mark. Unpleasant complications at a later date can be avoided in this way. Such complications could include:

- worthless filing costs
- useless expense for advertising, packaging, or the like
- possible confiscation and destruction of the products having an infringing sign
- stressful search for a replacement trade mark to fulfil an order and the delivery of products to Germany
- attorney and court costs
- contract penalties due to non-fulfilment of a delivery contract.

Compared to the risks mentioned with corresponding financial burdens, the costs for the mentioned searches is negligible, even if one includes the costs of an attorney for evaluating the search results. These costs are normally about € 300.- to € 500.- depending on the particular case.

2. Filing Costs (Trademark Application)

Speaking about costs, the costs for filing a trade mark application are always an initial consideration. In this respect, it is referred to the following fees schedule:

German Trademarks		
Filing Costs	Official Fee €	Attorneys Fee €
Representing and filing an application (1 to 3 classes)	300.-	600.-
Additional fee for each further class	100.-	90.-
Requesting accelerated proceedings	200.-	150.-
Filing formal Opposition	120.-	500.-

The attorney's fee shown here represents an average value. Some attorneys charge more while others charge less. It often occurs that additional consultation is required which goes beyond the filing and registration procedure for a new trade mark. In this situation, it is recommended that an hourly rate is negotiated upon with the attorney and that a cost estimate is being obtained for the legal consultation. As an average hourly honorary in Germany, one can expect about € 200.- to € 300.- for Patent Attorneys as well as Attorneys at Law.

Normally, this is also the basis for work performed in an Opposition proceeding before the German Patent and Trademark Office or the Federal Patents Court. The office fees and basic attorney fees illustrated previously will be charged in addition to the hourly attorney's fee.

H. Coexistence of Trade Marks

The German trade mark may coexist with:

- International Registrations under the Madrid Agreement (MMA) and the Madrid Protocol (MMP) as well as
- the Community Trademarks

1. Introduction of Madrid Agreement and Madrid Protocol

a. For more than a hundred years, the Madrid Agreement concerning the International Registration of marks has provided for the possibility of obtaining the protection of a trade mark or service mark in several countries by means of a single International Registration. It was adopted on April 14, 1891 and revised on several occasions, but its main features have remained basically the same during the past century.

b. At present 67 countries are party to the Madrid Agreement. They are mainly countries from continental Europe (including the Russian Federation and most of the former Republics of the Soviet Union), countries in the northern part of Africa and four countries in the Far East : China, the Democratic People's Republic of Korea, Mongolia and VietNam. A number of countries which are very important in terms of trade mark filing activity are missing. These are common law countries, in particular the United

States of America and the United Kingdom, and also the Scandinavian countries, most of the Latin American countries, as well as Japan.

c. Since the entry into force of the Madrid Agreement, some 680,000 International Registrations have been made. In view of the fact that each International Registration covers, on average, 10 countries, these 680,000 International Registrations are equivalent to nearly seven million national registrations. It should also be taken into account that the Madrid system is a multi-class system so that one and the same International Registration may cover several classes of the international classification. At present, close to 300,000 International Registrations are still in force. The oldest International Registration which is still in force dates back to March 27, 1893 (the famous Swiss mark LONGINES for watches).

d. In fact, among the participating countries, the Madrid Agreement has been and continues to be a big success. Trademark owners in the member countries largely favour the Madrid system route for protecting their marks abroad, in particular because it is very simple, cheap and efficient.

2. Main Features of the Madrid Agreement

The main features of the Madrid Agreement can be summarized as follows:

a. Firstly, the applicant must be a national of a country being party to the Madrid Agreement or a person having his domicile or a real and effective industrial or commercial establishment in such a country.

b. Secondly, the mark which is intended to be replaced internationally must first be registered at the national level by the Trademark Office of the country of origin of the applicant. That first registration is called the "Home Registration" and it must precede the International Registration.

c. Thirdly, there is no direct filing with the International Bureau (W.I.P.O.) under the Madrid Agreement. The application for International Registration must be filed with the Office of the country of origin, which will transmit it to the International Bureau (W.I.P.O.) in Geneva.

d. The role of the Office of the country of origin is not only to transmit the application for International Registration to the International Bureau (W.I.P.O.), but also to certify that the mark which is the subject of the application for International Registration is the same as the mark which is the subject of the Home Registration, and that the goods and/or services for which protection is sought are covered by the goods and/or services for which the Home Registration is registered.

e. Fourthly, the application form on which the international application must be filed must contain, <u>inter alia</u>, the list of the countries party to the Madrid Agreement in which protection is sought (the so-called "designated countries").

f. Fees are to be paid. Part of them belong to W.I.P.O. (and cover the expenses of the International Bureau in respect of the international procedure). There is also a designation fee which has to be paid for each designated country. It is called, in Madrid terminology, the "complementary fee" and its amount is the same for each designated country. In addition, if the list of goods and/or services for which protection is sought covers more than three classes of the International (Nice) Classification, the applicant has to pay a "supplementary fee" for each class of goods and/or services beyond the third class.

g. Fifthly, once all the required conditions have been met, including the payment of the fees, the International Bureau (W.I.P.O.) registers the mark in the International Register, notifies the International Registration to the Offices of the designated countries and publishes it in a monthly periodical called "Les Marques internationales". Under the Madrid Agreement, French is the only working language and all communications to W.I.P.O. (including the international application) must be in French; that situation is changed under the Madrid Protocol.

h. A mark which is recorded in the International Register - and this is the sixth feature of the Madrid system - is subject to the same regime in each designated country as a mark filed with the national Office of that country. During a period of one year, the Office of each designated country has the right to declare, in a notification of refusal addressed to the International Bureau (W.I.P.O.). That protection cannot be granted in the country concerned, in respect of some or all of the goods and/or services covered, to the mark which is the subject of an International Registration notified to the said Office by the International Bureau (W.I.P.O.). That refusal must indicate all the grounds on which it is based. Those grounds may only be grounds that would here be applied in the case of a national mark filed with the Office which notifies the refusal. Therefore, an International Registration under the Madrid Agreement designating Germany is to be considered the same as the German national registration.

i. Seventh, if there is no refusal of protection within the prescribed time limit, or where a refusal has been withdrawn by the Office of a designated country, the mark must be considered as registered in that designated country as of the date of the International Registration.

j. Finally, during the first five years from the date of International Registration, the validity of the International Registration is dependent on the Home Registration in the country of origin. If during those five years the Home Registration is cancelled, the International Registration no longer has any effect in any of the designated countries and it is cancelled at the request of the Office of origin. The same applies when national protection in the country of origin has ceased as a result of an action before a court, begun before the expiration of a period of five years from the date of the International Registration (Article 6(3)). The possibility to attack the International Registration through the national registration in the country of origin is very often referred to as the "central attack" feature of the Madrid Agreement, because it gives to the owner of a mark which is in conflict with the holder of an International Registration in several countries party to the Madrid Agreement the possibility of introducing a single action against the Home Registration in the country of origin, instead of introducing separate actions before the competent court of each designated country.

Repetitive: Main features of the Madrid Argeement

a) Applicant must be a national of a country to the MMA

b) Intended mark must first be registered at national level („Home Registration")

c) Application must be filed with the applicant´s national office

d) Office certifies identity and transmits application to W.I.P.O.

e) Application must contain countries where protection is sought

f) Supplementary fees have to be paid

g) Registration, Notification and Publishing through W.I.P.O.

h) Registered mark is subject to same regime in each country

i) Considered to be registered in designated country if not refused

j) During first five years dependent on validity of Home Registration

3. Necessity to Amend the Madrid System

Although, as said before, the Madrid system has been extensively used by trade mark owners of the member countries for more than one century now, the number of member countries has remained relatively low and has also remained geographically limited. This is so because a number of features of the Madrid system have proved to be obstacles to accession for several States. Those features are the following five:

    a. First, the necessity of obtaining, as a prerequisite to International Registration, a Home Registration of the mark at the national level, in the country of origin, and it is insisted on the word registration because, in many countries, the examination of a trade mark application takes a long time and a trade mark registration is not easily and rapidly obtained.

    b. Second, the relative shortness (one year) of the time limit within which the designated Office can examine the mark and issue a notification of refusal giving all the grounds for refusal.

    c. Third, the system of fees, in particular the uniform fee paid for the designation of a country, is considered by some countries having a high level of national fees to be inappropriate, because such a country would receive less money under the Madrid system than under its national system.

    d. Fourth, the fact that the International Registration remains linked to the Home Registration during five years and must be cancelled if the Home Registration is cancelled has been considered, in some countries, as being too strict since the grounds for cancellation of the mark in the country of origin do not necessarily exist in each of the designated countries.

    e. And finally, this is the fifth feature, the Regulations implementing the Madrid Agreement provide for a single working language, French.

Repetitive: Amendments to the Madrid System

> a) International application may also be based on a national <u>application</u>
>
> b) Time limit for refusal may be extended to up to 18 months by declaration
>
> c) MMA fee system and individual fee system may be choosen
>
> d) Conversion into national applications if Home application is subject to cancellation
>
> e) French is accepted as working language
>
> f) Possibility to intergovernmental organisation to join the Protocol

The Madrid Protocol addresses these issues, wherein the objectives of the Madrid Protocol are two-fold. Firstly, to attract new States to the Madrid System, in particular those member States of the European Community which are not yet party to the Madrid Agreement, but also countries like Japan, the United States of America and other countries in Asia and in America. And secondly, the Madrid Protocol aims to create links between the Madrid system and the Community Trademark system.

4. Innovations Introduced by the Madrid Protocol

In order to attract new member States, at present 9 states, the Madrid Protocol has introduced four major innovations into the Madrid system.

 a. The first innovation is the following. Whereas under the Madrid Agreement an international application must be based on a national registration in the country of origin, under the Protocol an international <u>application</u> may also be based on a national (or regional) application.

b. The second innovation is the following. Whereas, under the Madrid Agreement, any notification of refusal by the Office of a designated country must be sent to W.I.P.O. within a time limit of one year, the Madrid Protocol, while keeping that deadline as the basic deadline, provides for exceptions that are intended to allow accession to the Protocol by States that consider one year a too short time for the Office to communicate even provisional refusals. Under Article 5(2)(b) of the Madrid Protocol, any Member State can make a declaration to the effect that the one-year time limit is replaced by 18 months.

c. The third innovation introduced by the Madrid Protocol is the individual fee system. Under the Protocol, any Member State may choose between two fee systems. It can choose the existing Madrid Agreement system under which the designation of a Contracting Party is subject to the payment of a fee whose amount is the same for any Member State to which that system applies. But a Member State may also choose the so-called "individual fee" system which basically means that it can itself fix the amount of the fee which it wishes to receive whenever it is designated.

d. The fourth major innovation introduced by the Protocol is the possibility of transforming an International Registration which has been cancelled as a result of the loss of effects of the basis application, of the registration resulting therefrom or of the Home Registration (for example, in case of central attack) into national (or regional) applications in the designated Member States. The said national (or regional) applications would benefit from the registration date of the International Registration and from its priority date under the Paris Convention, if any.

e. The fifth innovation introduced by the Protocol is that English besides French is accepted as a working language.

f. As regards the creation of links between the Madrid system and the Community trade mark system, the Protocol gives the possibility to an intergovernmental organisation to become party to the Protocol where that organisation has a regional office for the purpose of registering marks with effect in the territory of the organization. When the European Community becomes party to the Protocol, which it is hoped will be very soon, it will be possible for an International Registration to be based on a Community trade mark application or registration and, on the other hand, Protocol applicants would be able to designate the European Community in order to obtain, via the Madrid system, the effects of a Community trade mark registration.

5. Examples of Registrations under the Madrid Agreement (MMA) and the Madrid Protocol (MMP)

a.   *MMA-Registration*

(151) 26.09.1997   680 227
(732) **HERMES INTERNATIONAL**
(Société en commandite par actions)
24, rue du Faubourg Saint Honoré, F-75008 PARIS (FR).

TOGO

(551) 16 Porte-chéqiers.
18 Articles de maroquinerie en cuir ou imitation du cuir (à l´exeption des étuis adaptés aux produits quíls sont destinés à contenir, des gants et des ceintures); sacs, à savoir sacs à main, de voyage, à dos; portefeuilles, porte-monnai en cuir, porte-cartes (portefeuilles), étuis pour clefs (maroquinerie), porte-documents; malles et valises; fouets, harneis, selles et article de sellerie.

b.   *MMP-Registration*

(151) **04.09. 1997**   680 609
(732) Cent holding ag
     50, Wickererstrasse, D-65439 Flörsheim (Germany).

(531) 26.1; 26.4; 27.1.
(511) 35 Business management, business administration, management consultation.
36 Financial affairs, monetary affairs, real estate administration.
35 Gestion d´entreprise, administration commerciale, conseil en gestion.
36 Opérations financières, opérations monétaires, administration de biens immobiliers

Based on these examples, one can see that within the territory of Germany, one must not only consider German trade marks, but also International Registrations deriving from the Madrid Agreement and/or the Madrid Protocol. These International Registrations are treated on the same footing as a German trade mark. Just as with a German trade mark, opposition and/or cancellation actions can be initiated with effect for Germany. However, if a Home Registration is being cancelled in part or in full, and if its corresponding International Registration is registered for less than five years, this International Registration will automatically be cancelled to the very same extent as the Home Registration (so-called "Central Attack").

I. Some Statistics

Total Number of Trademark Applications during the last 6 years

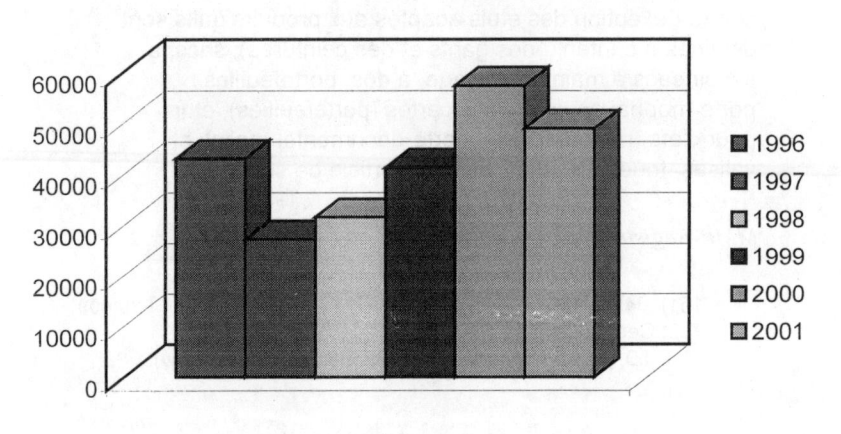

31.3.2002

Number of Trademark Applications of the Top 10 Countries

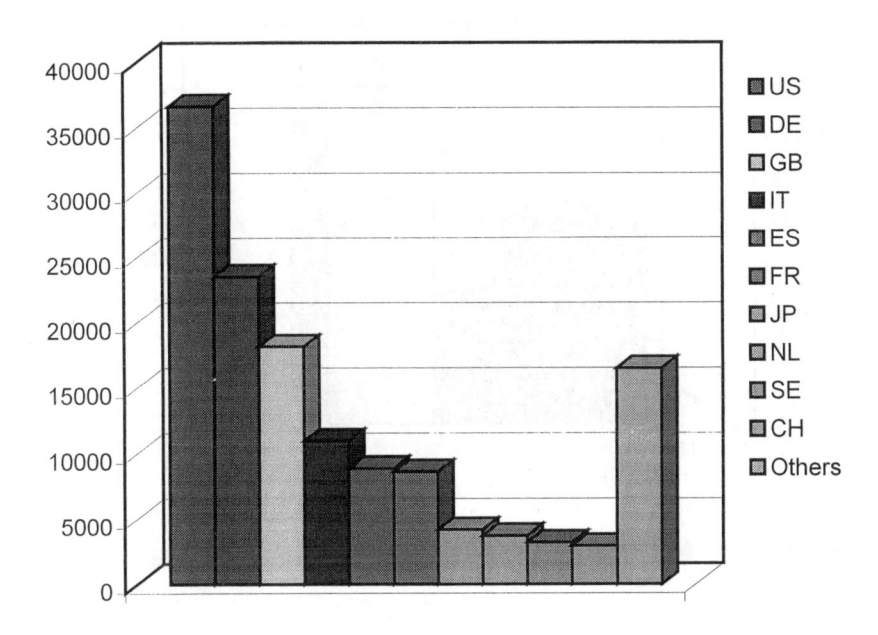

31.3.2002

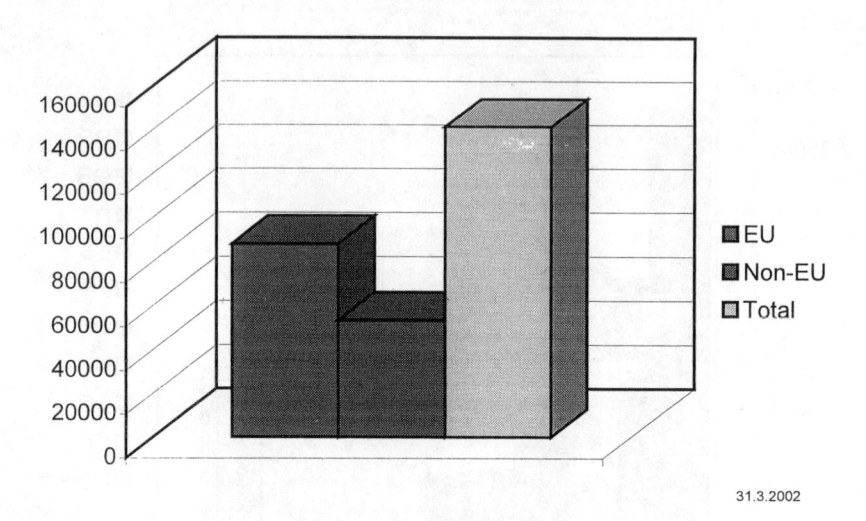

Total Number of Trademark Applications of Origin EU / Non-EU Countries

31.3.2002

Total Percentage of Trademark Applications of Origin EU / Non-EU Counties

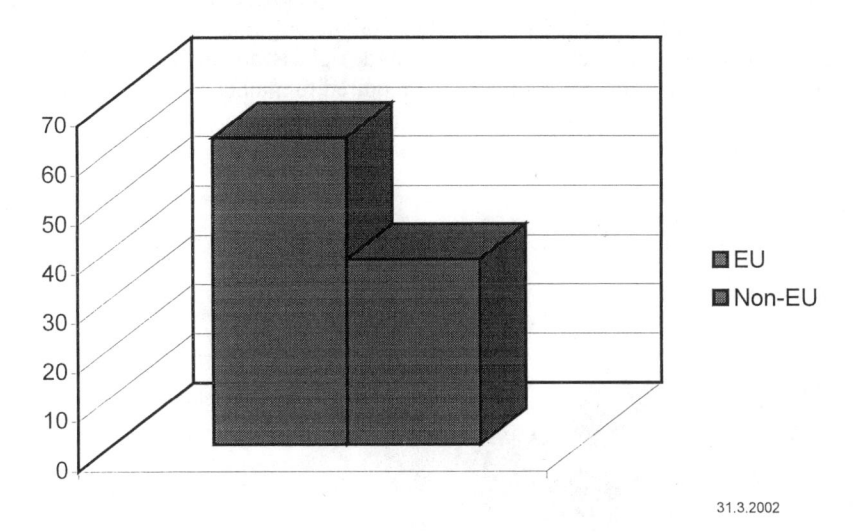

31.3.2002

III. Community Trademarks

The Community Trademark Convention provides coverage throughout the European Union on the basis of a single trade mark application. As opposed to the Madrid Agreement, there are no restrictions on the origin of Applicant; he may be an EU national or non-national. A trade mark right is obtained for all EU countries, while use in only part of the EU is required to maintain the right. Currently the EU member states covered include:

Austria
Finland
Italy
Belgium
France
Luxembourg
Germany
United Kingdom
Netherlands
Denmark
Greece
Portugal
Spain
Ireland
Sweden

The Community Trademark (CTM) system has been officially in effect since January 1, 1996, while the Trademark Office began full operation on April 1, 1996. The Trademark Office is located in Alicante, Spain, and is officially known as the Office for Harmonisation in the Internal Market (OHIM).

A. Application Requirements

Applicant shall be a national of a member State of the Paris Convention, however, need not be a national of a Member State of the European Union. Non-Europeans must be represented by a qualified professional.

A CTM application need not be based on an earlier national application, although filing will often be based on a priority claim. The CTM can be filed in any of the 11 languages of the EU Member States, while one alternative official language (English, German, French, Italian or Spanish) must be specified, for example for possible Opposition proceedings. The filing in Alicante can also be made by electronic mail or facsimile. In addition, applications may be filed at the national trade mark office of any Member State of the European Union.

Repetitive: Application Requirements

> a) Applicant shall be a national of a member State of the Paris Convention
>
> b) Applicant does not need to be national of the European Union
>
> c) Non-Europeans must be represented by a qualified professional
>
> d) No need for earlier national basic application, often priority claim
>
> e) Application can be filed in any of the 11 languages of the EU States
>
> f) Filing with OHIM in Alicante may be electronically or by facsimile
>
> g) Additional applications may be filed at the national Trademark office

B. Official Fees and Attorney's fees

are approximately as follows:

COMMUNITY Trademarks	Official Fee €	Attorneys Fee
Representing and filing an application (1 to 3 classes)	975.-	700.-
Additional fee each further class	200.-	90.-
Registration fee (1 to 3 classes)	1,100.-	350.-
Additional fee for each further class	200.-	90.-
Opposition	350.-	700.-

C. Examination and Registration

Upon registration, the OHIM will perform a search of prior CTM applications and registrations with respect to similarity with the filed mark. The results of this search will not be used for refusal, but are sent to the applicant as well as to the owners of the relevant CTMs found in the search. After publication of the application, the owners of these and other CTMs have the option of filing an Opposition.

The OHIM itself will not search national registrations, but the trade mark offices of several of the Member States will conduct a search for any earlier national marks which could lead to an objection and will communicate such marks to the OHIM in order for them to be included into the search report. Only the Patent and Trademark Offices of France, Italy and Germany do not provide a search report because these countries have a different principle in opposition, i.e., the Patent Office does not examine relative bars to protection of its own volition.

An example of a CTM publication is given below :

210 000168807

220 01/04/1996

442 17/11/1997

546

531 1.15.11, 20.5.15, 25.5.2, 27.5.13

731 C+D Consult & Design GmbH
     Im Mittleren Sand 48A
     65936 Frankfurt
     Germany

740 Meissner, Bolte & Partner
     Widenmayerstraße 48
     80538 Munich
     Germany

270 DE   EN

511 ES-25-clothing, in particular children's clothing, shoes.

D. Opposition

An opposition period of three months runs from the publication date, within which the owner of any prior conflicting mark may oppose the CTM registration. If refused in opposition proceedings, the application may be converted into separate national applications, for example in the countries where the prior conflicting rights do not exist.

If at least one opposition has been filed, an extendable "cooling off period" of initially two months commences in order to provide for time to negotiate a settlement of the opposition between the parties.

Repetitive: Opposition

> **Opposition**
>
> a) Opposition period of three months from publication date
>
> b) CTM-Application may be converted into separate national applications
>
> c) Extendable „Cooling off period" of initially two months

E. Seniority

To allow for a transition from national registrations to the CTM, a seniority claim is available. A CTM application may claim seniority from a previous national registration in any Member State. This will permit Applicant to make a CTM application covering all of the European Union Member States, while at the same time retaining his protection rights back to the filing date of his national registration. Having obtained the seniority right in the CTM application, the national registrations can be abandoned without loss of rights.

Repetitive: Seniority

> ## Seniority
>
> a) Application may claim seniority from a previous national registration
>
> b) Having obtained seniority right, national registration can be abandoned

F. Registration and Use

The CTM has a duration of ten years, after which renewal is possible without the necessity of filing proof of use. Validity of the mark requires use in any part of the European Union. The registration is subject to cancellation if it has not been used within the Union over a continuous period of five years.

Repetitive: Registration and Use

> ## Registration and Use
>
> a) Duration of 10 years, after which renewal is possible without filing proof of use
>
> b) Subject to cancellation if not used over a continuous period of five years

G. Litigation

Infringement and invalidity with respect to the CTM are dealt with by the respective national courts under national law. A CTM may be revoked in view of conflict with prior rights, including a prior right anywhere in the European Union. This may be the one disadvantage of the CTM system, however the CTM can be converted into national applications.

The CTM registration provides a single unitary right throughout the EU. Assignments or licences with respect to the mark are registered at the OHIM. Being unitary, the trade mark cannot be separately assigned to different parties for separate countries. However, it can be licensed to different parties for separate countries.

From these short remarks on the Community Trademark it can be recognized that such marks for Germany are just as important as national German trade marks. Actions can be taken against the Community Trademark out of prior national German marks or on the other hand, rights can be derived from Community trade marks against newer national trade mark applications.

In summary, the German trade mark competes in Germany not only with German designation rights, but stands on the same footing with:

- International Registrations under the Madrid Agreement and/or Madrid Protocol which designate Germany, as well as
- Community Trademarks.

Repetitive: CTM-Litigation

CTM-Litigation

a) Infringement and invalidity are dealt with by national courts and law

b) CTM may be revoked in view of conflict with prior rights in the EU

c) German Trademarks are equivalent to IR-Marks and CTMs

IV. Summary

A. What is a trade mark?

A mark distinguishes goods and services from those of another enterprise. Marks are the names, which "personalize" the product or service. A mark ensures the quality of the goods (guarantee and trust), the recognition of a product (advertising and origin) and the better quality (quality function).

The mark should also ensure the quality of the goods (guarantee and trust) as well as recognition of a certain product (advertising and origin) of the same or better quality (quality function) together with the technical advancement. The recognition function of a mark by the consumer and the control function of the owner of the mark was again confirmed by the European Court of Justice in the Ideal Standard decision dated June 22, 1994 (published in GRUR Int. 1994, 614 et seq.). The mark is therefore an instrument of consumer protection.

B. According to Par. 3 Trademark Act, marks can be registered in the following forms:

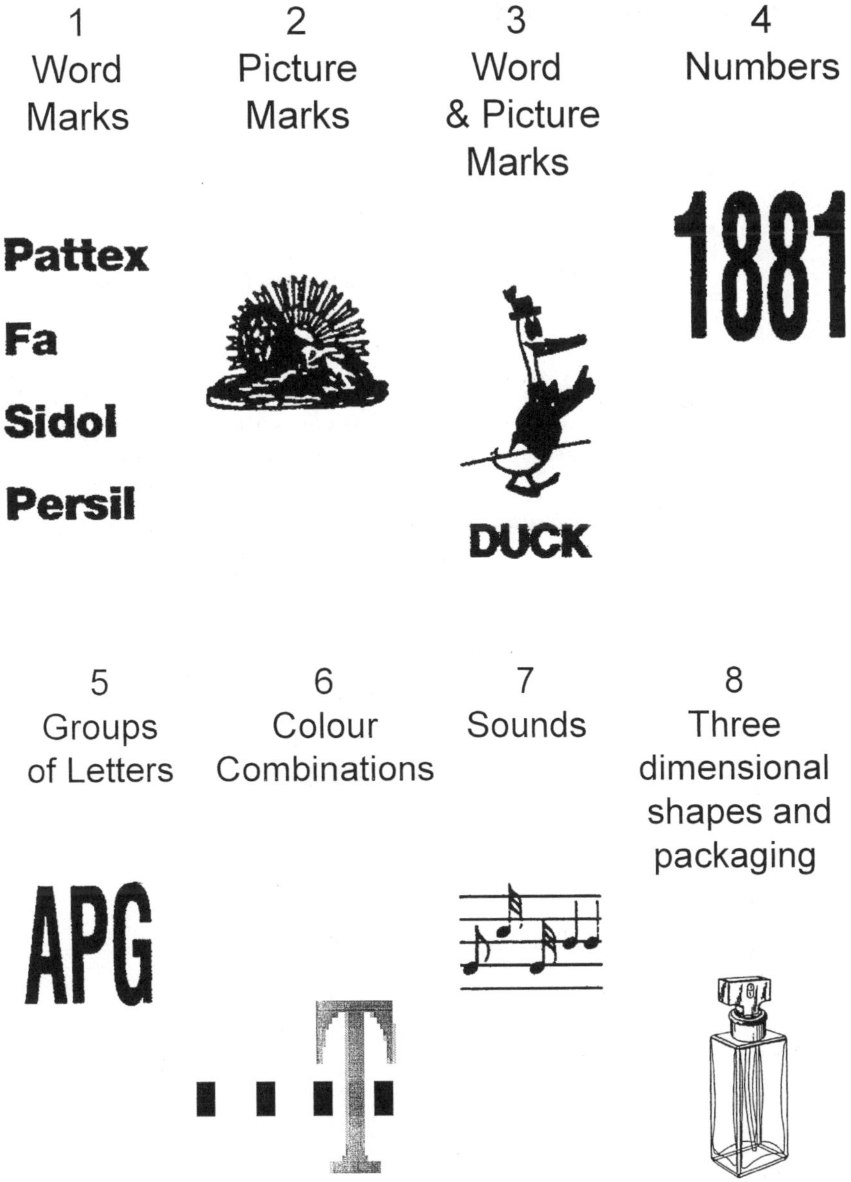

1 Word Marks	2 Picture Marks	3 Word & Picture Marks	4 Numbers
Pattex **Fa** **Sidol** **Persil**		DUCK	**1881**

5 Groups of Letters	6 Colour Combinations	7 Sounds	8 Three dimensional shapes and packaging
APG			

C. How does a mark originate?

Marks are born of the human imagination.

Persil — The name originates from **Per**borate and **Sil**icate (the prefixes of the names of chemicals).
It is interesting to note that the Imperial Patent Office did not consider Persil fit for protection. In 1917 the word Persil was registered on the basis of its notoriety. Today it would of course be assessed quite differently.

Henko — From the manufacturer Henkel

Düssan — From Düsseldorf (modification of geographical name)

Carclin — Modified spelling of CAR-CLEAN

Ata — Imaginary word

Word & Picture Mark — Comic figure with imaginary word Pril

D. How does trade mark protection originate?

Registered trade mark protection rights are obtained by application and registration at the competent authorities. Normally these are Patent Offices or Trade Mark Offices in the various countries. In Europe, the Community Trade Mark Office (OHIM) is also available for filing a Community Trade Mark (CTM).

In Germany, the German Patent Office in Munich with its branch office in Berlin is the competent office. Upon entry in the Trade Mark Register, a sign becomes a registered trade mark. The sign may (but need not be) marked with the sign ® which equals registered mark. For well known marks, the proprietor often does not use an ®, such as for Boss or Mercedes. However, for less well known marks, also with additional elements it is recommended, for example as follows:

Ferrolix®

STABILOX® PBS 1026

Ferrolix® 8350

Sekusept® plus

Balance®

For weaker marks, the ® should be used such that the presence of trade mark protection is visible. For example the trade mark Balance (registered by Goldwell AG, Darmstadt) appears almost descriptive especially when seen on the packaging or in advertising with the words "skin balance" or "maintains the natural balance", etc..

E. Why seeking Trade Mark Protection?

A registered mark provides industry with protection from mark pirates, infringers and inadvertant imitators. Mark pirates are extremely detrimental to the economy. Well known marks such as the Lacoste crocodile, Rolex, Prattex, Creme 21, Persil, etc. are often popular mark pirates' imitations. Concerning such imitations, see below:

Original   Imitations

Original   Imitations

Trademark Protection in Germany and Europe 323

Originals

Imitations

Original

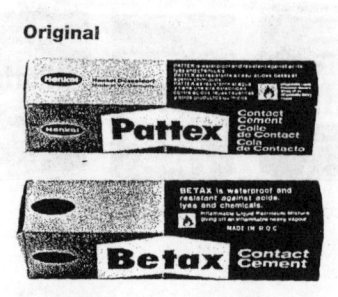

Pattex Contact Cement

Betax Contact Cement

Imitation

Mark piracy appears in many forms. While in some countries almost slavish imitation is rife, in western countries where the law is effective, imitations are more subtle. Leading market products are copied in such a way as to make the consumer think that imitations are another mark of the known manufacturer as can be seen from the following comparison between originals and corresponding imitations:

Perwoll
für Wolle und Feinwäsche

Original   Imitation

The trade mark protection law makes it possible for the owner to take legal action against imitators and pirates. The laws and their implementation are different in every country, however, the **registered trade mark** is the best means for defense. Thus, trade mark protection is very important.

As already mentioned, the trade mark also protects the consumer because he can expect the same or even better quality of the known product, especially for pharmaceuticals, etc.

Marks should not be ridiculed or satirized in such a way as to damage or exploit the goodwill associated with them.

F. What other Dangers Face Registered Marks?

Registered marks can lose their protection when they are used in a generic sense, e.g., the mark "Vasolene" for mineral fat was previously protected (still protected in the USA), the mark "**Kleenex**" for facial tissues or "**TEMPO**" for tissue-handkerchieves. The mark "**Nylon**" for synthetic fibre has also become a so-called "free sign" open to the public domain (generic designation), because the proprietor failed to prohibit third parties from use of the mark in describing similar goods.

Do you know for example that the word

"WALKMAN"

is a registered mark? Only the proprietor or licensee may use this sign on their products. The goods of other manufacturers use words such as walk player, cassette recorder, etc.

Thus it is actually detrimental to use a registered mark in the form of a verb, e. g. the mark "**PRITT**" in advertising as

"PRITT ALONG TOO".

PRITT is a trade mark for a glue stick. If used in the form of a verb, PRITT could one day replace the word "glue". Then trade mark protection would be lost!

As for another example, the company Henkel owns the mark "**MEGAPERLS**" for detergents. The detergents are presented in the form of small balls and look like little pearls.

The trade mark owner would be ill advised to speak of the newly developed detergent as the "Megaperls" in the descriptive sense of "Mega Pearls". In this manner, good trade marks can become generic expressions and, therefore, free to the public for use by the competitors.

List of Authors

DR. MICHAEL BIHLER
> Attorney at Law in Munich, Germany. He provides legal representation to large international corporations and distribution companies as well as to developers and mid-sized businesses.

DR. BERNARD BUECKER
> Attorney at Law in San Antonio, Texas. He received the Doctor of Jurisprudence degree from the University of Texas at Austin, was a Fulbright Scholar at the University of Heidelberg School of Law, Germany and specializies in German legal disputes. He was awarded the Service Cross of the Federal Republic of Germany in 1987.

HANS J. GORISS
> Tax Adviser and Business Consultant in Düsseldorf, Germany. His focus is on strategic tax policy for medium-sized and multicorporate enterprises, founding of establishments, apprising of investments of capital, controlling of investments, trusteeship, consulting in regard to incentives, going public, business consulting for managing boards and stockholders.

DR. MICHAEL KARGER
> Attorney at Law in Munich, Germany. His special areas of expertise include computer law and telecommunications law. He is a frequent lecturer on the law pertaining to the use of on-line computer services.

WOLFGANG C. LEONTI
> Attorney at Law in Munich, Germany. His special areas of interest include IT law, industrial property rights as well as commercial and corporate law. He handels business-law cases from the U.S.

ANDREAS MEISTERERNST
> Attorney at Law in Munich, Germany. His focus is on the drafting of contracts pertaining to the civil, commercial and corporate-law needs of his clientele.

DR. REINHARD NACKE
> Attorney at Law and Partner in the firm of Woedtke Reszel & Partner, Düsseldorf. His special area of expertise lies in the representation of foreign and German companies in legal matters with international background, including also the representation in legal disputes in and out of court or arbitration tribunals.

List of Authors

DR. EUGEN POPP
: Educated at the Technical University of Munich and Ludwig-Maximilians-University of Munich, he is a senior partner in the firm of Meissner, Bolte & Partner, Munich. His involvement in the wider interests of the profession recently were recognized as he was elected Vice-President of the German Patent Attorneys' Bar Association. He was the former President of the Bavarian Association of Patent Attorneys. He is also Secretary General of the European wide Committee of National Institutes of Patent Agents.

KAY RUPPRECHT
: European and German Patent and Trademark Attorney in Munich, Germany - Partner in the Intellectual Property Firm of Meisser, Bolte & Partner, Munich. He specializes in the prosecution and litigation of German, European and International (PCT-) patent and trademark applications and their registrations.

WOLF D. SCHENK
: Attorney at Law in Munich, Germany. His areas of special legal expertise include collective bargaining and individual labor law; industrial property and copyright law; drafting of corporate contracts, especially in regard to tax issues.

DR. BERND TREMML
: Attorney at Law in Munich, Germany - Senior partner in the law firm Wendler Tremml. He has many years of experience in the representation of foreign clients who wish to establish a subsidiary or purchase a business in Germany or in other European countries. Bernd Tremml is admitted to the Bar of the State of Texas as Foreign Legal Consultant.

RAIMUND E. WALCH
: Attorney at Law in Berlin, Germany. His special areas of expertise include IT law, commercial and corporate law and private construction law.

MICHAEL WENDLER
: Attorney at Law in Düsseldorf, Germany - Senior partner in the law firm Wendler Tremml. His primary focus is on the provision of legal representation to German corporations that operate globally and to foreign companies and associations concerning their business activities in Germany.

CHRISTIAN R. WOLF
: Notar in Kleve, Germany - Educated at the Ludwigs-Maximilians-University of Munich and the University of Freiburg. He specializes in corporate law and international business transactions, and in particular the formation and merger of business enterprises.

Glossary of German Terms and Abbreviations

A

Abgabenordnung (AO)	Tax Code
Amtsgericht	Court of Small Claims; municipal court
Änderungskündigung	a termination of a contract with the reserved right to renew it under altered conditions
Angestellte	employees; salary earners; "white collar" workers
Aktiengesellschaft (AG)	stock corporation
Aktiengesetz (AktG)	Stock Corporation Act
Aktionär	stockholder (of a stock corporation)
Aktie	a share of stock; stock certificate
Arbeiter	laborers; "blue collar" workers
Arbeitserlaubnis	work permit
Arbeitserlaubnisverordnung (AEVO)	Work Permit Regulations
Arbeitsförderungsgesetz (AFG)	Work Promotion Act
Arrest	Freeze Order
Aufenthaltsbefugnis	Authorized residence
Aufenthaltsberechtigung	residence entitlement
Aufenthaltsbewilligung	residence grant
Aufenthaltserlaubnis	residence permit
Aufsichtsrat	supervisory board of a company or corporation
Ausländer	foreigner; alien
Ausländergesetz (AuslG)	Foreigners Act
Ausländeramt	Foreign Nationals Authority
Außenministerium	Department of Foreign Affairs

B

Bergamt	mining authorities
Berufsgenossenschaft	administrative authorities in charge of providing social insurance due to occupational accidents
Betriebsaufgabe	abandonment of a business enterprise
Betriebsrat	works council
Betriebsverfassungsgesetz (BetrVG)	Employee Representation Law
Bezirk	district
BGB-Gesellschaft	see Gesellschaft des bürgerlichen Rechts
Bilanzrichtliniengesetz	Accounting Directives Act
Bundesanstalt für Arbeit	Federal Labor Office
Bundesarbeitsgericht	Federal Labor Court
Bundesministerium für Arbeit und Sozialordnung	Federal Department of Labor and Social Order
Bundesfinanzhof	Federal Finance Court
Bundesgerichtshof	Federal Supreme Court
Bundeskartellamt	Federal Cartel Authority
Bundesrechtsanwaltsgebührenordnung (BRAGO)	Attorneys' Fee Ordinance
Bürgerliches Gesetzbuch (BGB)	Civil Code
Bundesverfassungsgericht	Federal Constitutional Court
Bundesurlaubsgesetz (BurlG)	Vacation Act

D

Deutsche Angestelltengewerkschaft	White Collar Union
Deutscher Beamtenbund	Civil Servants' Union
Deutsche Bundesbank	Federal Reserve Bank of Germany
Deutscher Gewerkschaftsbund (DGB)	German Association of Industrial Labor Unions
Duldung	residence toleration
Durchführungsverordnung zum Ausländergesetz (DVAuslG)	Implementation Ordinance of the Foreigners Act

E

Einführungsgesetz zum BGB (EGBGB)	Introductory Act to the Civil Code
Einkommenssteuer	personal income tax
Einkommenssteuergesetz	Income Tax Act
Einzelunternehmen	sole proprietorship
Entscheidungen des Bundesgerichtshofs in Zivilsachen (BGHZ)	Decisions of the Federal Court for Civil Cases

Europäisches Patentamt	European Patent Office

F

Finanzamt	tax office; tax authorities

G

Gemeinde	community or municipality
Gerichtsvollzieher	sheriff's officer (official debt collector)
Gesamtbetriebsrat	combined or overall works council (of more than one business unit)
Gesamthandsvermögen	joint ownership (of the property of a partnership)
Gesellschaft des bürgerlichen Rechts (GbR)	(also: BGB-Gesellschaft) civil-law partnership
Gesellschaft mit beschränkter Haftung (GmbH)	limited liability company
Gesellschafter	shareholder (in a limited liability company)
Gesellschafterversammlung	shareholder meeting (limited liability company)
Gesellschaftsvertrag	articles of incorporation
Gesetz	law or act
Gesetz gegen den unlauteren Wettbewerb (UWG)	Unfair Competition Act
Gesetz zur Regelung des Rechts der Allgemeinen Geschäftsbedingungen (AGBG)	Law for the Regulation of Standard Business Terms
Gewerbeaufsichtsamt	Trade Supervision Office
Gewerbeordnung (GewO)	Trade Supervision Law
Gewerbesteuer	business tax
GmbH & Co KG	business organizational form which is a combination of a limited liability company and a limited partnership
GmbH-Gesetz (GmbHG)	GmbH Act (the law governing limited liability companies)
Grundsätze ordnungsgemässer Buchführung	principles of proper accounting
Grundsteuer	real-estate tax

H

Handelsgesetzbuch (HGB)	Commercial Code
Handelsgewerbe	commercial trade enterprise (owned and operated by individuals who are

	merchants by profession). Governed by the HGB.
Handelsregister	commercial register
Handlungsvollmacht (see also: Prokura)	full power of attorney (to represent an enterprise)
Hauptfürsorgestelle	Head Office for Public Assistance
Hauptversammlung	stockholder meeting (stock corporation)

I

Industriegewerkschaft (IG)	industrial trade union
Industrie- und Handelskammer (IHK)	Chamber of Industry and Commerce
Inhaberaktie	bearer stock certificate
Insolvenzordnung (InsO)	Insolvency Act
Interessenausgleich	compromise on issues of disagreement involving conflicting interests (for example, of employers and employees)

K

Kapitalertragssteuer	capital-yield tax
Kapitalspiegelmethode	literally: capital-mirroring method. The reflection of the actual net value of a partnership in its fiscal balance (as opposed to using the purchase price as the means of measure).
Kaufmann	merchant
Kommanditgesellschaft (KG)	limited partnership (for merchants)
Kommanditgesellschaft auf Aktien (KGaA)	limited partnership combined with stock
Kommanditist	limited partner (in a Kommanditgesellschaft)
Komplementär	general partner; personally liable partner (in a Kommanditgesellschaft)
Konkurs	bankruptcy
Kostenordnung (KostO)	Cost Regulation (for notary fees)
Körperschaftssteuer	corporate income tax
Kündigungsschutzgesetz (KSchG)	Termination Protection Act

L

Laienrichter	lay judges
Landgericht	Regional Court
Landkreis	county (approx. equivalent)
Leitende Angestellte	senior executives; managerial

Glossary of German Terms and Abbreviations 333

	employees (with the ability to hire and fire); literally: leading employees
Lohnfortzahlungsgesetz	Continued Payment of Wages Act
Lohnsteuer	wage tax

M

Mahnverfahren	summary proceeding for debt collection
Markengesetz	Trademark Act
Mehrwertsteuer	(MwSt) (also: Umsatzsteuer) value-added tax (VAT)
Mehrwertsteuergesetz (MwStG)	Value-Added Tax Act
Minderkaufmann	small merchant
Mitbestimmungsgesetz (MitbestG)	Co-Determination Law enabling employee representation in a company's management
Montan-Mitbestimmungsgesetz	Coal-and-Steel Co-Determination Law
Mutterschutzgesetz	Working Mothers Protection Act

N

Namensaktie	registered stock
Notar	notary

O

Offene Handelsgesellschaft (OHG)	general partnership (for merchants)
Oberlandesgericht	Court of Appeals

P

Personengesellschaft	partnership
Prokura	full power of attorney enabling company representation by an employee

R

Rechtsanwalt	attorney at law

S

Sachverständiger	public-appointed experts
Satzung	articles of incorporation of a stock corporation
Schachtelbeteiligung	intercorporate participation; mutual stockholding
Selbstbelieferung	the ability to procure goods oneself
Solidaritätszuschlag	solidarity contribution
Stammaktie	common stock

Stammkapital	nominal capital of a business enterprise
Steuer	tax
Steuerberater	tax advisor
Stille Gesellschaft	silent or dormant partnership
Stuttgarter Verfahren	Stuttgart Procedure (a way of assessing the value of a business, which was once the standard procedure in Germany but has recently fallen out of use due to its inaccuracy pitfalls)

U

Umsatzsteuer	value-added tax (VAT). Literally: sales tax.
Umwandlung	transformation of a business enterprise from one organizational form to another
Urhebergesetz (UrhG)	Copyright Act

V

vereidigter Buchprüfer	certified bookkeeper
Verfassung	Constitution
Vermögensübertragung	transfer of corporate assets and liabilities into public ownership
Verschmelzung	corporate merger
Verschmelzung durch Aufnahme	take over; a merger with at least one other company
Verschmelzung durch Neubildung	consolidation of one corporation with another for the purpose of forming an entirely new corporation
Vorschuß	retainer
Vorstand	board of management
Vorzugsaktien	preferred stock

W/X/Y/Z

Wirtschaftsprüfer	certified public accountant (CPA)
Zweigniederlassung	branch office